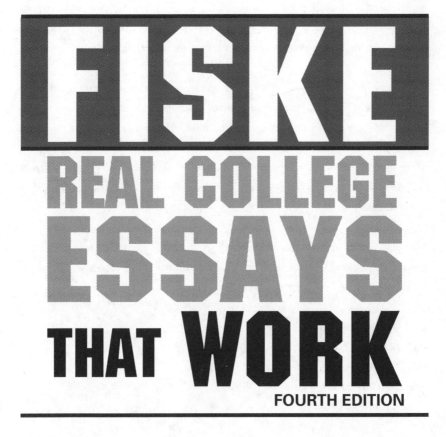

FISKE
REAL COLLEGE
ESSAYS
THAT WORK

FOURTH EDITION

EDWARD B. FISKE & BRUCE G. HAMMOND

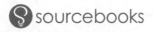
sourcebooks

Copyright © 2006, 2009, 2011, 2014 by FGC Associates, LLC

Cover and internal design © 2014 by Sourcebooks, Inc.

Published by Sourcebooks, Inc.

P.O. Box 4410, Naperville, Illinois 60567-4410

(630) 961-3900

Fax: (630) 961-2168

www.sourcebooks.com

Library of Congress Cataloging-in-Publication Data is on file with the publisher.

Printed and bound in the United States of America.

VP 10 9 8 7 6 5 4 3 2

Contents

Introduction: Why Couldn't I Just Write about Things That Make Me Happy? v

Part One: Writing a Great Essay 1
    Chapter 1: What Makes a Great Essay? 3
    Chapter 2: Rescue from Writer's Block 13
    Chapter 3: Crafting a Narrative 23

Part Two: Real College Essays That Work 33
    Academics 37
    Science and Science Fiction 51
    Hobby or Interest 61
    Athletics 95
    The Arts 105
    Camp Counseling and Community Service 141
    Racial or Cultural Differences 161
    Politics and Religion 193
    A Significant Experience 207
    Humor 223
    Family and Relationships 243
    A Moral Dilemma 257
    Personal Growth 267
    Travel 287
    Why I Love First Choice U. 311
    Appendix: The Search for an Opening Line 329
    Acknowledgments 349
    College Counselors Advisory Group 351
    About the Authors 353

Also by Edward B. Fiske
Fiske Guide to Colleges

Also by Edward B. Fiske and Bruce G. Hammond
Fiske Guide to Getting Into the Right College
Fiske Nailing the New SAT
Fiske Countdown to College

Why Couldn't I Just Write about Things That Make Me Happy?

When it was time to tackle my essay topic, I assumed that I needed to take the most emotionally gut-wrenching story from my life and work my way into a school by breaking the hearts of the admissions committee. If I couldn't pull that off, I figured that I should write the most intellectual five hundred words that I could get on paper. It would probably be a good idea to use lots of really big words and make allusions to really obscure works of literature, all the while analyzing why my (nonexistent) groundbreaking lab work was going to save the world. It took me a week-long essay writing seminar, an entire summer vacation, and several subsequent trips to the college counseling office to realize something that should have occurred to me in the first place: Why couldn't I just write about things that make me happy?

—Laura Cobb
Class of 2009
Washington University in St. Louis

On the list of life's most unpleasant experiences, writing a college essay ranks somewhere between getting a root canal and passing a kidney stone. Every fall, thousands of aspiring essayists spend hour upon hour staring into a computer screen. They wrack their brains for a clever opening line—always seemingly just out of reach—or a life-changing experience that they can presumably dust off and insert on cue. No wonder the process is such an ordeal.

We wrote this book to try to take some of the stress out of writing the essay. Not all of it, but enough to make writing the essay more bearable, and maybe even a little fun. As students like Laura Cobb eventually realize, a good essay does not necessarily need to be a Hemingwayesque literary masterpiece or a scholarly treatise worthy of Albert Einstein. The best essays come from high school students being themselves, with all the depth, wit, charm, and quirkiness that they bring to their daily lives. A good essay reflects the best qualities of its author—nothing more, and nothing less.

That said, getting your best self down on paper is not easy. To help with the process, we have gone to a logical source—students who have written a successful college essay and lived to tell about it. With the help of a network of high school counselors, we received hundreds of submissions from all corners of the country and chose 109 of the best for inclusion in this book. Many of the students also offered commentary about the writing process, and we think you will find their insights to be a valuable tool.

We should add that these are not the 109 best essays in the history of the civilized world. If you're a typical student, you'll have enough trouble psyching yourself up to write an essay without being demoralized by 109 of them that could have been written by Virginia Woolf. In compiling the essays, we tried to choose a variety that exhibit outstanding qualities but also represent an attainable standard for significant numbers of students.

We hope you will find this book to be browsable, and your first move may be to flip through it and sample some of the essays that catch your eye. Eventually, we hope you will find your way to Part 1, which includes three chapters that take you step-by-step through the writing process. Chapter 1, "What Makes a Great Essay?" gives a concise overview of dos and don'ts. Chapter 2, "Rescue from

Writer's Block," offers thoughts on choosing a topic and strategies for getting started. Chapter 3, "Crafting a Narrative," provides ideas on how to hook your admissions-officer reader at the beginning and keep him or her interested throughout your entire essay. We also give some pointers on how to avoid embarrassing mistakes.

The rumor mill aside, there is no single stroke that will get you into a selective college—not sky-high test scores, not great recommendations, not a truckload of extracurricular activities, not even a killer essay. Colleges weigh each application as a unified whole. But if you're a junior or senior in high school, your essay is the most important part of your application that is not set in stone. Among students with similar grades and test scores, essays are often decisive in determining who gets in, and who does not. No less than the director of admissions at Duke University has told us, "The better we get to know the students as people, the more likely that they will be admitted."

Laura Cobb figured as much when she wondered to herself, "Why couldn't I just write about things that make me happy?" She could, and she did.

> It all just hit me really quickly one Saturday…I was being lazy and my mind was wandering, and it suddenly wandered right into the first line of my essay. A lightbulb went off in my head, I repeated the line a few times, and then I sprinted as fast as I could to my computer. I liked it! As I typed it in, something clicked in my mind and the floodgates opened. The vast majority of my essay was produced within an hour.

Laura's essay, which begins with the fact that she won her school's pickleball tournament in tenth grade, is #70. Most essays take more than an hour to come together, but we hope that with a few helpful hints from this book, you can arrive at the same kind of realization as Laura did without the week-long essay seminar.

The key to a successful essay lies inside you, dear reader. Let's begin the process of finding it.

Part One:
Writing a Great Essay

What Makes a Great Essay?

Mention that you're writing a college essay and you'll probably get an earful of advice:

- "Write about your trip to Mexico," offers your mom. "You can show that you've broadened your horizons."
- "Community service always looks good," says Dad. "Talk about your work with Habitat for Humanity."
- "Write something funny," advises your best friend. "They love essays that make them laugh."
- "Make yourself stand out," says your school counselor. "In a pile of one thousand essays, yours should be the one they remember."

If you're lucky, you won't hear all of the above—at least not all at once. But the odds are good that you'll get some of it, particularly the one about making yourself stand out. How, exactly, do you accomplish that one? Have you scaled Mount Everest? Overcome a terminal disease? Saved a toddler from a burning building?

Of course not. Neither have 99.9 percent of the rest of us.

The best essays are seldom about a dramatic event or "significant experience" that changes the author's life. Real people don't get hit by lightning and suddenly realize that they should live their lives differently. Human development is a step-by-step, day-by-day process that happens almost imperceptibly.

Stand Out by Being Yourself

Instead of trying to be dramatic, be interesting. That's all a good essay needs to be—interesting to the admissions officers who read it. Forget the idea that your essay needs to be the one in a thousand that jumps out of the pile. That's too much pressure. Go for writing one that is among the 25 percent, more or less, that are reasonably interesting. It isn't as easy as it sounds. Among your first thoughts might be to tell about a trip, describe a community service project, analyze a political issue, or talk about the significance of your sport. Are any of these topics likely to be interesting? In the hands of a professional writer, they might have a fighting chance. In a college essay—even one written by a gifted student—these topics are likely to be painfully boring.

Fortunately, there is a solution that does not involve phony dramatics. Any of the topics above can be extremely interesting provided that you use them to talk about yourself. Hear that? *You* are by far the most interesting possible topic. If this sounds crazy, think of the most popular magazine in the United States. It has a one-word name: *People*. The magazine sells so well because people are interesting: their hopes and fears, their relationships, what they believe, and how their minds work. Call it gossip, the inside dirt—whatever. People are fascinating and you are a person. By happy coincidence, there is no topic in the world about which you are better prepared to write. If all the applicants in the country suddenly wised up and wrote about themselves, most would have good essays. Everyone is different, and people are endlessly interesting.

If you're still in doubt, think about the essay from the point of view of the admissions officers. They don't wade through all those essays to learn about the importance of self-discipline, or that persistence pays off. They want to learn about the applicants as people: their hopes and fears, their relationships, what they believe, and how their minds work.

In one way or another, every good essay is about the person who wrote it.

Details, Details

Your English teacher has told you one hundred times: if you want to write a good essay, you need concrete evidence to back up whatever you say. We'll take it a step further: you can't write a good college essay without details, by which we mean anecdotes, thoughts, and observations that are unique to you. Look at the 109 essays in this book. Every one of them crackles with specific references. In Essay 27, the author is an actor gazing out into the audience before a performance. He doesn't just see faces in the crowd. Nor does he see anything so generic as "a sea of faces waiting expectantly." Instead, he sees "the homely older women looking around the crowd for a familiar face" and "the seven-year-old whose parents dragged him along to the theater." In Essay 79, the author remembers an exchange student who lived in her home by "the tights scented with French perfume in my sock drawer." The author of Essay 101 writes about her trip to London. She didn't merely see Westminster Abbey, or even "the ancient splendor of Westminster Abbey." Instead, she was "moved almost to tears while wandering through Westminster Abbey, seeing the stained glass windows that had been pieced back together with such courage and diligence after being smashed during the bombings of the Second World War."

When stories involve people, a great way to make them more concrete is to use dialogue. Among the dozens in this book that use dialogue are Essays 3, 40, and 42.

The author of Essay 65 gets concrete by building her entire essay around the "256 steps" that it takes to walk from her mother's house to her father's house. She writes, "Twelve steps up the road, I see the crack in the pavement and I remember the first time I rode a tricycle—a hot pink contraption with a white wicker basket." Concrete detail is also crucial if you want to make your imagination become real, as the author of Essay 75 demonstrates:

There are two kinds of Perrier drinkers. There are those who are snobby and sophisticated who take small snooty sips from a glass while at a swanky café, and there are the free-spirited drinkers. I am the latter. I am one of the c'est la vie, I-have-class-but-appreciate-chaos, fine art loving, passionate drinkers.

Even the most mundane paragraph is more engaging if it is concrete, such as this passage from Essay 21:

No matter how tired I am, every Sunday morning I wake up, brush my teeth, put on my blue sweatpants and red sweatshirt, grab the keys to the car and head out into the driveway. Not even my puppy follows me outside; he likes to sleep till eleven o'clock on Sundays. I pull the car out into the driveway and position it just right so that the morning sun is blocked by the thick leaves and branches of the tall maple, and so that I can easily walk around the back end.

Not the most exciting paragraph you've ever read, but we'll bet that it held your attention.

Telling a Story

To translate our talk about concrete detail into slightly different terms, good essays use nouns and verbs while weak ones use adjectives. Strong essays "show" and weak ones "tell." Or again, good essays describe action while weak ones are a series of static images.

Allow us to explain. The adjective is a perfectly good part of speech, but only when serving strong verbs and nouns. An adjective by itself is an abstract category. If you say that your friend is "crazy," "zany," or even "off-the-wall," you haven't said much. But if you describe the time when she got out of her car and locked it with the keys still in the ignition, you're beginning to make progress. Or the time she got the hiccups during an assembly, couldn't stop laughing, and had to run out the back of the auditorium. If you describe the basketball game when she grabbed a rebound, raced to the wrong basket, and sank a shot, then froze in her tracks and exclaimed "Oh s_ _ _" loud enough for everyone to hear...

now we get the idea. After recounting a few anecdotes like these, you don't need to tell the reader that she is crazy because you have shown what she is like.

Strong verbs always drive interesting writing. But as essay writers grope and strain, too many of them reach instead for adjectives, as in the following:

> It was a chilly, grey twilight as the enormous stadium scoreboard announced the fourth quarter. I felt a damp, cool hint of dew under my aching feet. My muscles were tired but taut. The atmosphere was electric as the fans watched expectantly...

Though it is only a fragment, notice how this passage seems to move in slow motion. It is a series of images without much action (verbs) to link them. The overworked adjectives are not necessarily weak words, but they weigh down the prose. A trying-too-hard quality creeps in. Nothing is happening, but the author attempts to convey significance by lingering on every detail of the scene. The passage sounds forced and self-important.

A good essay consists of anecdotes and concrete observations that illustrate a story or make a point.

Think Metaphorically

Is your life boring? Does it leave you with nothing to write about? With metaphors (and similes), anybody's life can be the subject of an engaging essay. Consider Essay 93, in which the author likens his middle school years to the Dark Ages in Europe. He had been an active learner in his elementary years—which he compares to Greek and Roman antiquity. After a middle-school slump, he experiences a renaissance in ninth grade which he likens to, well, the Renaissance. By twelfth grade, he has undergone an enlightenment worthy of the Enlightenment and written an essay with real substance about his relatively typical school career.

There are numerous other examples in this book. In Essay 19, the author uses sailing as a metaphor for life. In Essay 69, the author describes being accepted as an adult in her family through the familiar experience of that first cup of coffee. In Essay 47, an author who grew up in the Caribbean imagines himself as a palm tree in conversation with a baobab tree that represents his African heritage.

Metaphors and similes show a student's ability to do big-picture thinking. If you're ever at a loss for what to write, think of analogies that apply to your life. Exploring such comparisons through simile or metaphor can transform mundane events into interesting ones.

WHEN PERSISTENCE PAYS OFF

I had a lot of difficulty picking a topic for my essay. I kept trying to find one aspect of my life that would represent me well, and eventually I realized that it was not going to happen for me like that. One day, after countless drafts of crappy essays, I finally sat down in front of my computer and did a stream-of-consciousness thing, typing down everything I saw that I felt represented me. I took this draft in to my history teacher, and we discussed what this meant. We came up with the idea of using my desk as a metaphor for my life, and showing my well-roundedness through the diversity of stuff on it. I rewrote this essay probably twenty or more times—an entire month's worth of second-period study halls was spent in my history teacher's office, discussing this essay and how to improve it! He was a great mentor because he understood me and was good at extracting what I was really trying to say out of failed attempts to do so.

—Christina Xu, Essay 22

How Long Should It Be?

We ask this question tongue-in-cheek—it drives teachers crazy. Students keep asking, of course, and the real answer is going to sound teacherly. An essay should be long enough to be good.

We can be thankful that Abraham Lincoln did not ask, "How long should it be?" when he wrote the Gettysburg Address. Generally acclaimed as the greatest speech in U.S. history, it went for all of 272 words. One of the best essays in this book, Essay 107, is also the shortest. In 78 words, the author explains why he hopes to attend Yale University. (He got in—and the admissions office made a point of commending the essay to his school counselor.) The longest, Essay 99, tips the scale at 1,172 words. How long should it be? Long enough to be good.

Sometimes, a length is mandated. Online, students often find that their cursors stop moving at the end of the allotted word count. Exhibit A of this reality is the Common Application, the primary vehicle for applying to more than 500 of the nation's best colleges. The "big" essay on the Common App must be between 250 and 650 words, no exceptions, and most of the supplemental Common App essays also have a mandatory maximum length. (Never heard of the Common App? Log on at www.commonapp.org to find out how it can save you time and aggravation in applying to selective colleges.)

Some colleges specify a word length but allow students to go longer if they choose. If the question says 500 words, then 520 words is probably okay, but not 720. When the question specifies neither a length nor an amount of space, a reasonable target for those in doubt is no more than 400 to 500 words. (Write less for a sidebar essay about your favorite activity or why you are interested in the college.)

There is an interesting footnote to the length issue that we must fess up about. In previous books, notably the *Fiske Guide to Getting Into the Right College*, we have preached the virtues of brevity, or at least of not going on forever. Yet in sifting through the essay submissions for this book—all from successful applicants to highly selective colleges, all identified as excellent by college counselors—we were surprised by the number of nominations that were longer than 500 words. (There were also plenty of short and sweet ones like our seventy-eight–word masterpiece.)

Our theory is that when an essay is outstanding—really outstanding—the reader doesn't mind if it goes on longer. Doing so gives the author more space to add the concrete details that make it memorable. You'll see a number of these longer essays in this book. (For examples, check out Essays 23 and 101.) We are at pains to add that the number of brilliant long essays is far outnumbered by the long ones that could be improved by cutting, sometimes ruthless cutting. If you're in doubt, consult a teacher who can give you feedback. We'll say more about that in Chapter 3.

There are good essays and bad essays of all lengths. We recommend that your first concern be writing a good one.

What Do You Want to Show?

Many applicants don't begin with a theme for their essays. They just write what comes naturally. Others choose a theme before they write. Either method can work, but at some point in the process, think about whether your essay conveys the qualities that you most want to emphasize.

One applicant we know intended to write an essay about her love of reading. She talked about some of her favorite books, but the essay turned out to be about how she used reading as a retreat from the world. The girl had many other outstanding qualities—she was a campus leader and one of the most adventuresome students in the school—but her essay made her appear much more withdrawn than she really was. The essay was well written and an accurate portrayal of part of her life, but it did not highlight her most appealing qualities.

There is, however, a balance to be struck. Some applicants are so worried about pandering to the admissions officers that they aren't true to themselves. Others are so packaged by college counselors or consultants that their voices are drowned out. Still others are so focused on their theme that they are heavy-handed and tell rather than show.

There are innumerable qualities that you might emphasize in an essay, including that you:

- have a sense of humor
- value diversity
- embrace learning
- notice the little things
- are deeply committed to an activity or idea
- can overcome adversity
- take initiative

Colleges want people who are passionate about life and learning, and who will add to their community with participation and leadership.

There are also qualities that can be real turnoffs. They generally appear unbeknownst to the author and can undermine anything good in the essay. Avoid any suggestion that you:

- are cynical
- think you are a finished product
- are likely to turn inward in college
- are depressed
- are self-destructive
- lack integrity
- tend to blame others

Colleges don't want people who are complainers, or people who will withdraw from a community rather than embrace it. Many students do all the "right" things but lack real passion, a fact that can be revealed by a passionless essay. Feel free to talk about the challenges in your life, including some that may be ongoing, but avoid giving information that could raise red flags about your mental health or the potential for destructive behavior of any kind.

Your essay may be the only time that the admissions office gets to hear your voice. Think of it as *you* on the page.

Rescue from Writer's Block

After all your reasons to procrastinate have been exhausted, you settle yourself in front of the computer to begin work on your essay. Again. The screen is just as blank as it was the last time you tried to get started. After ten minutes of vacant staring, your right leg begins to fidget uncontrollably. After ten more, you feel the muscles in your throat tighten. Your heart begins to race and your head jerks up to see a wild-eyed face in the mirror with teeth clenched in a silent scream. You grab the computer in a bear hug, and with one motion tear away the cables and lurch toward your bedroom window. As your arms feel the impact of shattering glass, you thrust the computer forward and watch it hurtle, cords and all, toward the pavement below. Just as you are about to dive headlong after it, the sound of your mother's voice gives you a start.

"This is the last time I'm going to tell you," she says in an exasperated voice. "Wake up now!" After several seconds of groggy confusion, you stagger out of bed and head for the shower.

We hope you manage to avoid nightmares about the essay, but if you do find yourself losing sleep over it, join the club. Getting started can be hard, even agonizing. To avoid a false start, give yourself thinking time before putting pressure on yourself to start writing. Chirps one of our student authors, "My personal statement was something that I had thought about for weeks, and when I finally sat down to write it, the words flowed straight out of my head onto the page. I finished in about thirty-five minutes." Some of the best ideas tend to come when you're in the shower, or after you've turned out the light to go to bed. Reason: you're more relaxed at times like these and can let your mind wander. To save the thoughts that occur at odd moments, record them using your favored electronic device as they come to you, or jot them down the old-fashioned way with pen and paper.

Know Your Assignment

Your first order of business is to preview the essays you'll need to write. Depending on how and where you apply, you'll probably need to write two to four "big" essays in the 500 to 600 word range and a handful of shorter ones in the 100 to 200 word range. If you are an applicant to selective private colleges, you'll probably start with the Common Application's 250 to 650 word essay. The Common App also includes Writing Supplements for most participating colleges. Some of these contain a second major essay assignment; others consist of several shorter essays. You'll also need to find out the essay questions for any college choices that are not on the Common. These include most state institutions and a few selective private hold-outs, notably Georgetown and MIT. Once you know your questions, be strategic. With luck, you'll have some colleges with exactly the same question. More likely, you'll find similar questions, or a choice topic for one college that allows you to write an essay that will satisfy another college's question.

In 2013–14, the powers that be at Common App overhauled the essay prompts for the first time in a generation. The range of topics was narrowed and "Topic of Your Choice" was eliminated as one of the options. Applicants must write the 250 to 650 word essay in response to their choice from the following:

- Some students have a background or story that is so central to their identity that they believe their application would be incomplete without it. If this sounds like you, then please share your story.
- Recount an incident or time when you experienced failure. How did it affect you, and what lessons did you learn?
- Reflect on a time when you challenged a belief or idea. What prompted you to act? Would you make the same decision again?
- Describe a place or environment where you are perfectly content. What do you do or experience there, and why is it meaningful to you?
- Discuss an accomplishment or event, formal or informal, that marked your transition from childhood to adulthood within your culture, community, or family.

Notice what all the prompts have in common. They are about *you*. Taken together, the prompts cover just about every imaginable angle from which you could write about yourself. Our advice is not to get too hung up on the details of the prompts. Instead, think about how you can use them as a jumping off place for reflecting about yourself, and for writing about what you want to share. Also, choose your prompt with an eye on your other essays to see if you can kill two birds with one stone.

College-specific prompts. Suffice it to say that the Writing Supplements to the Common Application, and the essay prompts from colleges not on the Common App, cover everything under the sun. Some examples from recent years:

- What matters to you, and why? (Stanford University, 250-word limit)
- What is one thing we won't know about you after reading your application that you haven't already reported in the Common Application "Additional Information" section? (Harvey Mudd College, 500-word limit)
- How are apples and oranges supposed to be compared? Possible answers involve, but are not limited to, statistics, chemistry, physics, linguistics, and philosophy. (University of Chicago, one to two pages)

- Describe the world you come from—for example, your family, community, or school—and tell us how your world has shaped your dreams and aspirations. (University of California, one of two prompts, maximum 1,000 words total)
- Why are you interested in attending the University of Notre Dame? (University of Notre Dame, 150 to 300 words)

Be sure to check the colleges' websites, and the Common App, for the latest updates.

From Prompt to Topic to Telling Detail

Finding the right prompt boils down to figuring out which one will put you on a topic that you want to write about. Our advice: think about your preferred topics first, then choose among the prompts. In turn, a good topic has two primary features:

- It is about you.
- You can write about it in concrete detail.

Choosing the right topic is the most important key to writing a good essay. Though each person's experiences are unique, some topics maximize chances for success while others yield a higher percentage of clinkers. Experiences in the arts tend to work well because they are about creative expression. Experiences in athletics produce a lot of bad essays because competition necessitates masking one's feelings. Religion is not a particularly promising choice, especially a description of one's beliefs. Political issues are also not the best; as a high school student, you are unlikely to add new insight to the abortion or gun control debates. Write about political issues only in the context of your personal experiences, such as participation in an organization related to politics. With these caveats, we refer you to our sections on "Athletics" and "Politics and Religion," where our student authors show how these topics can be handled effectively.

The best essays often use small things to illuminate big things as writers find themselves in the mundane details of life. One of our authors illustrates her personality by describing the act of buying a bottle of shampoo (Essay 72); another describes looking at her own face in the mirror (Essay 52). Other essays delve into why the author loves drinking Perrier (Essay 75), why the author bites her nails (Essay 76), why the author likes bowling (Essay 26), the author's various pairs of shoes (Essay 15), cleaning up vomit at summer camp (Essay 42), bringing underwear to college (Essay 77), and the home-spun wisdom of two pain-in-the-neck kids who were the author's counselees at summer camp (Essay 40).

TAPPING YOUR INNER DORKINESS

As for advice, I'd say write about something you really care about, even if others find it dorky or strange. My friends would always laugh at me for preferring old-fashioned snail mail to the phone. They rolled their eyes when I said I was writing a college essay about it. However, I knew that my true self would shine through if I wrote about something I was head-over-heels in love with, and writing letters is one of those things.

So if you tell someone else your idea for an essay and they think it's dumb, don't let that deter you. Sometimes the things that make us dorky or weird are the exact qualities that will make us stand out from a pile of fifteen thousand other application essays.

—Francie Neukom, Essay 17

In each of these essays, the insignificant surface topic is not the real point of the essay but merely an occasion for reflection. In Essay 52, the author is in a restroom looking at herself in the mirror. She reflects on herself and the fact that, as an international student, she is different from two classmates who enter the restroom. She ponders her immigrant status before the *whoosh* of the door brings her back to the present. In Essay 72, the author ponders buying a bottle of shampoo, which gives her a jumping-off place for various whimsical reflections about herself. In Essay 40, the author quotes the excuses and rationalizations of misbehaving elementary schoolers at summer camp, and in the process finds wisdom for his own life in an unexpected place.

One of our contributors hit the nail on the head when she wrote, "Some of the best essays I have read are descriptions of mundane events: people-watching at the mall, overhearing pieces of conversations in a restaurant, working out Saturday mornings before anyone in the house awakes."

Many of the essays in this book are about larger issues, but even these essays typically begin small. Essay 65 is about the divorce of the author's parents, but its title, "256 Steps," shows her approach. Rather than tackling the issue head-on, she describes sights along the 256-step walk between the houses of her mother and father as a way of reflecting on what the divorce means. In Essay 53, the author writes about the meaty issue of racial stereotypes, but she begins by discussing her love of equations and problem solving.

One of the pitfalls of the personal statement is to get bogged down in factual narration of a big event. Let's say you scored the winning goal in the state championship soccer game. You could narrate events—the ball coming your way, your charge down the field, teammates carrying you off the field, and so on. You could probably hold the reader's attention with a narrative like this, but what would he or she learn about you? Not much, other than that you are a good athlete, which would be obvious from your activity list.

Topic Ideas from This Book

For more words of wisdom about choosing your topic, we turn to our contributors. A number of them cite the importance of staying as stress-free as possible. Says one, "Sitting down knowing that you're writing a big, scary college essay can make your writing start to sound really wooden and formulaic. Instead, have fun writing about yourself, or remembering something important to you, in whatever your most natural writing style is" (Essay 90). Another student author believes that picking a topic isn't such a big deal. "I don't think the topic is as important as the tone of the essay. It's like two people can say the same thing, but you'll be attracted to the person whose personality shines even when they say a simple 'hello'" (Essay 59).

FIVE WAYS TO SHOOT YOURSELF IN THE FOOT

- **A Phony Life-Changing Experience**—Have you been a different person since the day you lost the big game while learning a valuable lesson? We doubt that you are, and so will the admissions officer reading your essay.
- **Making Everything Peachy Keen**—Avoid telling how you encountered a problem, found a solution, and lived happily ever after. Self-congratulation does not play well in an essay, and neither does the superficial sense that everything works out in the end.
- **Social Problem of the Year Bandwagon**—Remember Hurricane Katrina? Want to guess how many essays were written that year about responding to disasters and taking care of refugees? Don't touch global warming with a ten-foot pole and don't write about any issue that everybody else is talking about.
- **Melodrama**—Straining for the dramatic always ends badly. Do so, and you'll get something like, "the last gleaming rays of the sun bathed the field in a soft orange glow as we strode confidently from the huddle to begin the fourth quarter."
- **Quoting Pop Lyrics**—What sounds profound on your iPod may seem silly or trite in an essay. It's fine to quote Bob Dylan, Boxcar Willy, or something similarly out of the ordinary. With any quote, explain why it applies uniquely to you.

Even if there are many topics that could work, you still must pick one, or at least a way to open your essay. One of our contributors made a list of fifteen possible essay topics, then gradually eliminated choices until she had her topic (Essay 17). Another writes that she "reflected on what was important to me, and what aspects of my personality I felt were those most worth knowing" (Essay 51). Yet another student suggests using a stream of consciousness approach to brainstorming. "Write down things that make you happy, or random things that cross your mind, or that one weird thing that happened that one time," she says. "Get any and all ideas down on paper somewhere, and if one of them stirs your imagination, go with it" (Essay 70).

If you have plenty of time, consider beginning a journal to test out ideas. If you put down one hundred words a night, or at least every few days, the odds are good that you will hit on something interesting.

For those without a topic or any notion of where to begin, we offer the following five ideas to get you unstuck. Try writing about:

- **An article of clothing**—Many people have an item such as a favorite sweater, a beloved T-shirt, or a well-worn pair of shoes. One student author in this book writes about all the shoes in her closet, and how each pair reflects different facets of her personality (Essay 15). It is often possible to spin stories around an item that has been with you through many experiences, or that can be made to represent truths in your life.
- **The groups in your school and where you fit in**—Every school has groups of people who associate together based on common interests or traits—jocks, musicians, Goths, skaters, cheerleaders, "smart" kids, and everything in between. Not that you want to reduce anyone to a stereotype, but some perceptive comments about social life at your school can be very effective. Have you tried to bridge the groups? Ever gotten caught in a test of loyalty between them? One of our authors wrote a superb essay about how his mind was opened when some of the toughest football players in the school joined the choir (Essay 39). Another, a football player himself, writes about joining a drama group and expanding his circle of friends (Essay 33).
- **A family gathering or tradition**—You could pick anything from your family at the dinner table to an annual trip to the beach. You may decide to write about an extended family

gathering, and thereby give yourself more characters and interactions to describe. One of our authors writes about the morning cup of coffee with her family (Essay 69). Another writes about family vacations, and the lessons she draws are not the ones a reader—or her mother—might have predicted (Essay 98).

- **Your walk or ride to school**—Any trip that you take on familiar ground, day after day, is a good possibility. A walk through your neighborhood would allow you to reflect on experiences that you have had at each place you pass. Essay 65 is a classic in this genre. If you are a runner, another idea would be to describe a course that you have run many times, and your thoughts along the way. If you've lived in your house a long time, a look around the backyard could bring to mind good times with family or friends that might come together in an essay.

- **Your favorite things**—One of our authors writes about "Seven Wonders"—ranging from potter's clay to the dual-density midsoles on his shoes—and tells how each is meaningful to him. Another student describes herself via twelve items on her desk, from a piece of cheesecake to a copy of Stephen Hawking's *A Brief History of Time* (Essay 22).

An advantage of the topics here is that they give you plenty of opportunity to drop out of factual description and probe your thoughts and feelings. Whether you choose one of these or something else, make sure it is a topic about which you are passionate, enthusiastic, and/or otherwise entertained. In the words of one of our contributors, "If you can write about something you enjoy, the writing will be much easier and your voice will come through much better." No matter what direction you take, *you* are the real topic.

ANOTHER LOOK AT SHOW, DON'T TELL

If you really want to understand "Show, Don't Tell"—or if you simply need a hand in getting started—try the following exercise. Think of a friend and then an adjective to describe him or her. (Make the adjective as specific as possible.) Without using the word or any synonyms, write a paragraph that shows why the adjective describes the person. You'll be forced to use anecdotes to show why, which is exactly the sort of writing that you need for a college essay.

Crafting a Narrative

Once you've picked a topic and gotten a reasonable amount on paper, the real work begins. If you're a one-draft writer who cranks out perfect prose on the first try, more power to you. For most people, polishing an essay takes time and several pairs of eyes. If at all possible, get your first draft done at least two weeks, and preferably two months, before you plan to submit the essay. You'll need plenty of time to go over it—both for yourself and for any adults or friends who you recruit to help.

Your most important task is to make sure that the essay says what you want it to say with as much flair and pizzazz as you can muster. The second one, no less important, is to make sure that typos, spelling mistakes, and grammar errors are edited out.

The Opening Paragraph

We'll give you one guess as to the most important sentence in your essay. (The title of this section is a hint.) To understand why the first sentence, and the first paragraph, are so crucial, consider the plight of a typical admissions officer (AO). At the peak of application reading, she probably has a quota somewhere between thirty and fifty per day. Admissions officers spend as little as ten minutes per application, of which perhaps three minutes may be devoted to the essay. When the AO finally gets to your application, while munching on cold pizza at 1:47 a.m. having read forty-nine others that day, it is crucial that your opening paragraph grab her attention before she nods off. The way you begin will shape the admissions officer's perceptions of the whole essay and may even determine whether she reads or skims.

To get your juices going, turn to the appendix on page 329. There, you'll find the opening lines of every essay in this book. Each one is unique, but they fall into three basic categories:

- **An anecdote**—The most tried-and-true way to begin is to describe an incident or event that relates to your main point.
- **A zinger**—Some excellent writers don't need an anecdote. They may begin with humor, wordplay, or some other creative twist to grab the reader.
- **A straightforward statement**—Though good anecdotes and zingers are hard to beat, a simple beginning is preferable to a failed attempt at either of the former.

Many essays in this book begin with an anecdote. In Essay 48, the author describes volunteer work for an Indian cultural organization that often has her working late and neglecting homework: "I'm tired and a little bit desperate. My clock angrily glares at me through its neon green dial. It's 11:24. The biology exam tomorrow will be murder. I resolutely pass over my textbook, and instead return to the screen where Pandit Jasraj stares back at me."

Another of our contributors begins her essay standing at the blackboard in English class, drawing a figure to illustrate her reaction to a line in John Keats's "Ode on a Grecian Urn":

Now I was at the front of the classroom, using what little artistic coordination I had to draw a great big figure on the board: yes, those had to be eyes, an L-shaped nose, wrinkled eyebrows, a gaping "O" for a mouth. I added little stress lines on either corner of the cheeks, just to show how intent my hastily composed figure was on examining this

"Sylvan historian, who canst thus express a flowery tale more sweetly than our rhyme" (Essay 3).

Notice how deftly she relates a necessary fact—that she is writing at the board—without breaking the flow of her narrative. The essay continues with dialogue between her and the teacher.

It takes skillful writing to achieve a zinger opening, but a number of our authors were equal to the task. One student writes about the pitfalls of being known as a feminist. Her essay begins, "Sometime between waking up at the crack of dawn and fourth period I became a teenage werewolf. No, wait, I mean feminist." Another of our authors with an active funny bone turns his attention to the college search with this opening:

> Do you ever have those dreams where you've arrived at school and suddenly realize you've forgotten to wear pants? Well, for most high school seniors that dream becomes a reality, at least figuratively. We must bare our souls, not to best friends, or family, but to complete strangers who may not even want to hear about it and may even flat out reject us. What twisted institution would ever subject young adults in the formative stages of emotional growth to this experience? Oh, right. College (Essay 73).

Don't feel bad if you can't pull off a stream of consciousness like this; most of us can't.

Straightforward openings can work well when you have a lot of information to convey. One of our student authors writes about a robot he designed, opening this way: "'E2V2' was my own creation and I would drive it in BattleBotsIQ, a national robotics competition. I felt my body tense for the battle against the spinbot, Chromedome" (Essay 9). With most of the crucial information conveyed, the rest of the essay describes the battle between the two robots.

Another of our contributors writes about how his self-image changed when he decided to experiment with an acting class. The essay begins, "Before last year I had always thought of myself as a very shy, uncreative, introspective individual. And I was happy that way. I had found my little niche in the Kinkaid society. I was the jock who excelled in sports and also managed to make pretty good grades as well" (Essay 33). By outlining all of his preconceptions about himself up front, he sets the stage for talking about his change in attitude after taking a drama class.

A LAST-MINUTE DO-OVER

My writing process was actually extremely long and painful. I wrote an essay about my passion (art and painting) and worked on it for almost a year. I think I overworked it because it never seemed quite right. Then basically the night before I had to send in my applications, I decided to rewrite the essay from a slightly different angle that better answered the question. My essay is the product of four hours of work in one night. I was able to write it so quickly and well because I knew exactly what I wanted to say and even used many phrases and sentences from my original essay.

—Emily Stein, Essay 38

Managing the Flow

Once you've gotten the reader's attention with your opening, you should have a story to tell. But first, it is often necessary to pull back from the narrative to fill in background information. Beginning writers often struggle with how to manage the balance between describing an experience and reflecting on it, and how to create seamless transitions between the two. Beginning with dialogue is one of the most common attention-getters. Spoken words in quotation marks convey a you-are-there feeling to the reader. But too many writers let the dialogue go too long before dropping out to explain necessary background information. In most cases, one sentence or phrase of dialogue is all that is necessary. Below is one example of how it's done from Essay 87:

"So, you want this car or not?" Dr. Matt Petrilla asked again, in his simultaneously pushy yet polite manner. This smart, stocky man, a medical doctor and the father of a friend, had thrown me in a sudden state of blissful surprise: less than a minute before, he had offered me a free car.

Notice how quickly the author transitions from pulling in the reader with dialogue to providing necessary background information. Once he has explained the relevant facts—that the father of a friend has offered him a car—he can jump back into the dialogue or continue telling the story.

The ability to pull back from a narrative also comes in handy when you want to interject your thoughts and feelings, or if you simply want to broaden your scope to include more general reflections. In Essay 30, the author explains the significance of a figure in a Renoir painting that hangs on her wall and then begins a broader examination of dance, art, and creativity:

The lady in the red hat represents a side of myself not often seen, one that dances in the street without a care in the world...Renoir's painting constantly reminds me not to completely let go of that spontaneity.

Dancing is an act of passion; it is an act of freedom. Sometimes I search for this type of freedom in life, but at times, it can only be found in the subtleties of artwork.

It is logical to jump from an analysis of a Renoir painting to a more general discussion of art, but many students fail to make similar transitions that are just as obvious.

One of the surest marks of a well-written essay is a concluding "kicker"—a final sentence that echoes the beginning or provides an unexpected twist.

The author of Essay 1 ends with a particularly clever twist. In an essay about his love of languages, he begins with a quote from Charles V that refers (nonsensically) to speaking in German to his horse. "I don't speak German," the author begins, noting that he does not have a horse. After an essay describing his fluency in

Russian and Spanish, he ends by pondering which language he will learn next. "Maybe even German?" he muses. "Well, in that case, I'd better start saving up for a horse."

In response to a question about what she would do if given a year to spend any way she wished, another of our authors (Essay 2) responds that she would read books. Among them was Tolstoy's *Anna Karenina*, which, she writes, she has been "trying to finish for the last three years." After discussing other books, she concludes the essay with the thought that a year of reading would "not only expand my mind further—I could finally find out what happens to Anna and Count Vronsky!"

For more good examples of kickers, check out Essays 73 and 82.

Dotting the I's and Crossing the T's

If you're looking for the simplest way to improve your essay, we can summarize it in three words: edit, edit, edit. Then proofread and edit some more. Too many students spend countless hours on their essays, then get an itchy trigger finger and submit them before correcting obvious spelling mistakes, grammatical inconsistencies, words that have been left out—and worse. Don't underestimate your ability to make silly mistakes when you've been staring at your essay for a week. When students are under pressure they just want to be done, but to do your best essay it may be necessary to prolong the agony a little longer.

We'll assume that you've followed our advice about doing your essay in time to edit it properly. Once you get a draft we think you need at least two weeks. Set it aside for the first week without looking at it. When you do pick it up again, you'll be able to look at it with fresh eyes. Material that seemed to flow logically after you had been staring at it for hours may now seem disjointed. Errors that had camouflaged themselves will jump out. After you have gone over the essay yourself, get an adult such as your English teacher, guidance counselor, or parent to read it. Hopefully, he or she can give you two kinds of advice:

- Big-picture feedback about your ideas and whether your essay says what you want it to say.
- Micro-level feedback on details like typos, word choice, and spelling.

If you don't agree with the advice, get a second adult and see what he or she says. Though we respect the fact that some students want the essay to be theirs alone, we cannot overemphasize the importance of having another pair of eyes go over it.

MAKING A COLLAGE OR GOING TO COLLEGE?

Garden-variety typos are one thing, but goofs like the ones here are downright embarrassing. And if you think the spell check will catch them, don't be so sure.

Common Blooper	Correct Form
calculas	calculus
collage	college
councilor	counselor
financial aide	financial aid
honor role	honor roll
perspective student	prospective student
prepatory	preparatory
psycology	psychology

The following is a laundry list of things to look for when you edit:

- **Lack of a main idea**—The college essay is often a one-shot deal, and the impulse to cram in as much as possible can be strong. If you start out talking about why you love debate and finish with a discussion of your relationship with the debate coach—who also happens to be your English teacher—you may need to sharpen your focus and expand on one or the other.
- **Weak verbs**—How strong and precise are your verbs? List every one of them in your essay and see how good they are. Too many "to be" verbs are a bad sign, as in, "Jessica's dance across the floor was graceful." Better would be "Jessica danced gracefully across the floor." Best would be "Jessica

glided across the dance floor." Notice that a strong verb—"glided"—provides a much more vivid description than "danced gracefully" or "was graceful."

- **Passive voice**—Sometimes, the person doing the acting disappears altogether, as in, "It is clear that the job must be done." Even if the sentence were to say, "The job must be done by Tom," it would still be convoluted and passive. An active sentence would say, "Tom must do the job." Notice, too, that passive voice uses a "to be" verb. Avoid it.

- **Failure to use "I"**—Most students have had at least one teacher who told them never to use "I" in a paper. (Instead of "I think," you might say something like "One can conclude.") But in a college essay, always use "I" when you're talking about yourself. It is far more honest and direct than cloaking yourself in phony third-person omniscience.

- **Double-dipping adjectives**—If you describe a "cool, clear, sparkling mountain stream," you've overdone it. Instead of using two or three adjectives at a time, choose the one best, as in "the sparkling mountain stream." Go back over your essay and see how many times you used one adjective versus two or three. Were two really necessary? Sometimes the answer is yes, sometimes no.

- **Too many simple sentences**—A few simple sentences are great for effect—just make sure that your entire essay isn't made up of them. A bunch of simple sentences merely list disconnected ideas; compound and complex sentences establish relationships between those ideas and allow you to explore nuances. For instance: "I had a headache. I went home." Or again: "I went home because I had a headache. " Or finally: "Though I went home with a headache, it wasn't as bad as the one that sent me to the hospital last year." The first example makes no connection between the headache and going home; the second describes a cause-and-effect relationship; and the third retains the relationship while adding more perspective.

- **Wordiness**—Even good essays are full of words that aren't necessary. Any word that does not add insight or specificity should be cut. Likely candidates include clauses like "as you can see" and "it is obvious that" and words such as "basically," "perhaps," and "additionally." Scrutinize your essay one word and one clause at a time. Is everything necessary? If you think your prose is wordy but have trouble cutting, ask a reader to mark words and passages that seem superfluous. It is always easier to cut someone else's essay than to cut your own.

- **Messed-up tenses**—When in doubt, use the present tense rather than the past. When both the present and past are technically correct, the present is more immediate. When we refer to the essays in this book, we say that the author "writes" about a particular subject rather than "wrote" about it. While this may be a matter of preference, it is crucial to avoid inconsistency among tenses from one sentence and paragraph to the next.

- **Trusting the spell check**—It won't catch some of the most common errors, like when you write "an" and mean "and," when you leave out a word, or when you write "there" and mean "their." Definitely do the spell check, but don't make it a substitute for human editing.

- **Unwillingness to start over**—Sometimes it takes three or four hours of work, and maybe even a complete first draft, to realize that your topic isn't working. Some students can't bear to let what they have written go to waste, and end up with an inferior essay. Don't be afraid to cut out entire sections or chuck the whole thing—even if some of it is good material. Two really good pages that don't mesh will make a worse essay than one good page standing alone.

When you finally think you're ready to click "send," hit "save" instead and come back again for one last review. The vast majority of essays, even the good ones, include at least one misspelling, typo, or other error. A hint for your final review: read the essay backwards, a technique that can help you locate left-out or misspelled words that your eye might otherwise slide over. Only after you have proofread yet again, and found nothing, should you consider yourself done.

Part Two:
Real College Essays That Work

The rest of the book consists of essays from our 109 student contributors, each with a one hundred–word introduction from us. Where the essay was written in response to a particular question, we have repeated it in italics.

You may want to simply browse the essays, but for your convenience, we have divided them into fifteen categories according to their topic. The topics include:

1. Academics
2. Science and Science Fiction
3. Hobby or Interest
4. Athletics
5. The Arts
6. Camp Counseling and Community Service
7. Racial or Cultural Differences
8. Politics and Religion
9. A Significant Experience
10. Humor
11. Family and Relationships
12. A Moral Dilemma

13. Personal Growth
14. Travel
15. Why I Love First Choice U.

Not every essay fits neatly into one of these categories, and we could have included many of them in more than one. Our intent is not to pigeonhole the essays, but merely to help you locate them more easily.

You'll note that some categories include more essays than others. Rather than solicit essays in various categories, we simply sought excellent ones and let the chips fall where they would. The results confirmed what we already knew: that some topics are more likely, on average, to yield excellent essays than others. We offer our thoughts about each category in brief introductions preceding the essays.

We would like to call special attention to category fifteen, the "why us?" essay. In today's competitive admissions climate, many colleges want to know why you are interested, and they may use the depth of that interest in their decisions about whether to admit you. Too many students spend hour upon hour on their main essays and then crank out the "why us?" essay without sufficient thought and relevant specifics.

We recommend browsing the essays in all of our categories for ideas that may prove useful when you begin your own writing. Even the best writers are influenced by the work of others, and the essays in this book provide a broad sample of excellent material from which to draw. Take note of the techniques and themes that resonate with you. Experiment with the literary structures you see in these pages using material from your own life.

Though we hate to mention it, the same rules that apply to plagiarism in the classroom also apply here. Don't even think about copying paragraphs, sentences, or even phrases from the essays in this book. In addition to being wrong, it is counterproductive to try to graft the details of someone else's life onto yours. A book like this is a particularly bad place to plagiarize because it has wide circulation. But even if you are tempted to grab an essay from a dark corner of the Internet, don't do it. Every year, candidates who are otherwise qualified are denied admission because of doubts about their essays, or because phrases in them match those in essays in a book or on the Internet.

With that, we turn you loose on our smorgasbord of essays. Enjoy!

Academics

Nothing is more impressive than an essay that shows deep mastery of an academic subject. We mean the sort of mastery in Essay 3, which combines creative analysis of a difficult poem, superb writing, and an anecdote demonstrating the student's contributions to class discussion. Colleges are primarily academic institutions that covet the rare student who will make a significant intellectual contribution. One other pointer about the scholarly essay: it helps to write with a sense of humor, or at least with a hint that you don't take yourself too seriously.

SPEAKING HIS LANGUAGE(S)

A well-chosen quote can be a great way to start an essay, and author Ilya Alex Blanter provides a brilliant example in the one below. The opening is light, the body is serious, and the conclusion reaches back deftly to the beginning. On the surface, the essay describes Ilya's passion for languages. But a closer look shows that he uses the languages to illustrate various facets of his life, from his background in Russia to working with kids from an underfunded school. Above all, the essay shows Ilya's rare passion for learning that surely made an impression on every admissions officer who read it.

Essay by Ilya Alex Blanter

> "I speak Spanish to God, Italian to women, French to men, and German to my horse."—Charles V

I don't speak German. Horseless, and with two cats that understand only Russian, I never had the need. Besides, languages don't fall into neat categories for me as they did for Charles. But they do have a place in my life, and recently I have come to better understand just how important a place it is. As this year's High Holidays approached, it came to me: on those days, I would be using five different languages.

I love such days. Enclosed on both ends by my native Russian—the language of my family—and founded upon my probably even more "native" English—the language of my friends and school—those days don't stop there. They take me through Latin at school and Hebrew at my temple, two languages with such different histories: one that went on to seed countless others and has now all but vanished, the other battered for two thousand years to near extinction and yet now the vibrant language of millions of people. Those days also feature my fairly recent and much cherished addition, Spanish, the language that lets me connect with people in a small Mexican town and in a San Diego marketplace.

Now I love those five-language days, but it has not always been that way. Years ago, even two languages seemed to be more than I could handle. Fluent in Russian at the age of two, thrown into an English-speaking world, I was confused and disoriented. How much I hated English, and a year later, when it had become my own, with what vengeance did I turn on my Russian! Only relentless and often painful pressure from my parents kept me truly bilingual through all those early years. At the time, I resented them and their demands; only later did I realize how much of a gift they had given me.

Languages are my passion and they are my life. It amazes me that, having grown up speaking English, just last summer I could still pass for a native in Russia, where I have not lived in over fifteen years. I am thrilled that I was able to study *The Aeneid* in its original text; deeply moved that I could read ancient Torah scrolls at my Bar Mitzvah,

> **I am thrilled that I was able to study *The Aeneid* in its original text.**

the first person in my family in at least three generations to do so; and excited that I was given a chance to use my Spanish to teach math, science, and drama in a volunteer program for kids from underfunded, understaffed, and often just neglected Oakland schools.

I have made the transition from resentment to love, and these days I dream about going for more. I don't know which language lies next on my path, and, luckily, I don't have to make that decision now. But I do know that this is the path I want to take—through college and beyond, into my career and into my future. Should I explore Italian or Portuguese? French or Catalan? Maybe even German? Well, in that case, I'd better start saving up for a horse.

Ilya Alex Blanter attended Princeton University.

A CLINIC ON HOW TO BE CONCISE

The ability to write to a word limit can be an important skill in college admissions, and author Annie Sykes offers a superb example with the following essay. The question is Princeton's and calls for a "brief essay of about 250 words." In a mere 254 words, Annie gives a real sense for her love of reading as she packs in specific references to a variety of books and authors. Her kicker to end the essay is particularly deft; Anna and Count Vronsky are characters from *Anna Karenina*, a Tolstoy novel generally considered superior to his more famous *War and Peace*.

Essay by Anne R. Sykes

What would you do if you were given a year to spend any way you wish?

If I could have an entire year to do anything I pleased, I would spend it indulging myself in every book that years of required reading have prevented.

I have a long history of sneaking my pleasure reading; as a ten-year-old, my parents often caught me awake long after bedtime with a flashlight and an *Anne of Green Gables* book. More recently, my mother, knowing my weakness, actually bribed me with a stack of books from her book-club list—one book for every college essay I finished. With a whole year to read the books I choose, I could finally be open about my "habit."

> My parents often caught me awake long after bedtime with a flashlight and an *Anne of Green Gables* book.

Reading provides me a way to learn and to escape. I can read *Reviving Ophelia* and learn about the development of adolescent girls, a subject that fascinates me. I can read *Anna Karenina* (which I've been trying to finish for the last three years) and be transported to 19th-century Russia. I can finally find out why my sister laughs out loud when she reads David Sedaris's latest collection of stories. It's thrilling to me that just by opening a book, I can visit a faraway place, learn something entirely new, or simply forget the details of my everyday life for an hour or so.

While I don't deny that I've gained much knowledge through the reading I've done in school, with a year off to read the books I want I could not only expand my mind further—I could finally find out what happens to Anna and Count Vronsky!

Anne R. Sykes attended Wake Forest University.

3

THINKING OUTSIDE THE URN

Not many seventeen-year-olds can truthfully say that they are passionate about any poem, let alone one like John Keats's "Ode on a Grecian Urn." Author Kate Flanagan shows her passion with delightful creativity. Notice her skillful rhythm in using dialogue to drive her story forward: she opens with a paragraph of description, then uses a quote; then another paragraph of description, then a quote. All of the italicized lines are from the poem, as well as "beauty is truth, truth beauty." Says Kate, "I edited this paper as I have all my English papers. I read it out loud a few times, wrote alternative beginnings and endings, and worked with the length. The hardest part of all these application essays for me was the length factor. I overwrite everything."

Essay by Kathleen Flanagan

What can you bring to the Rice community, in past experience, background, etc.?

Now I was at the front of the classroom, using what little artistic coordination I had to draw a great big figure on the board: yes, those had to be eyes, an L-shaped nose, wrinkled eyebrows, a gaping "O" for a mouth. I added little stress lines on either corner of the cheeks, just to show how intent my hastily composed figure was on examining this *Sylvan historian, who canst thus express a flowery tale more sweetly than our rhyme.*

I sat down tentatively.

"Kate," my English teacher said, "I asked that the class draw the images Keats evoked inside the Grecian Urn."

I examined the board carefully. Figures of centaurs and trees and altars and young lovers in the heat of the chase were contained within the vessel she'd sketched a few minutes earlier. My figure loomed to the right of the urn, eyes open, sort of worried-looking now that I thought about it.

The class was silent. I'd done it again. I had gotten…*too creative.*

"Well, Ms. Erskine," I started hesitantly, "how could this urn mean so much if no one was there to observe it, to remember the history behind the *'marble men and maidens overwrought,'* to imagine the *'burning forehead,'* the *'parching tongue'*? Who would be there to feel the woe, the *'old age that shall this generation waste'*?!"

Silence, still. On top of being too creative, I'd gotten all passionate about it. My honors English class was looking at me as if I had an urn tattooed on my forehead. I prepared myself to live through it this time, just like the other times I'd gone out on a limb and fallen flat on my face, while the teacher looked at me as blankly as the students.

But suddenly, Ms. Erskine beamed. "I was hoping someone would say that! The point of this poem is to measure not just art, but time and our own humanity…"

I had gotten lucky that day—my teacher understood me.

I have to agree with Keats that *"heard melodies are sweet, but those unheard are sweeter."* My ideas are often considered unconventional; because of that I have learned to be brave, and to stand up for the way I see things. I can usually make my case, whether anyone else gets it

> My honors English class was looking at me as if I had an urn tattooed on my forehead.

or not. I have a commanding voice and I ask to be taken seriously. And while it is sometimes hard to risk the pride I've gathered over seventeen years for a single opinion, I get a rush when I put myself out there.

I'm always up for a challenge—be it taking an AP Biology class to a semester abroad in England, to working hands-on with a cadaver at a university summer school. It's not that I don't get scared, but being afraid motivates me to accomplish my goals. I value passion, dedication, and the quest for knowledge. My perspective is international; I find the glass ceiling of language and culture barriers easily broken, especially if you refuse to see them. Perhaps my attitude can be attributed to growing up in the most diverse city in the country;

but I think it has more to do with having an open heart and big eyes.

So, if I dare to put myself in a nutshell:

I am in a *"mad pursuit"* to understand life and education and humanity in the world, believing that *"beauty is truth, truth beauty."* If you are loyal to one, you'll find both. Let me add that to the Rice community. Let me grab the moment, taste the adventure, and immerse myself in the environment of a university renowned with a love of knowledge and the pursuit of truth. I'll take on whatever burdens are necessary to keep this spark alive.

Kathleen Flanagan attended Rice University.

A PASSION FOR LATIN

Latin is the last subject that most students would choose for an essay—which is why it's a great topic. Author Andrew Rist is a true Latin junkie, and he makes a convincing case for the importance of Latin in his life. Though his national honors are impressive, Andrew's commitment to Latin while attending three different schools stands out even more. Says Andrew, "The only advice I would give people writing essays is to follow their passion. Otherwise your essay will be lifeless."

Essay by Andrew Rist

I can say with certainty that there is nothing that has more of a positive effect on my life than Latin. Of course other things have grabbed my interest over the years, like poetry, math, singing, and women, but my true passion is for the Classics. I never would have thought that a civilization that lived over two thousand years ago could have excited me, but I have learned that many of the problems and concerns of Classical society are still widely applicable to our modern society. For example, in Plato's *Republic*, Socrates seeks the true definition of justice. Just like Socrates, we could never actually put such an abstract idea into a few words, but we still seek simplicity, as Socrates did. In Classics I see the basis for the majority of Western Civilization, and I yearn to explore it further.

I stumbled into this odyssey of classical discovery that I now call my life in the seventh grade. My Latin teacher was unusually eager to urge students into participating in Latin Club. I admit that she forced me into it, but from the very first time I competed I never regretted it. In middle school, Latin filled the void in my mind that was begging me to care about something, anything, so I kept working at the Classics, hoping I could keep the void full.

After middle school, I faced the inevitable transition to high school. My transition was rocky. Austin High is a huge school where I knew only a few people. On top of my trouble fitting in at this impersonal school, I found that the Latin program at Austin High was weak. My teacher had other problems to deal with and most of my classmates were too high to care. I realized how truly blessed I had been at my middle school. I decided to take more of a leadership role in the Latin program than I had in middle school. Unlike my middle school, Austin High tended to send only two or three people to Latin conventions. I was in charge of making sure the three of us got where we had to be during conventions. My freshman year was also the first year I won a spot on the state-bound Certamen team, which became a nationals-bound Certamen team when we won out over teams from San Antonio and Houston at the State competition. In this game of buzzers that tested both thumb-speed and Classical knowledge, I excelled, and our team took Third Place at Nationals. It was at Nationals that I had a close look at the students of St. Andrew's Episcopal School. Due to necessity, I traveled to Kentucky with St. Andrew's for Nationals. It felt like I fit with them. They impressed me with how close all the students were, both with each other and with their teachers, including one that, like me, was new to their community.

> **The only advice I would give people writing essays is to follow their passion. Otherwise your essay will be lifeless.**

By the end of that summer I knew that I wanted more than anything to be a part of the St. Andrew's community. I toured the school, but even before that I think I was decided: if at all possible I wanted to go to St. Andrew's. Thanks to the efforts of my parents and the Latin teacher I enrolled at St. Andrew's for my sophomore year, and I have never looked back. As a result of this change I started working harder in every subject at school, thus my grades went up, even in courses that were more intellectually challenging than the ones I had previously taken at Austin High. I also improved in my favorite area. At the Texas State Junior Classical League convention I was shocked to find that I had been named Texas Latin Student of the Year for having the highest score on the decathlon, a test that tested a range of subjects related to Classical civilization, such as Latin grammar, mythology, history, and literature.

My junior year was even better. Although classes were even more difficult, nevertheless I enjoyed the challenge and continued to excel. In Latin, where some thought I had little room to improve, I continued to climb. Again, I was named Texas Latin Student of the year; I got a 5 on the Catullus–Ovid Latin Literature AP; but the achievement I am most proud of came during the summer at the National Latin Convention in Richmond, Virginia. Not only did my Certamen team win first place, taking home the Maureen O'Donnell Traveling Trophy, but I had the highest score on the national decathlon, which came not only with a $500 scholarship, but also the title of Best Latin Student in the Nation. My parents, Latin teachers, and friends could not have been more proud.

Rome may have fallen 1,500 years ago, but I cannot help but think that the Classics live on. People still want to know the meaning of justice and they often consult Plato in their search. I want to find the answers in Classics like so many before me. The Classics may not have been my first love, but they will be something that will stay with me forever.

Andrew Rist attended Harvard University.

HEARING VOICES IN THE LIBRARY

For admissions officers reading essay after long-winded essay, Caroline Fulford's taut meditation on the printed word was undoubtedly a godsend. In her world, books speak—literally. Her essay is at turns playful and reflective, but it consistently highlights her reverence for books. She uses precise vocabulary without cramming in big words. The last sentence of her first paragraph is a beauty, but of the thirty-four words in it, the two longest ones are "authors" and "touched." Powered by verbs like "whisper," "echo," "flow," and "flipped," the essay forges ahead without unnecessary adjective detours. The point of the title becomes clear only at the end—a subtle touch that helps maintain interest.

"This Is My Signature, This Is My Name" by Caroline Fulford

Call me eccentric, but I've always thought libraries are some of the noisiest places on earth. The patrons may be polite and scholarly as they go about their business, but the books themselves make quite a racket. They whisper and murmur on the shelves, promising adventure, knowledge, and the meaning of life to anyone perusing them. Their stories echo across time and space in the voices of their authors, the men and women who one day touched pen to paper and said to the world, "This is what I think."

Literature not only immortalizes the names of its authors, but their minds and hearts, in a way that no other art form can. When I open a book, the words I read flow from inside a person I have never met but can commune with, regardless of little things like death or distance. The author's thoughts exist in an eternal present, never to fade away like their mortal creator.

I remember the first time I saw my name in print. Under an amusing little poem I had written was typed my name, in small black letters with my graduation year. I flipped back to the Table of Contents page to see it again, listed alongside the works I had contributed. I smiled and blushed with pride. Granted, it was in a high school literary magazine, but the feeling was just as profound, I think, as if it had been in the *New York Times*. Even now, I look for

> **I've always thought libraries are some of the noisiest places on earth.**

that first issue in my school library and wonder if another girl, sometime in the future, will stumble upon my words and hear my voice, speaking to her from across time. My thoughts would gain new life in her, no matter how long it had been since I expressed them.

More permanent than a signature and more enduring than a headstone, literature allows the human heart and mind to express themselves and to forever nurture the hearts and minds of the future. To put one's thoughts on paper is to overcome death.

Caroline Fulford attended College of William and Mary.

Science and Science Fiction

T his pair of topics may be akin to lightning and the lightning bug, but at the core of both is a love of science and technology. Essays in this category do not lend themselves to extensive self-analysis, but instead succeed or fail with the author's creativity and analytical insight. In this section, we include a recollection of a week at astronomy camp (Essay 8), the story of a student who built his own robot (Essay 9), and two of the University of Chicago's far-out science-fiction topics (Essays 6 and 7).

6

BEAM ME DOWN, SCOTTY

The following is a run-of-the-mill University of Chicago essay. In other words, it's about as wacky and way-out as you can get. If you like this sort of thing, U of C could be for you. Author Nolan Frausto says that he picked this question because "it was the only one I couldn't think of an answer for." Go figure. So how should you approach an essay like this? The same way Nolan does. Make logical deductions, imagine, tell a yarn, and generally go for broke. Throwing in a reference or two to Euclid or Karamazov, as Nolan does, would be a nice touch.

Essay by Nolan Frausto

In a book entitled The Mind's I, *by Douglas Hofstadter, philosopher Daniel C. Dennett posed the following problem: Suppose you are an astronaut stranded on Mars whose spaceship has broken down beyond repair. In your disabled craft there is a Teleclone Mark IV teleporter that can swiftly and painlessly dismantle your body, producing a molecule-by-molecule blueprint to be beamed to Earth. There, a Teleclone receiver stocked with the requisite atoms will produce, from the beamed instructions, you—complete with all your memories, thoughts, feelings, and opinions. If you activate the Teleclone Mark IV, which astronaut are you—the one dismantled on Mars or the one produced from a blueprint on Earth? Suppose further that an improved Teleclone Mark V is developed that can obtain its blueprint without destroying the original. Are you then two astronauts at once? If not, which one are you?*

The brain: an almost indecipherable (at least to me) mass of neurons. Some extend an infinitesimal distance in the brain while others run through the length of the body. Each neuron is constantly sending and gathering tiny electrochemical signals which travel along a nerve axon, shooting along at incredible speeds towards its destination. The signal travels towards the nerve ending and spreads quickly through the thin, branch-like dendrites extending into other cells. The electrochemical signal interacts with the cell connected to the dendrites and cues a reaction from that cell. This happens in billions of neurons every second, spreading out from the brain and spine, each neuron interacting with certain cells to obtain or transmit information. This entire system of electrochemical signals provides an interaction that, in total, induces feelings, thoughts, and a perception of the physical world.

If the Teleclone Mark IV were to make a perfect copy of me, with my memories and feelings and brain all exactly the same, there would in fact be another me, yet would this clone actually be me? This question essentially becomes: Is there such a thing as a soul? Is there a defining characteristic that exists in a person and makes him indistinguishable and nonreplicable? Is there a part of someone that acts as a link between the spiritual world and the physical world and is the source of all consciousness, character, and quality in any specific creature? I don't believe there is. The human soul is the human brain. Each thought, feeling, and perception of reality stems from the billions of nerve impulses traveling through the billions of nerve axons throughout the brain. Thus, the defining characteristic is not the soul but the brain. As

> **If the Teleclone Mark IV were to kill me and create my clone simultaneously, would I technically be dead?**

Francis Crick stated in his *Astonishing Hypothesis*, "You, your joys and your sorrows, your memories and your ambitions, your sense of personal identity and free will, are in fact no more than the behavior of a vast assembly of nerve cells and their associated molecules." If this is true, then the clone made by the Teleclone Mark IV from my atomic blueprint would in all reality be me. This seems to be the only logical and scientific conclusion that can be made.

Yet even so, there is something wrong with this conclusion. There is some base human awareness that screams "that cannot be!" Something seems fundamentally wrong with this concept, and my initial reaction was to think, "Wait a second...the clone would not be me, I'm me!" I once read a science fiction series by Tad Williams called *The Otherland Series* that dealt with the same subject. In the book there was the ability to create a digital brain, which a person could transfer his memories into and thus live forever. The whole concept of digital immortality as suggested by the book didn't feel right. Though it makes logical sense, my brain (or soul?) refused to accept it. If the Teleclone Mark V were to make a clone of me and leave the original me still intact, I know I would not be the clone. Our perceptions of reality would immediately diverge, and we would cease to be each other at that instant. My perception would still be through my own eyes and brain, not that of the clone. I would still exist in a singular awareness and thus perceive reality as my own self. Yet if perception originates from the brain, and the clone and I both had atomically identical brains, then what would define what *my* perception would be? What quality would differentiate me from my clone? And moreover, if the Teleclone Mark IV were to kill me and create my clone simultaneously, would I technically be dead? Logically no, but somehow still yes. The original me would have lost perception. Or would have he…or I…or it? Though my original brain would have stopped functioning, my brain would still exist. Wouldn't it? Does that matter?! What is going on!?!? WHERE AM I?!?!?!

It is, all in all, a very confusing situation.

The whole question inevitably settles on the existence of a god: a subject that is so far beyond me that I don't even know where to begin. I have often wondered about the nature of existence and reality, and, even though I'm almost eighteen, I have reached no definite conclusions. As Ivan Karamazov once said (and I agree), "[there are mathematicians and philosophers who] even dare to dream that two parallel lines, which according to Euclid can never meet on earth, may meet somewhere in infinity. I have come to the conclusion that, since I can't understand even that, I can't expect to understand about God." I, likewise, can't expect to understand whether it is my brain, soul, or God that defines who I am. But even though I may not know the answer to the question, I do know who I am at this instant, and that no one else has the exact same memories, thoughts, and feelings that I do. While I still continue to seek answers, that thought gives me comfort while I do so.

Nolan Frausto attended the University of Chicago.

7

WHAT ARE WE MISSING? THE SHRIMP KNOWS

The following essay offers a different take on how to succeed with a far-out prompt. Instead of spending the whole essay inside an imaginary scenario, author Anna Hundert plays with the prompt for a paragraph, then exits the dream world to talk about herself for the balance of the essay before circling back to the prompt at the end. "It was supposedly a prompt about what shrimp see, but I made it an essay about how the study of language affects one's (specifically, my) perception of the world," notes Anna. Another nugget: she mulled over the question for three months before sitting down to write.

Essay by Anna Hundert

The mantis shrimp can perceive both polarized light and multispectral images; they have the most complex eyes in the animal kingdom. Human eyes have color receptors for three colors (red, green, and blue); the mantis shrimp has receptors for sixteen types of color, enabling them to see a spectrum far beyond the capacity of the human brain. What might they be able to see that we cannot? What are we missing?

I once asked a mantis shrimp this very question. I repeated it to him verbatim from the University of Chicago writing supplement, and after he recovered from the initial shock of learning that I had only three types of color receptors, he attempted to explain to me exactly what I was "missing." Although this particular mantis shrimp was bilingual, he eventually gave up on me, because there was no accurate way to describe in English the extended rainbow of the world around him. He concluded that our individual experiences of the world were fundamentally different and proceeded to scuttle away with an air of intellectual superiority.

If only the mantis shrimp had stayed for a while longer! I would have begged him to teach me his language, the language of the mantis shrimp, so that I might be able to experience what he experiences, if not see what he sees. Each time I learn a new word, any word in any language, the scope of my perception of the world around me broadens by some unquantifiable measure. Although my retina fails to gain new rods and cones from such an experience, I can "see" more. The new word seems to appear everywhere in the following days, and suddenly I cannot imagine the world without that word, just as the mantis shrimp cannot imagine a world where the visible spectrum is bookended by red and violet.

When I learned the word "melancholy" around the age of nine, it changed the way I perceived sorrow. Nothing about exterior reality was altered, yet my own experience was broadened. Suddenly there were different kinds of sadness. There was sad and then there was melancholy, and I could identify these differences in my own emotions and in those of others. Some might argue that the difference was already there and I simply could not articulate it, but within my personal reality, the difference only arose at the moment I learned the word for it, in the same way that one does not notice key changes in music until learning what a key signature is.

If only the mantis shrimp had stayed for a while longer!

When I go to college and beyond, I want to "see" the world. Of course I can achieve this goal in the obvious sense through travel. However, in order to truly see in the sense that the mantis shrimp sees, I know that I must pursue my dream through the study of language and words. Whether they belong to English, Latin, Greek, or the enigmatic vocabulary of the mantis shrimp, words allow my vision to transcend the traditional rainbow and experience a world rich with colorful ideas. Therefore, I do not envy the mantis shrimp his sixteen color receptors. What he can see looking up from the ocean floor could never compare to what I can see looking up from a really good book.

Anna Hundert attends Brown University.

8

BACK IN ASTRONOMY COUNTRY

For true scholars, an essay about your academic passion makes perfect sense. It helps if there is a hands-on element to it, as demonstrated in this essay about going to Astronomy Camp. Author Chris Limbach has the love, and he also has experiences in which he is an actor rather than merely an observer. With references to planetary nebula and the SSP-3 photometer, he establishes his credibility. But the clincher is his second theme. He is a scholar, but also a social animal who appreciates camaraderie in his quest. A scholar who delights in sharing with others is much more appealing than one who stays sequestered in the lab.

Essay by Chris Limbach

After a pleasant early morning flight I had finally reached my destination. As I stepped out of the plane and toward the arrival gate I caught a gust of hot, dry desert air. I knew I was back in astronomy country, where over 80 percent of the nights are clear and the Milky Way's frothy band arches majestically across the black sky abyss. Another magical week of learning under the star-laden sky awaited; my return to Astronomy Camp was long overdue.

Hosted by the University of Arizona and organized by Dr. Don McCarthy, the camp draws young astronomers from all over the United States, and many times from countries beyond. My first venture to the camp was in June of 2002, after I had just completed my freshman year. The camp had been a godsend, reinvigorating my desire to study astronomy and the universe. In 2004 I returned again, this time more knowledgeable, ready to delve into the research projects that are the heart of the experience.

Early in the week I met with a small group of campers, and together we proposed three different research projects to the counselors. One studied the majestic dance of two binary stars through photometry with an SSP-3 photometer. Another focused on the light curve of a far-flung asteroid. The third sought to analyze the behavior of beautiful yet mysterious "flyers" in planetary nebula through spectroscopy. Each of these projects was researched throughout the week. Data was gathered and analyzed, and conclusions were made and presented to the whole group. The thrill of doing research permeated my thoughts during the whole camp, and the investigative experience was thoroughly satisfying. Even this, however, was not all camp had to offer. A large part of its influence on my character lay elsewhere.

> **Astronomy isn't just about what's in the textbooks. It's about people, and it's about everyone's search for the truth in our universe.**

Daytime activities gave me the chance to bond with other campers, and I became good friends with many teens who were strangers only a few days before. The love of astronomy brought us together, and it was a great source of fun and excitement. We participated in many activities, including the construction of a scale model solar system and imaging the sun at the hydrogen alpha wavelength. We also cooked and cleaned for each other, and supported each other's research projects. Without the sense of community, the experience would not have been the same. A love for anything cannot be sustained without someone with whom to share it, and astronomy is no exception. It was my fellow campers who had the greatest impact on me during camp, and they are fantastic people I will never forget.

Astronomy isn't just about what's in the textbooks. It's about people, and it's about everyone's search for the truth in our universe. No matter what one's experience level, there's a universe waiting to be explored. Investigation through original research marks the foremost thrill of inquiry and discovery. Often, however, is it the people investigating with you that are the most interesting and important of all. Astronomy Camp taught me that.

Chris Limbach attended the University of Arizona.

9

BATTLE OF THE ROBOTS

Engineers are not known for writing brilliant college essays, but if all of them had topics as good as that of author David Wu, they might do better. The story of E2V2's epic battle against Chromedome is hard to top, but most students of a science/engineering bent can tell about a lab experiment in their past that went well or horribly wrong. The advantage of writing about a lab—or a robot battle—is that both provide a sequence of events that gives structure to the essay. In the case of David's essay, the robot battle leads naturally to a discussion of making the robot, and then to the significance of the project.

Essay by David Wu

"E2V2" was my own creation and I would drive it in BattleBotsIQ, a national robotics competition. I felt my body tense for the battle against the spinbot, Chromedome. Before the match, I had reviewed and decided my strategy against spinbots—attack it before it spins up and then keep hitting it. I believed the two-pound titanium plate mounted at the front of my robot should be able to absorb the shock from the hits. The match started; I drove E2V2 quickly to strike Chromedome before its spinning shell reached high speeds. E2V2's agility and unrelenting ramming soon partially disabled Chromedome's weapon and drive system. Subsequently, E2V2's vertical steel blades severed Chromedome's electrical wiring and caused it to start smoking; the opponent was totally immobilized. After forty-nine seconds of collisions, flying sparks, and strategic driving, E2V2 was declared the victor.

My peers and advisors nominated me to lead this extensive robotics project. Creating a BattleBot was daunting. However, I willingly accepted the responsibility to be the team leader. My team and I analyzed weaknesses in our previous robots, watched videos of matches, and built prototypes. After exploring many options and understanding scoring strategy, my team decided to make a wedge-shaped robot with a pair of vertical steel blades to inflict maximum damage on opponents. We would adopt aggressive driving strategies to deal with different types of opponents.

> **I drove E2V2 quickly to strike Chromedome before its spinning shell reached high speeds.**

Besides using engineering design programs like AutoDesk Inventor and AutoCAD, I learned to use Feature CAM to write manufacturing procedures. There were instances in which I had to modify programs because of the incompatibility between computer software. My advisor instructed me in the use of the CNC Milling Machine. It was fascinating to watch the various drills and bits convert my computer programs into components for E2V2.

After initial assembly, our robot didn't function properly. The team spent a lot of time troubleshooting and consulting with advisors. Gradually, we identified the problems and corrected them accordingly. For example, we changed the location of the antenna to enhance its reception of radio signals from the controller. The team constantly explored options to solve problems and adopted necessary changes while assembling the robot. Pride and excitement can only partially describe my emotions upon the completion of the robot that consumed so much of my time.

Eventually, E2V2 placed seventh out of seventy-two participants. At the closing ceremony, the robot's polished titanium armor and steel blades reflected the flashes from cameras that celebrated the success of E2V2. And, I was overjoyed.

David Wu attended the University of Michigan.

Hobby or Interest

Essays in this category tend to be whimsical or low-key, though they can still contain important lessons. Among others, the range of topics includes sailing (Essay 19), stamp collecting (Essay 10), and watching old movies (Essay 12). Interest or hobby essays tend to be more successful than those about athletics because the goal of participation is self-fulfillment rather than winning. Two of our authors (Essays 13 and 22) chose to divide their essays into chunks by describing a series of things they like—a good strategy if you are at a loss to find an overarching theme.

10

WHEN STAMP COLLECTING IS COOL

This essay is for every applicant who thinks that having a near death experience—or making a diving catch in the championship game—is a prerequisite to writing a great essay. Alex Callen takes a mundane hobby, stamp collecting, and makes it come alive with skillful use of personification in his opening. The fact that stamp collecting is offbeat and a little nerdy works to his advantage because he can show himself to be a person who follows his passions regardless of what others may think. Among the hundreds of newspaper editors and varsity team captains, a stamp collector stands out.

Essay by Alex Callen

When I was ten years old, I met Vince Lombardi. I saw him at the post office. He was sitting quietly with George Marshall and Humphrey Bogart. Vince cast a triumphant smile in my direction. His excitement was so contagious that I could not help smiling with him. Mr. Marshall, however, seemed to stare right through me. His solemn gaze conveyed little more than that he had very important things on his mind. Then I looked to Humphrey Bogart, who, with a suave movement, simply cocked his head to one side, and sat there, just looking good. The three men seemed nice enough, so I took them home with me. Yes, they had all been dead for many years, but I didn't really mind. In my room, armed with a pair of tongs, I gingerly slid each of them into the slots of homemade album pages, next to stamps of bright blue jays, waving flags, bursting flowers, a crooning Elvis Presley, and scores of others, which I had acquired over the past two years.

Philately caught my attention very early in my life. My grandfather hooked me with a stamp from the 1960s that commemorated the sesquicentennial of the Erie Canal. I was drawn to the small colorful pictures like a crow is drawn to shiny objects. I started saving every stamp that I could find. The hobby quickly developed into more than a haphazard accumulation of pretty paper labels. A closer examination of each stamp revealed new cultures, new languages, new people, new geography; new worlds, each competing to quench my inherent thirst for knowledge, steering my imagination to new heights.

As a group, stamp collectors have been categorically branded as wealthy, reclusive, boring, moldy old men. However, I've been an avid philatelist since age eight, and, as a seventeen-year-old in high school, I don't fit the stereotype very well. It is true that few young people collect stamps. Though I know some exist I've never met another stamp collector my age. More often than not, my peers express disapproval for the hobby. In fact, when I told a friend that this essay would be about stamp collecting, he laughed and said, "Man, you're going to have a tough time making *that* sound cool." I pointed to a pile of trading cards on his desk and replied, "Hey, at least I don't collect Magic cards." (Magic is a fantasy card game similar to the Pokemon game that swept the country a few years ago.) I understand how some could perceive the slow, tedious processes associated with stamp collecting, like sorting, classification, grading, and organization, as exercises in monotonous futility. I, for one, not only welcome the procedural structure of these processes, but also embrace the rare opportunity for uninterrupted solitude that accompanies them, using it to develop my patience and allow my imagination to lead me through exciting childhood realms of exploration and adventure—winning Super Bowls, rebuilding post-war Europe, making films—which are markedly absent from the high school experience.

When I was ten years old, I met Vince Lombardi. I saw him at the post office.

I don't think I will ever be able to make philately "sound cool," but at the same time, I don't feel like I need to. It's not about being "cool." I'm a philatelist, because stamp collecting gives me pleasure and peace of mind.

Alex Callen attended Cornell University (NY).

11

WHY DEBATE? FUNNY YOU SHOULD ASK...

After devoting countless hours to the activity of their choice, many students come up blank when asked why they find it meaningful. Author Christopher Childers has no such problem. In no particular order, he tells us that debate a) gives him a better understanding of his father, b) helps him develop deeper friendships, c) allows him to have substantive discussions that he would never otherwise have had, and d) lets him compete on an even playing field with others from all walks of life. How many diving catches or game-winning home runs ever opened the door to all that?

Essay by Christopher Childers

Of the activities, interests, and experiences listed on the previous page, which is the most meaningful to you, and why?

My coach always tells me that there is some reason why we, as debaters, can take four weeks out of our summer vacation, away from our friends and our families, to enclose ourselves in lecture halls and cramped dorm rooms to learn the depths and intricacies of debate. He has never told me what this reason is, but now that I'm beginning my senior year and I have attended three of these camps, I think I finally understand why. Debate, by definition, is simply a discussion over opposing viewpoints. So what makes it so interesting? What makes it meaningful? Simply, it acts as a forum and a gateway into realms of discussion you would never encounter otherwise. No other activity exists where individuals of any age, any ethnicity, any background, any height, weight, sex, or color can voice their opinions on an equal playing field.

Debate has also affected me in other ways; I can't tell you how many times I get in debates with my father over controversial topics such as abortion, gay marriage, stem cell research, etc. These conversations, although intense and oftentimes frustrating, allow me to understand the assumptions my father makes, and often they provide me insight into my father's adolescence. I can trace his beliefs back to their root causes, and this ability has allowed me to finally understand what makes my father

> **Debate acts as a retreat from the daily discussions of, "Dude, did you see my new Mercedes?"**

tick. Being able to argue with somebody over opposing viewpoints allows you to create amazing relationships, whether they are friendships or rivalries. I value my relationships inside the debate community as my strongest. Finally, I think debate emphasizes and improves the art of conversation; debate acts as a retreat from the daily discussions of, "Dude, did you see my new Mercedes?" and, "Oh my gosh, did you see *The O.C.* last night?" and it expands our communication into deeper, more thought-provoking interactions. So when somebody asks me, "Why do you go to debate camp?" I simply smile, shrug my shoulders, and talk, until they can hear no more.

Christopher Childers attended the University of California, San Diego.

12

IN THE MOVIES, SHE FINDS HER OWN STORY

If you're looking for an activity to get you into college, watching movies is not high on the list. Unless you can write like author Kayla Lawrence, who vividly conveys a love of old movies in the essay below. She does not so much write about movies as imagine herself in them, with prose chock full of specific references that convey the depth of her knowledge. Along the way, Lawrence shows her interest not just in the movies, but in the cultural context that surrounds them, from drugstore lunch counters to the music of the Roaring '20s. She ends her essay with feet propped on a recliner, but she has taken the reader on an odyssey through decades of history and art.

Essay by Kayla V. Lawrence

I have always wanted to waltz through the foyer of the New York Public Library in the arms of Fred Astaire while Glenn Miller gently plays "Moonlight Serenade" on the balcony above. I wish I could gaze upon the White Cliffs of Dover at the side of Irene Dunne. Sadly, time has passed me by, and the closest that I will ever get to the likes of Fred Astaire, Myrna Loy, and Tommy Dorsey is through the music and films that they have left behind.

I remember the humid summer when I first stumbled upon the Turner Classic Movies channel (TCM). *Titanic*, my first love, was playing on a late August afternoon. The film which had been my first venture into the realm of historical movies made me want to learn more about the ill-fated liner. And I did. I read books, did research, and attended exhibitions. From then on, I sought out more history in movies. It was fate that the *Titanic* led me to TCM.

After the ship had sunk and the credits rolled, the programming turned to an old black-and-white film. As a child of the technological age, I twisted my face and looked around for the remote to change the station. But, surprisingly, before I knew it, my mind was completely engrossed in my first black-and-white film, *Libeled Lady*. It was so different from any movie I had ever seen. The actors were there to share their love of acting with their audience and the characters sought happiness, truth, and fulfillment. They held each other close when they were happy, sad, and excited and cherished moments as if they were their last. From that day on, I was addicted to classic movies. I turned my back on Technicolor and began hunting for new films, and new faces. I met Spencer Tracy and Katherine Hepburn, Ida Lupino, Barbara Stanwyck, and Cary Grant. I learned their genre, their voices, their style. I gobbled up film after film, hungrily searching for fresh films in libraries, movie theatres, and video shops. Each new film forced me to dig further into history, searching for answers to the allusions that my youth denies me. I saw that a nickel-odeon was not always a children's television network, but a precursor to movie theatres and that a drug-store lunch meant more than some beef jerky, a bag of chips, and a soda, but a full sit-down meal at a lunch counter. I learned history, music, and culture as I flew down to Rio with Fred Astaire and went to war with Cary Grant. I watched big time war heroes return to main street America following the end of WWII in *The Best Years of Our Lives*, and the hopes for a brighter economic future in *The Gold Diggers of 1933*. I depleted my list of must-see classics and sought out more reels, more history. I'd wake up in the midst of the night to catch silent flicks that are not shown during the day, to catch a glimpse of Charlie Chaplin and Douglas Fairbanks, Sr. in films from the late teens. I shunned the moonless skies, and the warmth of my bed night after night to revel in the beauty of RKO and Metro-Goldwyn-Mayer. I love the elegant costumes that grace the screen, the innocence that is scarce in today's media. These films made me love history as if it were a part of my own past. I needed more of it in my life and sought to explore the music of the time.

> **I turned my back on Technicolor and began hunting for new films, and new faces.**

Each decade's crooners sing with a different style, a different pitch, a different purpose. When I want to return to my summer afternoon spent frolicking through a hilly field, with nothing around but trees, birds, and butterflies, I turn to Billy Murray's gay music of the teens. When my energy is seeping out of me and oozing onto the floor, I turn to the lively swing music of the twenties, to kick my heels up high and dance the Charleston like Ginger Rogers. When all I can see is the gentle lapping of the ocean in front of me, on a bright starry night, where all I want to do is spin slowly around a gazebo in the breezy night I turn to the soft melody of "Moonlight Serenade." On evenings when the television in the living room is free, my schoolwork is done, and my eyes still awake I climb into my jammies and perch myself in the La-Z-Boy chair, turning the audio down low so that each film is a secret being whispered in my ear. As the film plays on, I close my eyes and let time wash over me. I have watched life pass by as if I were born in 1910.

Kayla V. Lawrence attended Princeton University.

13

A FEW OF HIS FAVORITE THINGS

For students who want to take an unconventional approach, consider what we call the "list essay." Below is one variation, in which the author takes "seven wonders" and tells why they are meaningful to him. In the first of these, he finds meaning in something that is seemingly mundane, a lump of clay, and thereby shows his unique point of view. There is a danger here: choosing a trite subject, such as hugs or chocolate layer cake. Instead, go with something like calluses or dual-density midsoles and tell a meaningful story about yourself.

"Seven Wonders" by Christopher John Hallberg

Wedged Clay.

Most people think that clay is clay, that mud is mud. Well, as a matter of fact, this is simply not so. Wedged clay is rolled and twisted at a factory to remove air. This clay is much smoother and easier to work with than ordinary clay. It's the best invention since sliced bread for the potter. For myself, working with clay on a potter's wheel is one of the most meaningful uses of my time. When working with a wheel, the clay must remain centered at all times. This centering action takes an infinite amount of concentration. As I transform the clay into a usable bowl or cup, I am reminded of my ability as a human being. That is the ability to create, whether it be something as simple as creating an eating utensil or creating a new interest in a needy child.

Calluses.

Beginning guitar players are often limited to the length of time they can play by soreness of their fingertips. This is caused by the force needed to press an unfriendly steel string against the fret board. Eventually, the body adapts to the steel string by forming calluses on the fingertips of the left hand. These calluses are wonderful for two reasons. The first is the immediate result that the player can now play for extended periods of time. For me, music is a way to relieve stress. With a demanding schedule, it is necessary to relax occasionally. Music helps me remain focused. The second is that music has a way of moving people by speaking to our hearts. It's nearly impossible to hear songs such as Bob Dylan's "Like a Rolling Stone" and not feel moved. Music provides a universal connection among all people that is undeniable.

The Internet.

My father constantly reminds me how lucky I am to be growing up in this time. With the explosion of the Internet so much information has become instantaneously available. My worldview has increased dramatically as a result. Now it is possible to access first-hand accounts of many important events in the world. Global communication has been completely revolutionized. It is now possible to have an electronic pen pal in a third world country. We are all able to benefit from its ability to connect us as a people.

Furnaces.

To be able to come home every day after school in the bitter Wisconsin winters to a warm home is something that I take for granted. Every year as it gets colder I often think about those that do not have a warm place to go at night. It becomes very apparent that it is a blessing to have a heated home. It's nice to know that I can go to sleep at night and not have to worry about waking up in the middle of the night freezing. Furnaces in Wisconsin are wonderful.

Dual-Density Midsoles.

A small minority of the running population suffers from a collapsed arch in one or both feet. I happen to be a member of that cursed minority. My legendary days as a track and field star came to an abrupt halt in third grade as I rolled my ankle coming off of a hurdle. I became flat-footed from that day forward and it became extremely painful to run more than a hundred yards at a time. Then I was introduced to running shoes specially designed for people who need arch support. They are equipped with dual-density midsoles. I am now able to run for miles without any foot pain. I consider running so important because it helps give meaning to my life. When I am out pounding the pavement at six in the morning, I know that something special occurs in the repetitive motion of running. It causes me to reflect and gives me joy in knowing that I am accomplishing something even though it is as small as traveling a route that I have traveled many times before. Through reflection I discover what brings joy to my life and where I need to change and grow.

> **My legendary days as a track and field star came to an abrupt halt in third grade.**

Smiles.

These are such an important part of our everyday lives! Everyone knows that being greeted with a smile is mood altering. Imagine how powerful flexing a few additional facial muscles can be! The best part is that smiles are free and universally accepted. In any language a smile can be felt in the heart.

Star-Shaped Stickers.

In second grade our teacher, like many others, would place star-shaped stickers on the wall next to our names when we accomplished something notable. I feel blessed because as I grow I realize more everyday how thankful I am for the great education and motivation which has been given to me. I often wonder what life will be like after high school. At Marquette High School our spirits are nurtured with many opportunities for growth. I know that as I leave MUHS I can only hope that I will continue to be blessed by a Jesuit education at Marquette University.

Together all of these wonderful items reflect who I am as a whole person. The wonderful items all relate to being a better person for others. The clay, music, and running help me to better understand who I am and how I can help others more. The Internet and furnace help me to see how fortunate I am and how I can work to make others just as blessed. Finally, smiles and star-shaped stickers, how could we live without them?

Christopher John Hallberg attended Marquette University.

14

A MAGICIAN CONJURES AN ESSAY

Author Evan Fenner wrote his first college essay about something BIG—a brain injury. After laboring for a month and a half with that, "I decided to sit down for an hour and write about something that you really couldn't know me without knowing. Magic." He made a mind-map of ideas connected by lines and began to write. "At the end of the hour, I had something I was almost as happy with as my first essay!" he recalls. Neat trick. What was the secret? "It was easier to write about something that I was truly passionate about."

Essay by Evan Fenner

Some students have a background or story that is so central to their identity that they believe their application would be incomplete without it. If this sounds like you, then please share your story.

The first magic trick I remember was something really simple. My uncle made a coin disappear and reappear behind my ear. It's a classic trick. He made a silk scarf disappear too. Simple things, but when I saw them I was amazed. First I asked, "How did you do that?" which was closely followed by, "*How did you do that??*" And then I became a student of magic.

I have always liked to know how things worked. I love taking things apart to see their inner workings even if I'm just going to put them back together again. With magic, it was completely different. Magic wasn't something I could take apart; it was something I had to learn and practice. When I was about seven years old, I bought a magic kit out of a catalog. They were easy tricks, but I learned the values of practice and keeping the secrets. After all, what is the point of knowing the secret if everyone else does too? After a while things started to get more serious. Magic transformed from an interest into a hobby into a passion, and in the process it transformed me too.

When I was little, I wasn't great at social interactions. I had my small group of friends, but beyond that I wasn't really good with people. Magic changed that for me. It taught me several critical skills. First, it gave me an icebreaker. It is often awkward to meet new people, but with magic, I had a new tool in my arsenal. I could open up with a magic trick and instantly lighten the atmosphere. People start to let their guard down and allow themselves to be more social. The second skill it gave me was confidence. A magic trick is not that different from a con game; some magicians even use derivatives of con games in their magical repertoires like the cups and balls or the three card monte. The con in "con game" stands for confidence. The performer has to believe that their trick will work or else the audience won't fall for it. The performer has to take risks and trust that things will work out. So I learned how; with each performance something could go wrong, but even if something did, if I recovered from it, the audience never had to know. That was how I learned my third skill: improvisation. The magician is always one step ahead. If something didn't go according to plan, I would have to skip a step to keep myself ahead and that meant staying on my toes. This, of course, is one of the primary skills of acting. In fact, in the words of the great magician Robert-Houdin, "the conjurer is an actor playing the part of a magician." I later became an actor in my own right, but my magic was certainly a gateway to it.

The skills of magic have been a great resource but they are not the reason I do magic, they are a happy by-product. I do magic for the reactions. I love to see people's faces light up when I show them a new effect, to see the wonder in their eyes. When they ask "how?" the same way that I did when I was little, it brings me back to the joy and wonder that I had then. People want to suspend their disbelief, to get wrapped up in the world of a story where magic exists. But then they ask for the secret. What they want to know is how the trick works. What they don't know is that the real secret of magic is that it does exist. It exists in the mind. For that brief moment before you think that it can't be possible, it is as real as anything else that you know to be true. *That* is where the real magic is.

The con in "con game" stands for confidence.

Evan Fenner attends Pomona College.

15

THE SHOES MAKE THE ESSAY

It's the simple stuff that makes a great essay. If you run out of ideas, try spinning a few stories out of the shoes in your closet. With each different shoe she describes, author Amanda Lewis reveals a different facet of her personality. On one level, the essay functions as an engaging way of telling about each of her extracurricular activities. But Amanda also demonstrates her ability to make creative analogies, and that she has an eye for detail in her closet and in her life.

Essay by Amanda Lewis

Don't you just hate those days where you find the perfect outfit, but don't have the right pair of shoes to complete the look? For me, deciding what shoes to sport depends upon which facet of my personality I wish to reveal or activity I'm about to partake in. Each day I face a dilemma—do I show the flashy, fun side or the conservative, chic side? When viewed compositely my eclectic shoe collection seems to create a convoluted image; but in reality they each represent an important component of my character. In order to better understand me, you have to simply look through my shoes. For instance, my saddle oxfords are not in the closet because I think they're stylish; no, they're here because they are a mandatory article of my school uniform. However, certain aspects of the shoes reveal much about my identity. As a student at Saint Mary's Hall becomes a senior, they experience the tradition of receiving their blue ties. This blue color represents the leadership and importance of being a senior, and therefore I wear this badge of leadership and connection to historical tradition in the form of my blue shoelaces. Other interesting shoes are my cowboy boots, since, of course, every Texan must own a pair of cowboy boots! These reflect the rugged nature of my personality, one that isn't afraid of ranch work or attending country dances with my friends. This infuses southern flavor and shows yet another dimensional and integral part of my persona.

Extracurricular activities, readily apparent in my volleyball shoes and dance shoes, also play a large part in my character. The scuffed volleyball shoes look worn from seasons of use and reflect my ongoing passion for the sport, which I've played since I was five. My variety of dance shoes reflects the different dances I've done—ballet, jazz, Flamenco, Irish. Ever

> **My pumps and complicated strap shoes show the vivacious girl who enjoys mingling and socializing.**

since beginning to dance in order to entertain my family at the age of three, dancing has become an important and defining trait of my identity, as can be seen by my collection of dance shoes. The final important part of my character is the fun and exciting side that appears during the weekends. My pumps and complicated strap shoes show the vivacious girl who enjoys mingling and socializing. Serving as a stark contrast to the flashy footwear, my clogs depict a person who enjoys comfort. Much of my time is spent in them, testament to my personality—despite having a busy and engaging life in many different ways I always find time to relax and enjoy life! A typical day progresses as I put on the saddle oxfords for school, changing into the dance shoes for dance during the day, prepare for volleyball practice with athletic shoes, and finally returning home to embrace the comfortable confines of my clogs. As you can see I utilize many of these shoes on a daily basis as I partake in different activities and show a variety of aspects of my personality.

Amanda Lewis attended Johns Hopkins University.

16

"BOOKS SMELL LIKE KNOWLEDGE AND COMFORT"

To find her topic for the following prompt from the University of Virginia writing supplement, author Emma Steele asked her family at dinner to identify her quirks. She began writing about a month before the supplement was due. Her preferred method, which she recommends to others, is to do a first draft without thinking about the word count, then cutting as necessary on the second. "Ignoring the word count allowed me to get all of my thoughts down. Going back and cutting out words helped me realize the important parts of my essay that I couldn't scrap," she recalls.

Essay by Emma Steele

We are a community with quirks, both in language (we'll welcome you to Grounds, not campus) and in traditions. Describe one of your quirks and why it is part of who you are (roughly 250 words).

When our family travels, my suitcase is always the heaviest, not because I pack multiple pairs of shoes, but because I bring physical books, not digital copies. This is my quirk: I don't read books electronically. There's something satisfying about turning pages, seeing the progress I've made and how much I still have to learn. Books smell like knowledge and comfort, a smell that has always been a part of my life: one no fancy gadget can duplicate.

My passion for physical books is contradictory to the digital person I am in all other aspects of my life. I have never visited a bank; I do my finances online. I have never used a card catalogue to look up information; I rely on the Internet for research. My aversion to electronic literature is not a resistance to conformity, but a pull to sentimentality. My childhood was shaped by lugging books to and from the library, teeming with the excitement of cracking open a new world. Though it was impossible to encounter talking bears, "mad" tea parties, and a wizard with a lightning-bolt scar all in the same day, with the flip of a page, anything was possible. When I finished an adventure, I would walk to the bookshelf and tuck the worn copy into its place, giving myself a sense of closure that cannot be done with an electronic reader. Even now, the endless number of pages turned, knowledge learned, and books returned remains an important part of my life.

> **My aversion to electronic literature is not a resistance to conformity, but a pull to sentimentality.**

Emma Steele attends University of Virginia.

17

A LIFE IN LETTERS

Just as a preference for bound books is noteworthy in the digital age (Essay 16), so too is a fondness for the old-fashioned art of letter-writing. Author Francie Neukom eloquently conveys her love of handwritten communication as she describes her interactions with various pen pals. Says Francie, "My friends would always laugh at me for preferring old-fashioned snail mail to the phone. They rolled their eyes when I said I was writing a college essay about it. However, I knew that my true self would shine through if I wrote about something I was head-over-heels in love with, and writing letters is one of those things. Sometimes the things that make us dorky or weird are the exact qualities that will make us stand out from a pile of fifteen thousand other application essays."

Essay by Frances Patricia Neukom

My mom is already telling me that I will have to clean out my room and throw away most of what fills my desk drawers. I am a very sentimental person and keep large quantities of what friends have given me over the years, so it will be hard for me to decide what to discard. The one thing I will never throw away, though, is my letters.

I first began seriously writing letters when I was in fifth grade and found my first pen pal, a cheery girl named Cate from Virginia. We were referred to each other through a magazine and began avidly writing. Cate was not much like me, as she loved horses and hiking while I preferred dogs and writing. Our geographic differences amused us—she couldn't believe I'd never seen a snow storm and I was perplexed when she started playing lacrosse, a sport seldom heard of on the West Coast. But we learned about each other through our letters and I grew close to her—this girl I'd never met who lived three thousand miles away.

She was followed by many others: a girl who lived in West

Virginia, another Kate but spelled with a K, who wrote me a letter when she read a story I'd published in a kids' magazine; an elderly lady I knew from Kentucky, Ginny; an old friend from camp, Georgina. I wrote to Frances (named after me), the daughter of a Welsh pen pal my mom had when *she* was my age. I even began writing to a girl who left my school in eighth grade and lived right over my back fence. Although I saw Sarah occasionally, the way we described our unfolding high school experiences to each other was through our letters. She described her public high school events, like making Homecoming floats, while I told her of my small-school happenings, like the annual lip sync. In my letters, I expressed more and more of myself, igniting my lifelong love of writing. My letters were always keys to self-discovery—I learned who I was through those scribbled sheets. And I kept almost all of my pen pals' letters.

In this world of word-processing computers and instantaneous e-mails, letter writing seems a bit quaint to most people, an activity of yesteryear. But I never see it that way. I have always told everyone I can write much better than I can speak. Sometimes when I need to discuss a serious subject with a friend, I find it easier just to sit down and write a letter. With a letter, you have time to reflect on the issue at hand, mull over the precise words to use, and eliminate the constant need to keep the conversation going. Letters are permanent things—they don't vanish into the air like the spoken word. If someone pays you a compliment in a letter, you can save it for when you need it.

I don't type letters. As much as I love computers for their many advantages, typing seems so impersonal. Everyone uses Times or Helvetica to aid the reader in legibility. But letters don't need to have every word be understood—they speak for themselves. You can tell more about someone by their handwriting than printed papers. For instance, my Welsh pen pal would always adorn her curvy handwriting with doodles in the margins, something you couldn't do on a computer. Besides, question marks and exclamation points are so much more effective in handwritten form.

My friends would always laugh at me for preferring old-fashioned snail mail to the phone.

My letter-writing ability has carried over into other aspects of my life. At the end of the year, everyone wants me to sign their yearbook, for I am able to recount the private jokes I've shared with my classmates better than most. People are delighted to receive my postcards, even when I have spent only a weekend in Lake Tahoe, because I don't waste space telling them the lake is beautiful and wishing they were there. One time I got an eleven out of ten on an assignment from a particularly demanding teacher because the assignment was to write a letter from someone else's point of view.

I have lost pen pals over the years. Cate didn't write me for a while and then wrote back recently, describing in detail how she'd gotten drunk at a Creed concert. I felt as if she had become a different person than the girl I grew to know through letters and didn't write back. The elderly lady died a few months ago, and I still cry when I come across cat note cards of hers, filled with her distinctive cursive handwriting. My Welsh pen pal had family problems and never wrote back, no matter how many letters I sent her, pleading for a response, even a short one. (Her mom even stopped writing to my mom.) But I've kept a lot of them, and added some new ones. I am dreading next year a bit, considering how many friends I will want to write long letters to, even though most of them will probably send me only mass e-mails. But I know I will never join their ranks, for letters have allowed me to discover more about myself and other people than any activity ever has. My letters I could never throw away.

Frances Patricia Neukom attended Stanford University.

18

"MAMMON MAY BE IN LEAGUE WITH THE YANKEES"

Author Evan Brooker is not the first writer to make a morality tale out of the Boston Red Sox and the New York Yankees, but he manages to provide a fresh take on this baseball blood feud. With tongue firmly in cheek, he describes the travails of being a Red Sox fan in Yankee country. The essay soars highest in the third paragraph, in which he segues from baseball to delicacies such as Linguica sausage and "heaping plates of Jagacito." It is a measure of his skill as a writer that he can turn baseball into a metaphor for so many facets of life.

"Red in a Blue State" by Evan Brooker

Slammed into lockers without warning for years. Verbally assaulted from Manhattan to Madrid. The constant object of unadulterated hate and derision most of my life. No matter: it has been worth the burden. A product of a mixed marriage, I should be "mauve," less red at least. But I am stolid in my defense of red principle, merit, and tradition. Go Red Sox!

I was born in Manhattan and raised all my life four train stops northeast of Grand Central. So why am I a Red Sox fan? Was it truly worth taking the abuse and being on the "outside" for so many years? What drew me to the Sox, on reflection, was a sense of place and pride, the paying of homage to family that left blood on Brookline High's football field, built bits of Boston, and served the people of New Bedford, Massachusetts—my grandmother's rough cut hometown. I learned in conversation with my grandparents that Fenway Park was a refuge from tough times. How superior Boston was to New York intellectually, physically, and morally. How the Red Sox were to the Yankees as Athens was to Rome. That Mammon may be in league with the Yankees, but the powers on high surely bless the

Red Sox. So, yeah, it's been worth it. You develop a great sense of self and satisfaction through the ability to stake an early claim in the world, defend a belief, and "to thine own self be true."

Game for game, over the last sixty-four years at least, the Bosox have consistently taken our breath away with the quality of their play. Yet, the Red Sox are, for me, as much about baseball as about pilgrimages to trace family trajectories and view personal monuments. The "Sawx" are walks on Beacon Hill, or consuming—during the Portuguese "Feast of the Blessed Sacrament" in New Bedford—succulent, over-sized chunks of grilled beef "Espetada"; links of thick, greasy Linguica sausage whose orange-red color somehow adds to its rich, gamey flavor; and heaping plates of Jagacito—humble rice and beans made sophisticated through now forgotten empire. The Red Sox are my proxy for exploring memories, touching history, and appreciating a great cultural mix.

> **The Red Sox are my proxy for exploring memories, touching history, and appreciating a great cultural mix.**

I am not obligated to hate the Yankees because I have a connection to Massachusetts. I understand what a privilege it is to grow up in New York. My focus on Massachusetts and the Sox closed the physical distance between me and my father's family. Baseball fandom, like citizenship, is about so much more than loyalty to a locale. Baseball fans are passionate but only occasional idiots. They are thinkers, strategists, and usually in control of themselves. This is how I see myself—and my fellow citizens. I used to get a kick out of the insanely foul-mouthed, belligerent, and unpredictable passion of Boston fans. Until I realized I was confusing passion with loutishness. Yankees fans, in turn, know how to reciprocate any and all antagonisms along the Red/Blue divide. These days, I would rather just enjoy nine innings without the burden of hard feelings.

The interaction of too many Red Sox and Yankee fans reminds me of current political discourse in the United States. We're forgetting anew the rules of the game, how good the game has been to us and why we play it. Every team and locality is entitled to pride of place, history, and tradition. Think St. Louis, Cincinnati's "Big

Red Machine" and today's Tampa Bay. No locale should be so self-absorbed or selfish that they forget to respect other's abilities, contributions, and the good of the game. I will study political science and economics in college, with the intention of eventually entering the public arena, or at least its policy debates. When I do, I will remember the lessons I learned as a Red Sox fan, when I merged passion, self-discovery, civility, and higher truths into a better understanding of my world.

Evan Brooker attended Johns Hopkins University.

19

A SAILOR SURVEYS THE HORIZON

A lot of overworked metaphors make the rounds in college essays—as in "I realized that the big game symbolized my quest for meaning in life"—but such essays can be good when they are done right. Author Christopher Pirrung masterfully explains his love of sailing—and convinces the reader that it is a pretty good metaphor for his life. He understands the importance of using terms like "outhaul," "boom-vang," and "jibe-turn" even if most readers won't know what they mean. Notice, as well, the graceful way in which he weaves in comparisons of sailing to charting a path in life. He doesn't belabor the metaphor at the beginning. Instead, he makes a brief reference to it in the third paragraph, subtly setting the stage for more extended reflections in the last paragraph.

Essay by Christopher M. Pirrung

Leaning backward in my one-man laser, I hike out hard in an attempt to keep the sailboat from capsizing, the tiller clutched hard in my left hand and the main sheet sliding through my right. These strong thermal winds are exciting yet challenging. I have been waiting for them for some time. As I leave the protected harbor and venture out into the bay, the swells grow and the horizon appears. Sailors know that Little Traverse Bay is one of Lake Michigan's best protected harbors, yet the horizon to the west gives the impression of vastness equal only to an ocean.

The race is about to begin as I try to assess the wind shifts and puffs. Everyone has the same boat and most racers are equally experienced; the key to winning resides in tactics. The right side of the course appears better because of the ten-degree wind lifts, but the windward mark is slightly to the left. What is the shortest course? Which side does the wind favor? There are a thousand options. I must tighten the outhaul, downhaul, and boom-vang to change the sail shape to de-power up the sail; the winds are strong today. So many variables make small-boat racing the most exciting and rewarding challenge.

Just like a sailor, I am at the real beginning of my life. Decisions I make now will affect who I shall become. Although slightly jittery, I must go forth with confidence and hope. On that race day, the wind favored the right side so I head out on port tack. Before long I noticed the wind shift left and I took the lead. Feeling proud of my successful tactics, I am the first to round the windward mark. Downwind, however, is anybody's game. You never know what a wind puff will bring. The left looked windy, so I pointed the bow slightly left. I caught a puff and enjoyed the ride for some time but when the puff died, I decided to jibe-turn the boat suddenly and unstably. The race makes me think of the infinite variables I face at this time. Sometimes I become passionate about my physics class and decide to dedicate my life to the study of hydrodynamics and naval architecture. Not long after, however, I may meet a prominent man and become inspired to be an entrepreneur.

Feeling proud of my successful tactics, I am the first to round the windward mark.

Sailing is a metaphor for my life right now because there are so many variables and paths to take, each of which can produce successful results. So many options lie at the beginning of a race, yet a sailor who initially heads right may cross the line within seconds of a racer who headed left. There is no correct path to take, just knowledge mixed with gut feeling. I may catch a puff and head right, but as the puff dies I must decide to push forward or tack. Once you start a race each decision affects your place but one thing is for sure: you can't finish a race on one tack only. Small-boat racing is a process of intellectual exploration where knowledge and curiosity lead you; a university should be no different.

Christopher M. Pirrung attended the University of Virginia.

20

BART, MTC, AND ME

When a student is passionate about an interest, and has taken the initiative to pursue that interest, an essay can almost write itself. Author Chris Ramirez is an excellent writer, but he merely needs to describe what he has done to learn about, and work on, issues related to public transportation. How many high school students attend public hearings or participate in conferences dealing with long-term transportation goals? Chris is already a functioning professional in his field of interest, which gives him all the fodder he needs for the ultimate "show, don't tell" essay.

Essay by Chris Ramirez

It was a thrill to land my dream job this summer as an intern with the Metropolitan Transportation Commission. As long as I can remember, I have been fascinated with everything associated with transportation. My commute to high school on the Bay Area Rapid Transit System (BART) and the city bus system puts me on the front lines as a user of public transit. This daily use has increased my awareness of how transit systems work and the impact transit policy decisions have on people. Last year in Journalism, my concern prompted me to interview other student commuters and write an editorial for the school newspaper on how proposed reductions in transit services would affect our own school community. I also wrote an English essay in support of equality in policymaking and environmental justice when allocating access to public transportation services.

Outside of school, I have been a member of several transit advocacy groups consisting of people from all walks of life. I have attended multiple public hearings and participated in the Transportation 2030 Conference, which set transportation goals for the nine-county San Francisco Bay Area for the next twenty-five years. Because of my involvement, I was featured in the Metropolitan Transportation Commission's annual report. Although it was exciting to see my photo on the cover, more importantly, this experience led to my summer internship at the regional planning agency.

At MTC headquarters my assignment placed me in the Legislation and Public Affairs Department working primarily on the awards program, honoring people and projects that have helped to make transportation more efficient. I solicited nominations, wrote summaries for the awards jury, and coordinated the many video shoots for the film featuring award winners. Working with the nominees and hearing their personal stories gave me a first-hand view of their perceptions on current transportation issues as well as visions for the future. At the same time, I served as an intern with BART in the Amtrak Capitol Corridor Management Section. My position enabled me to gain marketing experience working on their "Kids Ride Free" and "Capitol Corridor Month on BART" promotions. Both internship positions provided a great opportunity to work with transportation professionals. Instead of looking from the outside in, as a transit user, I saw the process from the inside out. I learned that operations and management solutions are more complex than fixing one immediate problem, and that one must consider the ramifications the solutions have in the broader context. My internship allowed me to attend meetings with commissioners, write articles for the agency newsletters, and observe policy decisions being made. This experience convinced me that a career in a transportation-related field is something I want to pursue.

To help make this dream into a reality, I intend to major in Urban Studies or Public Policy with an emphasis in transportation. Transportation issues encompass environmental, political, socio-economic, legal, and economic concerns. I plan on taking courses in these areas as well as researching successful transit systems in other countries. Gaining this broader perspective will be important to my

> **I served as an intern with BART in the Amtrak Capitol Corridor Management Section.**

understanding of how mass transit can improve our lives by reducing congestion and improving air quality.

The "smart growth" concept that is currently gaining attention interests me. The idea is to create "transit villages" that will provide a variety of housing options and services within walking distance of public transportation. I feel this is a critical time to make good and equitable transportation decisions and believe the University of California, with its wide range of focused disciplines and commitment to quality education, will provide me with the knowledge necessary to participate in making those decisions. I am excited to be a part of the future transportation planning challenges.

Chris Ramirez attended the University of California, Davis.

21

TAKING CARE OF HIS BABY (WITH WAX AND A POLISHER)

Author Pavel Sotskov has written what is known as a process essay. In his explanation of how he cleans and waxes his car, Pavel shows logic, dedication, and attention to detail. Process essays naturally lend themselves to specifics, and Pavel gives us plenty. For instance, we learn that he washes the top of the car first because the water will flow down and loosen the dirt on the lower parts. A little compulsive? Perhaps. But anybody who devotes this much thought and effort to a car will probably excel in other areas, too.

"How I Use the Orbital Polisher" by Pavel A. Sotskov

Every Sunday morning until the weather drops below freezing and my parents do not let me use the hose, I wash my car. This may seem like an ordinary job to some, but to me washing a car requires a distinctive technique.

No matter how tired I am, every Sunday morning I wake up, brush my teeth, put on my blue sweatpants and red sweatshirt, grab the keys to the car, and head out into the driveway. Not even the puppy follows me outside; he likes to sleep till eleven o'clock on Sundays. I pull the car out into the driveway and position it just right so that the morning sun is blocked by the thick leaves and branches of the tall maple, and so I can easily walk around the back end.

I then attach the longest hose I can find in the basement of my house to the water spigot, and fill my large gray bucket with just enough soap that when agitated by the pressure from the hose the mixture I am left with is half a bucket of water and half of foam. I let the multicolored sponges soak for two or three minutes. Each sponge is used for a specific task: the yellow for the car body, the red for the wheels and tires, and the orange for cleaning the squashed bugs off the bumper. When the sponges are properly saturated I use the hose to soak the car and begin washing. Contrary to what my parents believe, there is a specific order of washing that must be kept in order to achieve the best quality wash. First, I wash the roof, then the hood, trunk, and only afterwards do I scrub the doors, bumpers, and finally the wheels. In this order the soapy water flows off the top of the car and loosens the dirt on the lower parts, which are then easier to wash.

> **Not even the puppy follows me outside; he likes to sleep till eleven o'clock on Sundays.**

After everything is washed and rinsed I dry the car off using a white towel to make sure I have not missed any dirty spots which would rub off onto the bleached towel. At this point, the sun is already higher in the sky, so I move the car forward to escape direct rays which warm the paint.

When the car is completely dry I begin to apply the wax again, starting from the roof and working down towards the bottom of the car. The wax dries in two minutes, which gives me just enough time to wax the car if my arm is working at close to the speed of sound. Normally, it takes me a bit longer than that to wax the whole car, so I finish with the waxing in closer to fifteen minutes. I use the orbital polisher to polish the hood, roof, and trunk, while the rest I do by hand, as the polisher does not do a good enough job on curved surfaces. After polishing, I buff the whole car by hand until the paint sparkles, the wheels shine, and the tires look wet.

I vacuum the interior, and clean all the map pockets which accumulate fascinating rubbish throughout the week. I rub lotion into the dashboard to protect it from the sun and I wash the windows where my puppy has mashed his wet nose while riding on the seat.

I keep this precision and order every Sunday.

Pavel A. Sotskov attended Dartmouth College.

22

LIFE AS A MESSY DESK

If you can't figure out one angle from which to describe yourself, try three. Or twelve. That's what author Christina Xu does in this essay, which surveys various items on her desk. The fact that she is of Asian descent allows her to explore the relationship of typical American items to those of the East, and thereby delve into her dual identity. She also manages to touch on her interest in philosophy, science, art, and music, with specifics about each that bolster her credibility. Says Christina, "I rewrote this essay probably twenty or more times—an entire month's worth of second-period study halls was spent in my history teacher's office, discussing this essay and how to improve it."

Essay by Christina Xu

Display dagger. Teddy bear. Cheesecake.

I love cheesecake. In fact, a slice of this delicious dessert is on my desk right now, impaled by a pair of chopsticks. These odd juxtapositions of East and West occur frequently at my house; my mother puts peanut butter into her moon cakes, and my dad uses the coffee maker to boil chrysanthemum tea. My two halves, however, have created a greater whole. I am able to think in both Eastern and Western terms, and I am comfortable with the philosophies of Plato and Lao Tzu alike, though I do admit to dicey moments in *The Republic* and the *Tao te Ching*. Raised in two cultures, I am able to connect to many others. I can be at home at a football game, a Chinese karaoke party, a Japanese tea ceremony, or a French soirée. I am capable of shoveling snow with Buddha.

Jade necklace. Post-it notes. *School of Athens.*

On the other side of my desk lies a copy of *A Brief History of Time*. When I was younger, my room was littered not with dolls, but with books about every topic. I idolized the versatile Leonardo Da

Vinci, who seemed capable of everything. As I've grown older, I've sometimes felt like a penniless artist forced to meet the expectations of a patron rather than work for my own interests and needs. It is difficult to emulate Da Vinci in a society that emphasizes specialization. Artistic creativity, however, is not a thing to be controlled and confined—and neither is my mind.

Dancing vampire doll. *Rush Hour*. Army Men.

Last summer, I went to an astronomy camp in the hills of North Carolina, even though it had no significant "practical value." There, I saw the Milky Way for the first time. While listening to a professor point out constellations with familiar names and alien shapes, I marveled anew at the joy of learning for its own sake, with no agenda and no assessment. When I am asked about what I want to do with my life by friends, parents, and college applications, I imagine Da Vinci tinkering with this invention, sketching out that painting, examining yet another plant; choosing a major probably would have driven him insane. I may have been born six centuries too late, but no career can possibly define who I am. I will be the business major who can solder a circuit and paint portraits, the engineer who can recite British poetry and speak in five languages, the artist who knows calculus and can break two boards at once. I will be a Renaissance woman.

> I rewrote this essay probably twenty or more times—an entire month's worth of second-period study halls was spent in my history teacher's office.

Newton's thermometer. Sheet music. CD spool with two discs remaining.

"We Didn't Start the Fire" is a work of genius—each line corresponds to a year of Billy Joel's life, and the major events of each year are organized with rhythm and rhyme. A good songwriter like Joel weaves together all the disparate tones, beats, and lyrics of the song into a melody that organizes but does not constrain. As I look through my CD collection, full of the delicately beautiful strains of Prokofiev and the head-banging bass beats of Rammstein, I am reminded that my life, too, must have a melody to keep it valid. Each of my tunes is a singular cacophony, but united they make great harmony. I am composed of many passions, many faces, many reflections, and the Tao teaches me to let my different parts go their own way. I am neither yin nor yang. I will simply stay in the center of the circle and direct the symphony.

Sheets of white paper. Keyboard. Me.

Christina Xu attended Harvard University.

Athletics

More lousy essays are written about sports than any other subject. Part of the problem is that sports are not about personal reflection or expression—like, say, the arts—and attempts to find lessons on the playing field tend to ring false. It is no coincidence that only four of our writers make athletics a central theme. Essay 23 is by a football player who gains self-confidence and a new identity from being a respected member of the team. Essay 24 is by a soccer player who is also an artist, and who makes the case that soccer really is like art. Essay 25 describes how a water polo player makes the best of the fact that she is not a particularly gifted player. Essay 26 is a refreshing twist on the typical sports essay, written by a varsity bowler.

A "5'5" NOBODY," AND HOW HE BECAME A TEAM CAPTAIN

Essays about athletics often fall flat, but that doesn't mean it is impossible to write a good one. Author Michael Asmussen's essay succeeds partly because of obvious sincerity: he has no great epiphanies after the championship game, nor does he offer any platitudes about hard work and self-discipline. Michael felt like a nobody until success in football made him feel like somebody. His story is endearing partly because he is so self-effacing—as when he was shocked to be named a team captain. And if you're going to write a football essay, it never hurts to talk about the time you cried.

Essay by Michael Asmussen

When I first came to St. Andrew's-Sewanee, I had pretty much led a common life for a child in my area. Athletically, I played baseball, basketball, and soccer. There was peewee football down the mountain in the valley, but on top of our little plateau there never was much interest in getting a team together. So I entertained myself by playing pick up football with my friends. I played soccer in the fall and it was always fun, but there was always something missing. It wasn't until I first came out for football during my eighth grade year that I finally discovered something that created a spark inside of me. In soccer, I had played every position, and there was not one niche for me. However, in football, I was a lineman. That was the one position that I played, and it was a position for which I was well suited. I had finally found something that could be all mine. This was my chance to do something on my own and to finally follow my dreams.

I had always been somewhat big as a child. So when I joined football it was only natural that I would join the linemen. My friend was a lineman, and I did not see any reason why I shouldn't play that position too. There was still only one problem. Although I was big for my age, I still wasn't all that big. At five foot five, and one hundred and fifty pounds, I was dwarfed by all the players that I went up against. My first year was frustrating because I did not get a lot of playing time. It was not until my freshman year that I finally began to get playing time, and bit by bit I improved. Finally, in my sophomore year, I cracked the starting lineup. When our starting noseguard was injured, my coach called upon me to fill the spot. I took over that position and held on for dear life. I never relinquished my spot on the defensive line, and worked as hard as I could to fend off any challengers. I was the lone sophomore starting that year and it created in me a sense of pride. That feeling of accomplishment inside of me carried into my junior year, where, after an intense summer, I took over the job of being the starting center on the offensive line. I was one of the iron-men of our team. I would start both ways and would get very little break from my jobs. I held these titles proudly as I knew that with them came a certain level of respect from both the coaches and other players. It was not until my senior season that I realized exactly how much respect I had earned from both the coaches and players. When the results from the elections were tallied, I was told that it was almost a unanimous decision that I had been selected as one of the three team captains. I was shocked to hear this because in years past the captains had often been the more popular players, which was a group that I never saw myself a part of. My coach told me that he was totally confident that the players had chosen the absolute best examples for them to follow. This was when I realized how much of a different person I was in comparison to when I began on the team as an eighth grader.

I almost never came to this realization. When I came home as a seventh grader and told my parents that I wanted to join the football team, they bordered upon adamancy in their desire to keep me from playing. Their biggest worry was that I might get hurt because I was so small. It took a great deal of coaxing and cajoling to get the permission that I desired. And once I got this permission my journey was not over. That August, when my first preseason started, I was utterly unprepared for what I was about to face. It was easily the hardest three weeks that I have ever experienced. To this day, I still remember constantly thinking of how I could be at home with my friends rather than suffering under the hot sun on the practice field. But, before I had started, I had made myself a promise that I would see this commitment through. I would treat it like all the other commitments that I make and never give up on it. The first year was almost as aggravating as the three weeks of preseason. Every game, I would stand on the sidelines and

But when it came time to peel my soiled jersey off my shoulder pads one last time, I cried.

watch as my friends were constantly sent in to give the starters small breaks. By the end of the season, I had begun to have serious doubts about ever playing again, but my friends told me that I just had to put the time in, and someday my time would come. When my time finally arrived, I experienced the greatest sense of accomplishment that I have ever felt. I had worked hard and shown all those around me that I deserved notice. Every time I pulled the jersey over my shoulder pads, I felt that maybe something great was about to happen. I had earned everything that I had gotten and done it all on my own. This was my accomplishment and nobody else's.

I think, however, that the biggest realization came when I took the jersey off my shoulder pads for the last time as a St. Andrew's-Sewanee Mountain Lion. It was the hardest thing that I had ever done as a player. I had been able to last through the three weeks of sheer hell of that first preseason. I had even been able to play through discouraging games when we were not only out-manned but also out-sized. But when it came time to peel my soiled jersey off my shoulder pads one last time, I cried. I cried because I realized how important football had been in my life. Football was the first pursuit that I had ever made on my own. Everything else that I had done had always been tried by my older sister and older brother first. But football was my own special accomplishment. I had spent five years of my life devoting myself to something that was entirely my choosing. I think that it had the most impact on my life over everything else I have done. It taught me to follow my dreams, and that through hard work and determination anything is possible. But most importantly it had become an outward and visible sign of my inward and invisible determination. After all, who would have thought that a five foot five nobody could have developed into one of the most respected players on the team? I certainly never did, and I am sure hardly anybody else did either, but that is exactly what I think drove me to succeed.

Michael Asmussen attended Dickinson College.

24

SCORING POINTS WITH ATHLETICS

We've warned you about the pitfalls of sports essays. Here's one that avoids them. The author gives a fluid description of scoring the big goal in the big game, but what comes later is at least as interesting. Games and goals are not of lasting importance, and though the author speaks of familiar standbys such as hard work, camaraderie, and teamwork, they aren't the bottom line, either. "The game of soccer is not so much a sport as an advanced art form," he writes, and proceeds to show how soccer "is an amoeba of continuous, fluid motion." Through the game, the author becomes a much more interesting person than the run-of-the-mill player who kicks the winning goal.

"The Beautiful Game" by Sam James

Glaring floodlights illuminated the brisk autumn night, steam rose from the sweaty players, and screams rang from the abnormally large crowd. With less than ten minutes left to play, the game remained a scoreless draw. I was the only freshman on the field, and I had been running on sheer adrenaline for nearly the whole second half. The ball floated into the penalty box, and I instinctively

> The game of soccer is not so much a sport as an advanced art form.

darted to meet the beautifully arching cross. With a slight jump and a deft touch off my right cleat, I watched the ball as it sailed just beyond the outstretched arms of the goalkeeper. That goal proved the winner as we rallied past the top-ranked team in the state.

Rarely does success and meaning in life come without toil. While last-gasp goals and hard-fought victories stand out in my memory, the importance of my soccer experience cannot pertain to any one set of events. It includes countless hours in the backyard, early morning timed runs, hard-fought losses, agonizing poor performances, and all the small but sweet accomplishments on the practice pitch. I have cherished the entire evolution of my twelve-year career, and the lessons I have learned that transcend the game of soccer. My experiences with soccer have taught me the importance of dedication and perseverance, the value of camaraderie and teamwork, and the ways to harness raw emotion. More importantly, however, my involvement in soccer has provided me with valuable insight on life. The game of soccer is not so much a sport as an advanced art form. It requires a combination of mental, physical, and technical ability, accentuated by instances of innate skill and creativity. Whereas most sports require strict rules, carefully calculated plays, and numerous breaks, soccer is an amoeba of continuous, fluid motion. On the field, soccer players are given the liberty to be artists, perpetually adjusting and tending to the movement of play. Life itself is continuous motion. The "beautiful game" has taught me to be an artist in everything I do, forever tending to and sculpting the events of my own life.

Sam James attended Tufts University and the School of the Museum of Fine Arts.

25

HARD WORK PAYS OFF (SORT OF)

If we had a nickel for every essay that talks about the importance of hard work to achieve a goal, we'd be too rich to worry about writing this book. But what about when hard work doesn't pay off? That's the predicament in which author Michelle Tessier finds herself. Michelle's soul-searching in response to failure is much more interesting than exhilaration in response to success would be. In the end, Michelle discovers goals other than winning or being the best, and in the process, she learns (and tells the reader) something important about herself.

Essay by Michelle Tessier

After deciding it would be fun to play a sport in high school, I joined my school's water polo team as a freshman. Although I had never been particularly athletically inclined, I threw myself into the sport with total energy and enthusiasm, hoping to be a starting player. I worked incredibly hard, arriving at practice early to swim extra laps, and staying after everyone else had left to work on my technique. But no matter what I did, I was still only an average player. Why couldn't I score more goals? In school, I knew that when I completely immersed myself in the material and devoted extra effort to my classes, good grades usually followed. I had become accustomed to my hard work and dedication being rewarded. So I was naturally disappointed when devoting the same tremendous amount of effort to water polo did not yield similar results.

> I realized that if I really wanted to participate in an activity I loved, I could not let my embarrassment or false pride stand in the way.

I began to ask myself, why was I doing this? It was embarrassing and even somewhat humiliating for me to participate in an activity that I couldn't do as well as others could. I could not help but be frustrated when my coach yelled at me during practices, benched me during games, or when I saw the weekly sheet of statistics being tacked up by the pool for all of the players to see. I even began to wonder whether participating in water polo was worthwhile if it were something at which I could not excel.

However, I would never allow myself to quit. For even though I was not the best player on the team, I am not a quitter and the truth was I love playing water polo. I enjoyed the physical challenge it gave me, swimming as hard as I could until every muscle in my body ached. When I didn't get to play, I took pleasure in analyzing our game strategies, sometimes discussing ideas with my coach, even going so far as to very subtly suggest his strategy was wrong. I was amazed to learn I could actually enjoy the time I spent on the bench, often inventing cheers to support other players. I realized that if I really wanted to participate in an activity I loved, I could not let my embarrassment or false pride stand in the way. And because I refused to give up, participating in water polo has been simultaneously one of the most frustrating and yet rewarding experiences of my life. I found the determination not to walk away from something that was especially difficult for me. And although I was raised with the notion that every goal was within my reach if I simply worked hard enough, I now understand that I don't have to do something better than everyone else in order to be successful.

Michelle Tessier attended Georgetown University.

26

HOW TO SUCCEED BY NOT TRYING TOO HARD

After reading countless essays that belabor the significance of a soccer game or a school play, admissions officers will welcome the following one from author Scott Pelletier. He uses his enjoyment of that most mundane sport, bowling, to write an interesting essay that succeeds partly because it doesn't break a sweat. In no particular order, the essay shows that Scott a) cares about others, b) has a good sense of humor, c) can tell a good story, and d) doesn't take himself too seriously. Only near the end does he relate that his performance really does matter a great deal—he was very nervous during Sectionals—and that bowling has helped him build self-confidence. After his understated essay, it is a believable conclusion.

Essay by Scott Pelletier

A ball is rolled down the lane. Confidently, I turn around; there is no need to see the result. A perfect strike. I stroll back to the bench, receiving high-fives from not only my teammates, but the opposing team as well. Bowling has been my most satisfying extracurricular activity. Turning with a smile on my face to my teammates knowing I threw a strike, without having to see it, feels amazing. On the other hand, it can prove a little embarrassing when a pin is left standing.

> It is the only sport I know of that you can eat french fries and play cards during practice.

When I was in ninth grade, I tried out and made the freshmen basketball team. Spending almost the entire season on the bench was not an enjoyable experience. While my spirit to play was strong, my height of 5'2" was an impediment. The next year I decided to try bowling instead of putting myself through another year of warming the bench. Bowling is an equal opportunity sport, where it doesn't matter if you're short, fat, or even deaf, dumb, and blind. It is the only sport I know of that you can eat french fries and play cards during practice. Bowling matches and practices are always fun as we never have to do strenuous wind sprints and no one ever gets injured. My teammates and I get to relax and have fun.

On good days, it is satisfying to know that I can throw a strike on any shot. My best game to date is a 266. On the other hand, I have also experienced the "agony" of getting a gutter ball. We often joke with each other about throwing gutter balls; claiming it "hit my leg" to use as an excuse.

It is amazing to see how although as individuals we don't have a lot in common, yet as teammates, we bond. The team is very supportive; we cheer when someone does well and give encouragement when one of us throws a bad shot. I have never quite experienced that kind of team sportsmanship before. As a varsity bowler, I enjoy helping the younger JV bowlers perfect their game. I have spent numerous practices working with one freshman in particular to improve his approach to the shot (unfortunately, my efforts had limited success).

My own game has improved as well. Sophomore year, when we went to the Westchester/Putnam sectionals, I was really nervous and I did not bowl up to the expectations I had for myself. In contrast, junior year, we qualified again and I averaged fifteen pins better than my season average. My skills, along with my confidence, had significantly improved. This newfound confidence has spread to other areas of my life. Recently, I had to give a speech for Mu Alpha Theta (Math Honor Society) and I was pleasantly surprised with the ease I felt at delivering the speech. While bowling is not as glamorous as football or basketball (no cheerleaders), for me it will always be a wonderful way to spend an afternoon.

Scott Pelletier attended Columbia University.

The Arts

Some of the best essays in this book are about art, drama, or music. The arts are a vehicle for personal expression, and writing about them can be a great way to reveal an author's personality and passions. Performers, in particular, have great material because getting on stage is itself a dramatic moment. Our authors are mainly actors and musicians, though one student (Essay 39) writes about the effect of a performance that he saw.

27

MAKING THE ESSAY YOUR STAGE

The following essay is a superb example of the you-are-there genre. Author Ross Bercun writes of making the audience live his "Actor's Nightmare" (the title of the play), and through his essay, he transports the reading audience to his shoulder for the performance. From "the moment the light hits my eyes," Ross's concrete description of being on the stage *shows* his passion for drama more effectively than he could ever tell about it. His writing is full of skillful touches, such as when he loops back at the end to give a second mention to the cute girl, the old woman, and the seven-year-old. Says Ross, "My advice for future students is to write about something they are passionate about because it will make the words flow out of them."

Essay by Ross Bercun

There I sit, just having eaten a big bucket full of butterflies. They are fluttering about inside my stomach. A warm ball of energy gathers in my chest, and all other problems of the past day, week, and year disappear. All that exists is my moment and I.

Most people despise the winged creatures stored inside their bowels; I, however, believe they give me the energy to pull upon every skill I have, all the potential in my system, to come together and put on the performance of a lifetime. I peek around the corner of the dark, velvet curtain like the corner of a dog-eared sheet of paper, ever so slightly. I see family, friends, teachers, neighbors, and strangers. I see the cute girl in the third row turning off her cell phone, I see the homely older woman looking around the crowd for a familiar face, and I see the seven-year-old whose parents had dragged him along to the theater. I will speak to all of these people; make them live in the world I do. For one night, these people will live my *Actor's Nightmare*.

With the starting note of the opening music, the stage goes dark, and the audience takes a collective breath. They enter into my world. For every second that passes until my entrance, the butterflies double in number. Then finally, I enter. My ears connected by my smile and my muscles moving by rote, the light hits my eyes and the audience disappears; only memory lets me know that they are still present. I breathe in a diaphragmatic breath and release my voice, letting my breath and tongue conduct the symphony that is my song. The ensemble of this piece works together as one, our voices in sync with each other and our harmonies immaculate up until the final note. The stage returns to the blackness that had occupied it only minutes before; the difference is the audience. They are no longer silent, but have erupted into an awaited applause.

Without one remaining butterfly, I return to my place back-stage with a hum in my body that could only be created by a thrilling performance. My anticipation tells me that the fire has not left my system; I am ready for the encore that is my next entrance, my main entrance.

Up until then I am dragged through the play without my conscious mind, though it has been playing my upcoming scene in my head over and over ensuring perfection. The previous performances had been good, better than I had expected. But this was closing night, and I had to be perfect. In what seems like a split second, it is my turn to go on. The lights dim and rise again like the trail of the sun on fast-forward.

> **For one night, these people will live my *Actor's Nightmare*.**

I close my eyes, breathe, and then step onto the stage, back into the light. The audience's silence notifies me that I have their undivided attention. I am no longer Ross. I am George, living in a world unfamiliar to him. The audience is no longer in the theater. They are backstage with me, living George's nightmare—living my nightmare. With every panicking nerve in George's body I act my part. I am my part.

Before I know it, it is time for a soliloquy. My soliloquy. No other person on stage, no prop on stage. All alone, just me and my audience. I deliver every line from my soul; I don't have to struggle to remember my lines because I say them naturally. They flow like glass water down a plastic stream. I connect with the homely old lady, I connect with the cute girl, and I connect with the child who no longer would need to be dragged by his parents to the theater. A drop of sweat drips into my eyes and stings, a pleasant sting. I drop to my knees to end my monologue, and the silence from the audience tells me that I have succeeded in creating their life within the play. For this night, they only exist in my play.

Looking back, I was always upset that I didn't get a final bow, but that's how it is written in the script. Sure, it bugged me the nights before that I wasn't allowed a bow, but those were merely *good* performances. Tonight I needed one—I needed a bow. As the audience applauded the other cast members I could hear the restrained applause that was being saved. Saved for me. At the moment I was to bow, the applause would tear free like an angry dog from a weak leash. I never got to know what those dogs sounded like. I remained still, "dead" on the floor as the cast gestured to me. The lights dimmed for the final time and a disappointed audience fell silent.

Ross Bercun attended the University of Arizona.

28

WAXING POETIC, TAKING A RISK

Occasionally, adventuresome applicants submit poetry as part of their applications. Then there is Abby Fleeter, who created the poem below with two distinct viewpoints and submitted it to all of her colleges as an additional essay. Was it harder to write than a conventional college essay? You betcha. Getting it right to Abby's satisfaction "took draft after draft." Why do it? Well… if you need to ask that question, poetry probably isn't for you. One other nugget from Abby: "Ask two different people for advice on your writing: one person who knows you well (and can therefore confirm that your writing reflects you as they know you), and one person who does not know you as well (so that you can see if their thoughts match what you hoped a stranger would learn)."

Essay by Abby Fleeter
A Poem for Two Voices
(*This is a poem meant to be read by two different people, with two distinct viewpoints. It is a poem of fiction, not an autobiographical work.*)

She whispers silent words
To the surrounding emptiness,
An emptiness that represents relationships
She has selfishly severed,
In an attempt to disappear slowly
From a world she once yearned to experience.

I can speak to the pale, wispy clouds
The towering maple trees
The crisp, crimson leaves quietly cascading
Towards my heavy, burdened feet.
I can sing silently to the cool, autumn air
And imagine that I am endlessly alone.

Her unfocused eyes flit about
Desperately searching for help
Before finding security in the ground
Once again.
She is here,
But is she really present?
You can see her...
But she can never be reached
Her skin is armor

Goosebumps creep up my spine
As the pitying stares of the naïve
Pierce me like sharpened knives.
They have labeled me an outcast,
A wilting weed amongst
Beautifully blossoming roses.
But only their assumptions
Have made this label authentic.
They don't understand
The relief of escaping
To the corners of my mind,
Or the liberation
Of being engulfed
By my sea of dreams.
When I am alone,
I can taste freedom

She's clearly not normal
Something is busted, broken
There is no alternative explanation
For her isolation.
Perhaps it is her fear
Of potential vulnerability
Maybe she is punishing herself
For failed friendships of the past
Her trust must have been shattered
Countless times before.
There is no alternative explanation
For her seclusion

They look at me, seeing a girl
Smothered by the thick cloak
Of depression,
Battling with the pain
Of loneliness.
But in the mirror, I see a girl
Spreading her wings
Preparing to soar
Through the sun-streaked sky,
Reaching altitudes that escape
Judgment's cruel clutches.
I am not the lonely girl
Who everyone else blindly sees.
I am not the same helpless girl
Who isolates herself
Out of a fear of failing,
Out of the pain of punishment.

She does not realize   They do not realize
What a mistake she is making   What a mistake they are making

By allowing loneliness   By assuming that I am suppressed
To suppress her   By loneliness

She is alone,   I am alone,
Surrounded by people   Surrounded by people

                                                            But it is a choice—
                                                            It is *my* choice
                                                            To make time
                                                            For self-discovery

I am not the lonely girl
Who Everyone else blindly sees.

Abby Fleeter attends Macalester College.

29

TRYING NOT TO SING OUT OF KEY

The first thing to notice about Alex Petterson's essay is how well it answers the question. Few people are comfortable writing about failure, but Petterson has the confidence to do it honestly. The essay is all the more impressive because Petterson is a science person for whom drama could easily be an afterthought. He'll never be a particularly outstanding performer, but he finds as much meaning in his performances as any star actor or soloist. He concludes by noting that though he has grown as a performer, he is still not particularly comfortable on stage. Yet he continues to perform, and to grow as a well-rounded human being.

Essay by Alex Petterson

Describe how you have grown in one area over time. Explain your motivation, successes, and failures.

"Whenever you're ready," a voice echoes from somewhere in the seats. For the first time, I am on stage, alone, auditioning for a role in the musical *Nunsense*. Well, sort of. There are no male roles in the musical, so the directors added a chorus. I shake, and my voice quivers as I proceed with the required monologue, acting a part I have not found a way to relate to. When it is done, I nod to the accompanist and he begins to play. I sing an excerpt from "We Go Together" I have practiced for weeks. And I go off key. I leave the stage and bike slowly home, expecting to be cut.

There are few things I struggle with as much as public speaking and performance. Even after ninth grade speech class, being alone in front of an audience scares me. I only auditioned because my teacher encouraged me and I love music. On the way home, I thought over my apparent failure and made a decision.

"How will I get anywhere in life if I'm afraid of this?" I asked myself. My plan is to be a scientist, and even the most reclusive scientists need to be good public speakers to get funding and convey findings. From this point, I chose to force myself into performance or speech situations in order to practice and become more comfortable. On a broader scale, I committed never not to do something just because it scares me. To my surprise, I was accepted as part of the chorus in *Nunsense*, but I still wanted to improve.

My next opportunity to do so came in the following summer at the Frontiers of Science Institute, where I was reminded of just how important public speaking would be in life as a scientist. After six weeks of preparation, my partner and I presented our research on how to use experimentation on enzymes in a freshman chemistry lab. That experience was still scary, but we must have done well because we received an award for our research and presentation.

When I auditioned for the next school musical in junior year, I managed to be in the chorus again, but I also received an invitation from the director to join a theater class for the next semester. This would be a test; I would be in front of the class every week. Even with four AP tests to study for, I decided that the class would be well worth my time; and it was. It allowed me to practice in front of an audience and helped me become more comfortable on stage.

> **To be honest, I still do not enjoy being on stage, even if I am not terrified of it anymore.**

The pressure from performing also crossed over into more privately set auditions off stage. Ever since *Nunsense*, I have tried out for every solo in my choirs, but so far I have not been awarded any of them. My voice and body continue to quiver and shake, trying to catch up with my brain. I also auditioned for All State Choir, Band, and Orchestra. I did not succeed in those auditions either. In the case of the choir, I probably would have been accepted if I had not had a slight case of nerves and stopped singing for three seconds. I was discouraged to see only a small difference between my score and the cutoff.

Finally, this past summer was my chance to focus on nothing but music and performance, free from the stress of additional classes. I auditioned for and was accepted to the Lutheran Summer Music

Academy and Festival for both voice and clarinet. There I practiced long hours with experienced teachers and opted for solo recitals in both of my instruments. These performances were successful, even though the time preceding them was very stressful. The last few rehearsals had a few technical issues, and my last vocal lesson had to be canceled due to a scheduling conflict. Even with stress, I felt better about the two recitals than I had about anything I had ever done alone and almost everything I had done as part of an ensemble. I left feeling more confident and more musically competent.

To be honest, I still do not enjoy being on stage, even if I am not terrified of it anymore. I love the people, the music, the practice, and the aftermath, but not the act itself. But I want to be better at it, so I continue to perform. Nothing comes without practice, particularly not confidence, and if I eventually become a chemistry professor, I will have the skills I need both to teach and to ask for funding. As a senior, I am again auditioning for the All-State groups, our musical, and choir solos. So far I've been given a solo in jazz choir. I'm confident I can succeed in even more ventures.

Alex Petterson attended St. Olaf College.

30

FINDING YOURSELF IN A PAINTING

Most people have at least one print hanging in their bedroom, but few scrutinize it to the extent that author Kate Newton has reflected on Renoir's *Dance at Bougival*. It helps that she also had it on the wall in her elementary school art room, but this essay is all about Kate's ability to identify with the woman in the red hat, and to see her idealized self in the image. Note the nice kicker in the last sentence that gives the essay an exclamation point. Says Kate, "When you are writing about something that is personal, you have to go with your gut first. You can always go back and fix what needs to be fixed."

Essay by Kate Newton

Choose and describe a particular piece of art and explain its significance to you.

All six of my elementary school years were spent in the same art room. Miniature tables and chairs sat surrounded by walls covered by prints of paintings and sculptures created by some of the greatest artists of all time. When my young eyes wandered around the room, which was often, I found my attention constantly drawn to a painting of a woman in a red hat. Something about it heightened my curiosity and it became not only my favorite painting, but my fascination. Upon leaving elementary school, I bought a print of my own to hang in my room at home.

The longer Renoir's *Dance at Bougival* hung on my wall, the more hidden details I noticed, and my once inexplicable fascination with this particular work of art became more apparent. The lady in the red hat represents a side of myself not often seen, one that dances in the street without a care in the world. She embodies passion and love of life through such simple touches as a red hat and her expression of contentment. She dances on for the world to see, completely absorbed in the moment. Living for the moment and for the sake of loving life has always been a wish of mine that I continue to bury in the back of my mind because I've been told it's not "practical" or "responsible." Renoir's painting constantly reminds me not to completely let go of that spontaneity.

Dancing is an act of passion; it is an act of freedom. Sometimes I search for this type of freedom in life, but at times, it can only be found in the subtleties of artwork. Renoir's *Dance at Bougival* was created when Impressionism was a prominent form of painting, my favorite period. Paintings were not meant to be perfect or precise; they were merely meant to inspire feeling and movement to try to capture the essence of life. The vibrant colors speak for themselves and the brush strokes display the passion felt by so many during the late 19th century. As I look closer, the background slides out of focus and the floor seems to blur below the figures, giving the painting a weightless, dreamlike quality where time seems to stop in that one blissful moment.

> **When you are writing about something that is personal, you have to go with your gut first.**

Even when school becomes stressful or events in my life don't come out just right, I will forever hold a piece of myself in that painting of the lady with the red hat. She exists in a small world of color and light, where time and space have no meaning. All eyes are drawn to her as she floats freely across the canvas, the red strings woven through her dress like the passion her life embodies. Even though some days I walk right by it without a second glance, deep down I know that her life in that painting is sometimes the one I secretly wish to explore on the most dreary of days when all I really want to do is wear a bright red hat and dance like no one is watching.

Kate Newton attended Wake Forest University.

31

"AN OVERWHELMING HUMILITY AND ARDOR"

It is easy to sound forced or self-important when writing about a memorable moment. Too often, applicants get bogged down recounting facts or straining for meaning. Dawning Welliver shows how to write a full-length essay about one moment without being repetitive. She starts with the big picture in the first paragraph before zooming in to describe her feeling as the music rises. But then, crucially, she pulls back to recount important experiences that brought her there. Each of the first three paragraphs offers a different, complimentary perspective on the moment. Welliver uses the rest of the essay to explain nuances in her thinking before concluding with an echo of paragraph one.

"My Most Memorable Musical Experience" by Dawning Welliver

It was the end of a lot of things. It was the end of my freshman year, and the end of my youth orchestra's concert season. It was the end of my time living in Philadelphia, right before I was to leave all my friends and the home in Swarthmore that I loved. It was the end of our last concert; it was the last page of Mahler's Titan symphony.

We were reaching a triumphant passage, and I remember glancing up from my music, looking around at the orchestra. It was the heat of the moment, and I felt a surge of pride so strong that, although I had long before committed the music to memory owing to the many hours we had worked on it, I almost completely lost any sense of orientation in what I was doing. I was proud that I was there, sitting right up front in an orchestra that I had come to, two years before, at just the right moment in my life.

The intensity of my emotion, I'm sure, was amplified by the fact that, not long before joining the orchestra, my musical life had hit a low point. Ever since the age of four, when I picked up and pretended to play a toy violin with a chopstick for a bow, my life had been thoroughly shaped, defined, and enriched by music. I loved the violin. But I had changed teachers from someone who was phenomenally kind and wonderful with young students to someone new who, while an excellent violinist, was not able to reach and inspire that part of me that needed nurturing. For over a year I felt an increasing sense of loss, as though I no longer belonged to the music world. Fortunately, though, the combination of a new teacher and falling in love with chamber music at a wonderful summer camp changed everything. And now I was part of an orchestra that meant everything to me.

> **For over a year I felt an increasing sense of loss, as though I no longer belonged to the music world.**

I was not only proud of my return to the glorious music world. I was proud of my section, for working so hard and learning how to become one conjoined wave of sound. I was proud of the whole orchestra, for how far it had come, how many hours we had all spent together, feeling at times frustrated, at times rewarded, but always so inspired by the music.

But the feeling of pride and ecstasy was soon joined by another feeling that was much harder to understand, harder to interpret to myself. It had the outward signs of an aching sadness, yet there was something deeper and purer within it. It wasn't just that I would miss my friends, who were so motivated and encouraging, so accepting and amusing, and it wasn't just that I would deeply miss my conductor, the selfless mentor whose enthusiasm, expertise, and love for music radiated so powerfully that no musician was left untouched. I realized, at some point afterward, that the true emotion I was feeling was not sadness about leaving these dear friends, but rather an overwhelming humility and ardor in the face of the music that we were creating, the product of all that we cared about, worked for, and loved, wrapped up and packaged into a gift that we, and our families, and the audience, would take away and cherish. More than anything, it was a deep yearning to carry forward the pure essence of everything we had attained.

It was the end of a lot of things. But it was the beginning of something very important. There, with the concluding passages of Mahler, my ears and heart saturated with the ringing of the horns and the timpani, came my realization that I wanted to follow a path of music, for my whole life.

Dawning Welliver attends Vanderbilt University.

32

THE ORGANIZATIONAL MAESTRO

For a textbook example of organization, check out the following essay. It begins with a snapshot of the moment of completion with the author, Steve Hall, reflecting on a year-long series of arts productions that he has organized. The second paragraph steps back in time to trace the development of his involvement in music, and then his transition from performing to organizing. After recounting his impressive experience as producer, he concludes by going back to where he was in the introduction, thinking about his next project. Says Hall, "My advice is to place yourself in the shoes of the reader. If you were reading about two hundred applicants, what would make this person different?"

Essay by Steven H. Hall

While standing backstage sipping my nth cup of coffee, forty hours awake and counting, I tried to think of what I'd do next. A year's efforts organizing Breakin' Curfew would soon draw to a close with the fall of the curtain; after this last band finished and the packed theater emptied, I'd have to begin again—with nothing. What would I do with myself? An hour later, I was sitting in the middle of a big empty stage with pad and pen, wheels turning on the next project: new ideas, new work, new people, new bands, new music. More music. Even better music.

I can remember no time in my life in which I was not making music. When I was young, I played *all* the time. In second grade I began piano lessons; by seventh it was drums and guitar. Guitar and drums. All the time. Drums and guitar. By thirteen I was a budding musician with an insatiable appetite for performance.

High school provided me with a world of opportunities to play. As a freshman, I played drums in the top jazz combo. We rehearsed constantly, played competitive festivals and endless gigs. I soon joined a rock band of upperclassmen and began to write, record and perform with them as well; every night that wasn't a jazz gig became a rock show. Several good bands needed a drummer, so I joined another. Then another and another. By my junior year, I'd played with twenty-three bands, appeared on thirteen albums and sold a thousand copies; I was going to be a famous musician, no doubt about it.

As my passion for music grew and evolved, so did my enthusiasm for academics. I had the good fortune to attend Ann Arbor's Community High School, a school which is very supportive of the arts, but academically demanding too. My teachers helped me find a balance between performance and classes; time-management became a full-time job. I excelled in most subjects, developing a particular passion for English and literature.

Through performances and recordings mid-freshman year, I learned about a remarkable organization called The Neutral Zone—a multifaceted local teen center that provided a substance-free environment with a focus on art, slam poetry, and lots of music. They sponsored a Youth Owned Records program, which produced albums and hosted shows. I came to hold a variety of positions in the organization, finding great rewards in producing and promoting younger bands. Through developing my management and organizational skills, I discovered that this work provided me even more satisfaction than performing did.

> I can remember no time in my life in which I was not making music.

I started to focus on becoming an organizational mastermind, proficient in structure, communication, and problem-solving. More and more engaged in community service, I became Facilitator of the Teen Advisory Council and, then, the Teen Fellow on the Board of Directors and Executive Committee, for which I even received a nomination for Ann Arbor Young Citizen of the Year. The more work I did for the community, the more my desire for performance faded.

Then came Breakin' Curfew. Now my largest endeavor, Breakin' Curfew is a collaboration between The Neutral Zone and the University of Michigan Musical Society (a venerable fine arts presenter with a 136-year tradition) to present the flourishing local youth music, poetry, and dance to the community. I joined as a Teen Curator last year. As the year progressed and the curatorial process evolved, as I booked acts and directed rehearsals, wrote press releases and distributed fliers, hawked tickets and designed light plots, I began to find my niche: to encourage talents greater than my own—to bring things together and make things happen.

I've started producing Breakin' Curfew again for this year. Moreover, I created my own class based around an internship I have with the University Musical Society, learning their methods for producing concerts and shows while refining my own. Coming from a school such as Community High, I'm applying to Brown University because I'm eager to find my new balance between education and music in a more diverse setting, to expand my academic interests, and explore a new artistic environment. I'm not sure where these past experiences will take me, but isn't that the way to approach the adventure of college? I'm eager to make things happen, to work like a dog, to get out the pad and pen, and get the wheels turning—to begin my next improvisation and see where it goes.

Steven H. Hall attended Brown University.

33

A FOOTBALL PLAYER GETS OUT OF HIS RUT

Everybody knows the groups that populate a typical high school: the jocks, the nerds, the artists, and so on. By the time students apply to college, most know their comfort zone and are reluctant to leave it. That is why author Will Thanheiser's story is so impressive. He begins with a remarkably self-aware explanation of why, as a smart athlete, he really didn't see himself as an actor. Despite his limiting self-image, he soon discovers that he enjoys acting and might even be good at it. He doesn't claim to have had an immediate transformation—who in real life actually does?—but instead stresses that his personal growth is an ongoing process.

Essay by Will M. Thanheiser

Before last year I had always thought of myself as a very shy, uncreative, introspective individual. And I was happy that way. I had found my little niche in the Kinkaid society. I was the jock who excelled in sports and also managed to make pretty good grades as well. But I wasn't an artist. I hadn't taken an art class since eighth grade, and I only took it then because it was required. I didn't think I was good at acting, or drawing, or playing an instrument. So I never did. Truthfully, it was because I was way too insecure about myself to risk humiliation. I was a perfectionist. I wasn't accustomed to failure, and didn't really see a point in trying it out now.

However, it is required that each student receive a fine arts credit before graduating from my high school. So, I decided to take Children's Theatre my junior year. A couple of my friends were going to do it with me, and I had heard that hardly any artistic ability was needed. So I gave it a shot. I started out very timidly, not volunteering for improvisational exercises or looking for a big part in our major production, *Charlie and the Chocolate Factory*. I didn't want to make a fool out of myself. But for some strange reason, our teacher saw some sort of hidden talent inside of me. She had seen me play football in front of thousands of people, so she knew she could rid me of my stage fright. And besides, how could I be intimidated of children less than half my age? Slowly the whole acting thing grew on me. I went from speaking in my own deep-toned voice to adopting the personality and traits of one of the central characters in the play, Grandpa Joe. I found myself really enjoying performing for elementary students from my school as well as some underprivileged schools around Houston. And besides, they made me feel funny. They had no idea that I really wasn't a good actor or funny at all. They just enjoyed the show.

> They had no idea that I really wasn't a good actor or funny at all. They just enjoyed the show.

My newfound artistic confidence encouraged me to try other new things as well. I became a much more social person. Whereas I used to just hang out with a select group of friends, I began trying to associate with more and more members of my class, as well as meet new people from other schools. I began opening up more to my family instead of keeping everything bottled up inside of me. Now this didn't just happen right away, and I still hang out primarily with my same group of friends. In fact, our relationships were made even stronger. However, I am really trying to become a more approachable and personable young man. And I think I am doing a pretty good job up to this point. But this "transformation" is an ongoing process, and I hope the college experience will only help to facilitate its development.

Will M. Thanheiser attended Princeton University.

34

"THE MASS OF MIDDLE-AGED STRANGERS"

Author Claire Askew vividly captures the experience of participating in a poetry reading with a group of middle-aged adults. She impresses by the mere fact that she is there. Claire lets us see the audience through her teenage eyes by noting the "salt-and-pepper beards, wedding rings, and some crows' feet." Her vocabulary is precise, but she never uses fancy words when ordinary ones will do. And she doesn't end the essay with a heavy-handed meditation on trusting oneself or having the courage to persevere. "I told the story I wanted to tell," says Claire, "It can be tempting to think about what admissions counselors want to hear and what would sound the most impressive, but if you don't really care about your topic, your writing is going to fall flat."

Essay by Claire Askew

"Let your passion rise, let your passion rise," she sang, letting her hands twirl and float up towards the ceiling. "See that beast run free, see that beast run free!"

For the first time, I was visiting Kansas City's castle of word-smithing, the Writer's Place. It was the day after New Year's. I was barely seventeen. It was an open mic—my first—and I was nervous. The woman who was running the show continued to sing, drawing the writers away from the tables of homemade cornbread and leftover Christmas decorations and back to the makeshift stage area. They were captivated. I had come thinking this would be a casual, laissez-faire sort of thing. And, in a way, it was. Everyone there seemed to know each other, and seemed to be old pros at making their written work come alive. The only problems were that I was a stranger there and had never shared any of my writing out loud with anyone in public.

The time came when the MC asked me if I wanted to read

anything. I was so nervous I almost shook my head. But I had brought my tattered, red, wallpaper-covered writing notebook with me for a reason, and I knew that if I didn't take the risk, I would regret it all week.

"Uh, yeah…" I said. He handed me the clipboard with the day's schedule, and a black gel pen. *Claire Askew*. It was done. About fifteen minutes later, it was my turn. I slunk up to the microphone and, naturally, it fell off its stand before I had the chance to introduce myself. I fixed it, perched on the stool and looked out at the crowd, noticing salt-and-pepper beards, wedding rings, and some crows' feet.

"My name is Claire and I'm seventeen and this is my first time at the Writer's Place. I'm going to read a few poems I wrote." I breathed. "This is called 'Singing Maidens.'" I had written it six months earlier, but it was one of the first I had written that I was proud of and excited about. It felt comfortingly familiar up there against the mass of middle-aged strangers. My voice was shaky as I began, but line after line I grew more relaxed. So what if my audience had manuscripts for sale in this building, if they had read here a hundred and twelve times before. They were people who loved writing, reading, and the word-full life as much as I. We were not so different.

I told the story I wanted to tell.

I read another poem. My nerves dissolved, and I even began to have fun. I read another, now sure of heart and confident of voice. By the time I was finished, though my heart was pounding and my cheeks tingling, I was happy. My audience applauded.

With a small, strong smile growing on my face, I stepped out of the warm building, with its smells of black-eyed pea soup and old library, and into the crisp January air.

Claire Askew attended Lewis and Clark College.

35

AN ANCIENT CATHEDRAL AND THE GRATEFUL DEAD

The key to author Harry Russin's essay is the fact that it is really about him, not about the Chartres Cathedral or the Grateful Dead's "Dark Star." The foundation of his essay is the ability to make an unexpected comparison between two reasonably well-known but very different works of art. His intellect makes the essay interesting, but his passion makes it soar. "I would hardly count listening to the Grateful Dead as a life-changing experience, but exploring that music is an artistic celebration for me," says Harry.

Essay by Harrison Russin

Describe a character in fiction, an historical figure, or a creative work (as in art, music, science, etc.) that has had an influence on you, and explain that influence.

Two works of art have made me shiver. Chartres Cathedral in France and "Dark Star" by the Grateful Dead continue to fascinate me every time I think of them. As art, the two specimens are completely opposite to each other. Chartres is a masterpiece of human ingenuity, architecture, creativity, and order. "Dark Star" is an exercise in improvisation, a constantly evolving work of group invention and lateral thought. However, both compositions represent me as a person and as a thinker.

I recall the first time I saw Chartres in an art history video. The cathedral's spires rose out of the television screen and I beheld the gothic cathedral as if it were frozen in time. Like a Bach fugue, the flying buttresses and vaulted arches contain intricate designs that made me wonder if their complexities were due solely to the architect's genius and planning. The colors in the stained glass windows are simply irreproducible, their kaleidoscopic light playing on the limestone floor. Although each window by itself contains a relatively simple rendering, thousands of the windows create a complex scene that is crowned by the rose window with its incredible Chartres blue. The symmetry and complexity of Chartres appeals to my analytical mind, but the Transcendental and creative features invite my soul to appreciate the cathedral as a work of art.

From my viewpoint as a musician, "Dark Star" is not as much a song as an experience. After starting to play the album *Live/Dead* for the first time, I felt as if I had wandered into a previously unknown part of my mind. The opening notes made me think I was eavesdropping on a concert that was just starting. Immediately my ears entered orbit and I was trapped between Phil Lesh's bass and Jerry Garcia's growling guitar.

> I was trapped between Phil Lesh's bass and Jerry Garcia's growling guitar.

I entrusted my mind to the band, and they treated it to an improvisation that was so orchestrated, so complex that I did not believe it was a spontaneous performance. The palette of the electric guitar painted fantastic peaks and subtle valleys of modal, dorian riffs and harsh-sounding chord progressions. Every time a new theme was introduced, the band played until the motif evolved into a work of art that cannot be frozen in time. "Dark Star" does not include the complex planning of a cathedral, but I cannot attribute its artistic value solely to genius; like Chartres, there is something more. I am not claiming that Chartres and "Dark Star" are equally enduring works of art, but juxtaposing a gothic cathedral and a piece of modern popular art makes me recognize different interpretations of different art forms.

Chartres and "Dark Star" stand contrary to each other. However, I am composed of both elements—order and improvisation. I have a need for organization and subjectivity. I used to be in love with science because solutions are either right or wrong. I still admire science, but literature, history, and the arts have captivated me. The power of the mind enthralls me because, through science, it defines life; but through art, it relishes life. I have realized that, as Ralph

Waldo Emerson wrote, "Empirical science is apt to cloud the mind." My mind is not formulaic, but I still need standing ground—a floor or launch pad. I have entered the labyrinth of the arts. I still marvel at the intricacies of Chartres, but I am longing to improvise.

Harrison Russin attended Swarthmore College.

36

MAKING A MUSIC ESSAY SING

A short essay about a "meaningful activity" can easily become run-of-the-mill. This one avoids that fate because the author, Peter Liu, delves beneath the surface of his involvement in music. At age seventeen, it takes a big man to admit that he listens to classical music; Peter shows a sophisticated understanding of how various forms of music can make him a better musician. Forming a new band is always more impressive than playing in an existing one. Without bragging, Peter makes clear that he is a guiding force behind his band. Says Peter, "Creativity can't be rushed; it's best to let ideas stew and mature in your head before sitting down to write."

Essay By Peter Liu

Of the activities, interests, and experiences listed on the previous page, which is the most meaningful to you, and why?

I started playing piano at the ripe old age of ten, but there was an advantage to learning music when I became more mature. Classical music is an acquired taste, and the time to develop that taste enabled me to tolerate the unavoidable lessons on basic notes and rhythms.

> **Their wide-eyed, teeth-gnashing antics onstage encourage me to be more spontaneous.**

While many fellow pianists struggled to stay interested, I found that I could motivate myself by choosing pieces I enjoyed listening to, which led me to accept more and more challenging material. Although my friends teased me endlessly for listening to classical music, the habit exposed me to the greatest of my hobbies. I would try to learn the pieces as well as I could, and play along on the piano as I listened on the headphones.

Many selections required finger technique far beyond what I was able to do, but the result was often too moving, too lithe to keep me from trying!

Last year, my friend and I started a new funk band at school. This was particularly exciting, because I could finally use my ability to play popular music. After listening to Duke Ellington for years, I look forward to being able to improvise on the keyboard, without following sheet music. Fortunately, there were enough eager electric guitarists at school for us to form a five-man group. Although the guitarists never had formal training, I feel we make a perfect fit: their wide-eyed, teeth-gnashing antics onstage encourage me to be more spontaneous, while my classical training helps give structure and musicality to our pieces. I believe Fat Cat Fusion has been a hit at school functions because of our dedication, if not outright talent.

Peter Liu attended the University of California, Los Angeles.

37

WHEN DAD MAKES LIKE JOHN TRAVOLTA

No potential essay topic is richer than the relationships with your parents. The trick is not sounding labored or predictable. No admissions officer wants to read one more essay about how much somebody's dad means to him or her. And since the essay should really be about you, not somebody else, you don't want line after line of description about your parent. The following essay sings because in the process of telling about her dad, the author actually tells about herself; her enthusiasm, her sincerity, her patience, her joy in dance, and her affection for her dad are all lovingly conveyed.

Essay by HollyAnne Farris

"OH MY GOSH! I have a whole new appreciation for the art of dance!"

Who said that? The voice sounds familiar, but those words… they didn't just come out of the mouth of my dad, did they? They did, and wow, how long have I waited to hear something like that from him? Years…fifteen to be exact!

For fifteen years, the only things my dad has known or said about my life at McMillan School of Dance were things like "You mean you're only going to wear that thing for one night and we have to pay for it? Why can't we just rent it!" or "This recital is too long. We can't leave after your dance?"

That all came to a screeching halt the day I asked him to dance in the "Daddies" dance during our annual Jazz Shoppe Winter Recital.

Jazz Shoppe is a select group of dancers who train rigorously two days a week for approximately four months to learn twelve to fourteen different dances. This is in addition to the regularly scheduled classes we attend to prepare for the spring recital. Jazz Shoppe consists of a mini company, a junior company, two senior companies, and the infamous Daddy Company. I have been a member of the senior company for five years and this year, my dad officially became a member of McMillan School of Dance—Daddy Company.

As hard as we try to make each of the dances entertaining, the most popular dance of the Jazz Shoppe is the "Daddy Dance." It's hard to compete with eight or nine middle-aged dads, all dressed as John Travolta wanna-bes, complete with gold chains and open collars, shaking it to the Bee Gees's "Saturday Night Fever!" Some people come just to see the dads perform.

How he came to be a member of the Jazz Shoppe—Daddy Company is just short of a miracle. One night, on a whim, I asked him if he would be interested in dancing in the Jazz Shoppe, thoroughly expecting him to take one look at me and say something like "You're kidding, right?" But much to my delight and amazement, he said yes. I figured what better way to incorporate the one man who has always remained faithful to me into something that I love and take pride in!

So, in October, the practices began!

Every Tuesday, the daddies would go to the studio for an hour and a half to learn their ONE dance. Practices seemed to get more frustrating as they slowly learned more and more sections of their ONE dance (keep in mind I was learning twelve). Needless to say, there I was, attending their practices and videotaping our teacher. Each night I would pop the tape into our VCR and review, rework, and re-teach the Saturday Night Fever number with my dad.

> The audience went nuts! They even had a few catcalls made to them.

Finally, it was performance night! While I was busy making sure I had my suitcase full of my own costumes, my dad was busy making sure each of his gold chains, which we had picked out exclusively at our local Super K-mart, were positioned just right and that his collar was standing up at precisely the right angle.

Then it was off to the auditorium!

While backstage, I glanced over and I could hardly believe what I saw. My very self-confident and self-assured father, pacing up and down in the wings. He was nervous. Finally we were experiencing some sort of role reversal. Now I was the one calming down his nerves and reassuring him that he was going to do just fine. I even heard myself saying to him, "Just go out and do your best and everything will be fine!" Where and from whom had I heard that before?

And then, the end result of many long days of practice was finally here! It was time for the infamous "Daddy Dance." The lights dimmed, the curtains opened, and there they went, eight "John Travoltas"—gyrating across the stage, nailing the dance! The audience went nuts! They even had a few catcalls made to them.

In less than three minutes, the dance was over, but a change of a lifetime occurred. Not only was he the best one out there, it was as if he became a different person on that stage. It was then I knew he could finally relate to me and my passion for dance. He now knows how I feel when the lights go down and the curtain parts and I become one with the stage and one with the audience. Who would have thought that the appreciation of dance would become a common link between us?

It was so great to be sharing something so special with someone I love, my dad. I was so proud that that was my dad out there, shining in the limelight! We will always share that memory of Jazz Shoppe together and will continue to do so as long as we both dance!

HollyAnne Farris attended Texas A&M University.

38

AN INFATUATION WITH ART

An intriguing title gives an essay extra pizzazz, especially when the title is echoed by a line in the main body (that usually comes near the end). Author Emily Stein chooses some particularly nice words, such as when Mrs. Reed "glides" to the front of the room, or when her mind "swam" with visions of beautiful colors. The last paragraph is the longest, and not coincidentally, where Emily builds toward an emphatic statement of her passion for art. In her last six sentences, she offers a textbook example of how to begin with the concrete and move to the abstract.

"Lavender" by Emily Stein

I tentatively grasped the plastic blue handle of the fattest brush. Its firm but compliant bristles tickled as I pulled them along my palm. I looked around nervously, waiting for my first oil painting class to begin. The intimidating, white primed canvas rested on my easel, boasting its potential. Fresh, plump paint tubes in every color but black sat in a neat line, echoing the rainbow. My water cup was half full. I was ready.

I thought about the conversation that had resulted in my registration for the class. A month before, my mother and I had discussed what a long, boring summer it would be without anything scheduled. So I had decided painting would be the best waste of my time. I had always enjoyed art classes in school anyway.

At noon exactly, a woman with spiky red haircut close to the scalp glided to the front of the classroom. Her neck and wrists were suffocated by silver bands inlaid with jade, and a vibrant French scarf was wrapped carelessly around her neck. She was the teacher, Mrs. Reed.

Promptly, she introduced the paints. As instructed, I squeezed thick pearls of each color onto my palette. Mrs. Reed began moving her brush delicately, dipping it into her water cup, dropping a few beads of water onto her palette, and mixing a touch of aquamarine blue into the small pool. Then she introduced other colors to the melee, her wrist making loose, consecutive circles. Somehow she managed to produce the most beautiful lavender I had ever seen. Mrs. Reed firmly placed the tip of her brush, which was now saturated with watery paint, at the top left corner of her blank paper and pulled it down an inch.

"Lavender," she explained. I looked at the paper, at its glistening purplish-white stripe. Suddenly my fingers itched to make lavender, too. And this was only one shade of one color. My mind swam with how many beautiful colors must exist, waiting to be solidified on a canvas. Mrs. Reed set the other students and me free, challenging us to see how many colors we could discover. Then we learned how to sketch and block in still lifes, to see the delicate contours of the apples, and the tiny details of the iris's petals. I began to see everything around me in a different way. I had found my euphoria. Stepping into that classroom, I had not known what an addiction I would have to painting. Yet even now, three years, many paintings, and a few awards later, I am still the last to leave the art room. I go into art stores just to run my hands along canvases and admire fat new tubes of paint. My world has morphed into landscapes as I drive, still lifes as I eat, and portraits as I sit in class. Through colors and shadows I have become more alive. I am grateful to my mother for making me attend that first class. It has changed my life forever.

As instructed, I squeezed thick pearls of each color onto my palette.

Emily Stein attended Barnard College.

39

WHEN JOCKS JOIN THE CHOIR

Author Alex Wellman writes deftly about his surprise at seeing senior football players "singing about being someone's buttercup." Everyone knows the role that cliques play in high school, and it is impressive when a football player such as Alex shows an awareness of the need to broaden his horizons. On his first reference to his significant experience, Alex does not write that his attitude was changed forever, but rather that he was "reminded of the importance" of being his own person. It makes sense to be low-key at first; after he has shared more of the anecdote, he can be more believable in making claims as to its significance.

"Me, Myself, and I" by Alex C. Wellman

It has been about eighteen years since I was born in New York City, and I have spent roughly the last eight of those years in what I still call a new home, here in Charlotte, North Carolina. My life has followed the clichéd and semi-charmed life of a teenager growing up in a very nice American neighborhood. I spend my falls playing football, and my springs running track. I spend my weeknights doing homework and my weekends at movies, parties, and friends' houses. Where I tend to stray from the cliché of the typical teenager is in my ability to be myself. It is with thanks to three random individuals, people to whom I never thought I would owe anything, that I was reminded of the importance of never compromising who I am just to make somebody else happy.

Somehow, standing 6'3", 200 pounds, and playing two sports religiously makes me fall into the category of the stereotypical athlete. Historically, high school athletes are supposed to make jeering remarks at kids who do not play sports and act differently from them. They are even supposed to poke fun at the kids who play sports, but do not get the playing time. I was never one to agree with this sort of thing, however, I almost did back in my sophomore year, because all of the other athletes were doing it. Well, all of them except these three seniors on the football team. These were all guys that were going on to play college ball somewhere and it is to them that I owe what will probably be the greatest lesson that I ever learned as a teenager.

It was during assembly, and all I was concerned about was getting to my break period, which was next. That was when Mr. Stallworth, the director of the drama program at my school, got on stage and said that there would be a special performance by the chorus. The audience groaned, because they knew this meant that break would be cut short. The stage lights kicked on, the curtain dropped and I will *never* forget what I saw next. The three burliest, meanest, and best seniors on our football team had decided to join the chorus. Seeing them up there singing about being someone's buttercup made me want to laugh until the tears ran, but I quickly decided it would not be wise to do so for fear of what might happen to my little sophomore self come practice that afternoon. What overcame me next was a sensation of profound respect for those guys. They had crossed a line that the Hollywood gods and the higher-ups in society had dubbed as a taboo. I had always thought of them as being the stereotypical jocks, but seeing them belting their lungs out on stage proved to me that they were indeed more than just athletes.

What those seniors do not and may never know is that they changed me for a thousand lifetimes over. Seeing them up there with students who I never thought they would associate with made me realize that the only barriers the human race struggles to cross are the ones it creates. Since I saw that performance, I have made a point of talking to and hanging out with kids who I would not have normally associated myself with because of that invisible line. Today, I realize that if I had held myself back from different people, I would have been going along with the crowd. In essence, I would have compromised my own morals and values because someone else

> Seeing them up there singing about being someone's buttercup made me want to laugh until the tears ran.

thought that they just were not good enough. Thanks to those three seniors, I know that it is ok for me to be the king of my own life, instead of the pawn of someone else's.

Alex C. Wellman attended Middlebury College.

Camp Counseling and Community Service

Working with kids, and learning from them, are the unifying themes in this category. Several of the following essays describe tutoring or mentoring children. Yet as Essays 40 and 42 remind us, the kids often teach valuable and unexpected lessons of their own. If you are involved in tutoring or community service, keep the focus on what you gain from the experience rather than what you give.

40

WISDOM IN UNEXPECTED PLACES

Colleges love applicants who can learn from those who are different from them. By highlighting lessons from the mind-set of elementary schoolers, author John Ivey Eagles finds an ingenious way of showing that he can learn from anyone. This sort of openness is solid gold to institutions that place a high value on diversity. Direct quotes from his "teachers," a couple of wayward kids, add the concrete detail (and humor) that make this essay sing. Says Eagles, "I found it very helpful to put out a draft that I felt pretty good about and then leave it alone for three or four days and come back to it as a reader, rather than as an editor, to see what I thought."

"Alfred and Bill: Role Models for Life" by John Ivey Eagles

I have spent the past four summers working as a volunteer and counselor at a summer camp for kids ages four to ten. Each week presents new challenges, opportunities, and surprises and I am often amazed at the wit, intelligence, and confidence that elementary schoolers can display. This year, it was the bright faces of two campers, Alfred and Bill, that provided the most humor, challenge, and surprise to me and the rest of the staff. While no child consistently behaves in a manner appropriate for adults, they often offer interesting and unconventional insights that have inspired me to try to redefine how I view the world.

Bill's father wore NASCAR T-shirts, hats, and socks, and he spoke with a thick southern accent; despite Bill's short hair, one could not look at him without seeing (imagining?) the faintest hint of a mullet peeking out from underneath his cap. Upon being asked his name, Bill would reply, his boyish, drawling voice raised to a yell, "I'm Bill who doesn't play by the rules," and in a much softer

> **Thus I am striving to be "John Ivey who doesn't play by the rules...too much."**

tone, as if beginning an unrelated sentence, add, "too much." It clearly articulated a desire for freedom, while not creating an inconvenient commitment to rebellion. I support questioning authority, finding your own path, and civil disobedience. However, occasionally the status quo deserves credence. Thus I am striving to be "John Ivey who doesn't play by the rules...too much."

Like Bill, Alfred was not one to be hemmed in by society's expectations. With amazing consistency, he would come in to camp with his pants or shirt on backwards, and sometimes he would return from the bathroom missing one, the other, or both. He spoke with an astonishing vocabulary and a voice that sounded like he had just learned to talk. The incident with Alfred that I found most inspiring followed his biting another camper's ear. The camp director was talking to Alfred, who was in time-out, explaining that he would have to call Alfred's mom. "No! No! Dat would be *tewible...Can't* you call my dad's fwiend? He knows our famiwy vewy well." Alfred knew he was beaten, but he never gave up. After his dad's friend, he suggested two grandmothers before the director ended the conversation. His persistence was impressive. No matter how far out an idea might have seemed, he was ready to suggest it as an alternative to something he found disagreeable. I have found that too many people are willing to give up too quickly on issues that are important to them. Like Alfred, I believe we should always suggest even that which seems impossible or laughable. The effort might turn into a compromise, or even be the best idea in its own right.

Alfred and Bill each demonstrated admirable qualities. Their behavior showed that kids often approach problems and questions from angles older people cannot imagine. The way children absorb and react to life can provide others with interesting ideas on how they can take the best and most unusual notions of children and apply them to make their lives more interesting and fulfilling.

John Ivey Eagles attended Haverford College.

41

DOING WELL BY DOING GOOD

There have been a lot of bad essays about the problem of homelessness. This one stands out because it chronicles personal experiences. Not many high school students have the moxie, as author Marisa Kaley did, to step into the role of coordinating a homeless shelter, even if it was only for one night per month. The first two paragraphs skillfully set the scene as the reader realizes only gradually (or perhaps not until the third paragraph) that she has entered a homeless shelter. Says Marisa, "My advice is to have someone you trust proofread the essay. No matter how many times you read it yourself, there will be mistakes that you miss."

"Hillcrest House" by Marisa Kaley

After climbing a set of dull looking concrete stairs, I entered the kitchen/dining area, a small space complete with a television and curtained windows. Two tables were set for the guests. Down a hallway were two bathrooms, one marked "Men," the other, "Women." In the second room were two rows of freshly made twin beds, each topped with a neatly folded pair of pajamas, robe, and slippers. A partition separated each bed from the next, ensuring at least a bit of privacy. My parents and I began heating dinner as we waited for the guests to arrive.

And arrive they did, crammed into one lonely van. Many knew the routine, entering with a shy, almost whispered hello and then proceeding to the showers. One by one, men and women took their seats at the dinner table, eagerly awaiting a home cooked meal. Each was extremely appreciative of our efforts as hosts and no one forgot to use their manners. From my conversations, the guests were cognizant of current affairs and television programs, wanting to watch a variety of different shows while they ate. Everyone was easy to engage in conversation and seemed to want to talk, need to talk.

Two years ago, I became the Freedom Plains Presbyterian Church coordinator for the Dutchess County Coalition for the Homeless Overnight Shelter. The shelter provides temporary, emergency housing for adults who are homeless, based on the simple philosophy that no one should have to sleep on the street. Our church is responsible for the fourth Wednesday of each month. A group of volunteers cook a meal for fifteen people. Two additional volunteers bring the food to the shelter and spend the night, during which time they serve the meal, do laundry, make breakfast, and otherwise take care of the guests.

As coordinator, my most challenging responsibility until last September was finding volunteers to stay overnight at the shelter, since many adults work on Thursday mornings. I had been fortunate to find volunteers as I could not host overnight until I turned eighteen. I was, however, still able to make a difference in my community. I wrote letters, called church members, spoke about the program at church services, cooked meals, organized donations, wrote church Bulletin and Herald inserts, participated in a training program, and visited the shelter during the day. In September, the host hours changed from all night to eight to eleven p.m. but the other tasks remain. I have since hosted on three nights with my parents and have had a much easier time finding volunteers.

Everyone was easy to engage in conversation and seemed to want to talk, need to talk.

I have gained a great deal as a result of my involvement with the shelter. I am working to increase awareness of the needs of the men, women, and families who are homeless to our church members and also to my fellow high school students. Last November, I organized a very successful supply drive at my high school and on Thanksgiving eve delivered two van loads of towels, sheets, blankets, pajamas, slippers, and toiletries to the shelter. I hope that my next supply drive will be even more successful.

Many of the shelter guests are the working poor. I have learned that their problems go beyond not having a place to live and include substance abuse problems, mental illness, and past incarcerations. I have realized how sheltered my life has been and that I have taken so many things for granted. I like knowing that I can help people in my city and feel more grateful for the things that I am so lucky to have. I can prove to those older and to myself that I am responsible, can handle a challenge, and can help improve people's lives even though I am just one person, and a teenager at that. I have been raised with the idea that those who have received talents and benefits need to give back. I am lucky to have had and to continue to have experiences that enable me to gain new perspectives and to develop additional skills. I have received so much more than I have given in volunteering in my community.

Marisa Kaley attended Wellesley College.

42

MAKE ME BARF

We won't spoil the final twist of this essay, but suffice it to say that sometimes an essay merely needs to be a story well told. The personality of the author, Sarah Lindsay, comes through loud and clear in her description of being a counselor at summer camp. Instead of lapsing into heavy-handed moralizing about camp and everything that it taught her, she shows the importance of camp by relating an anecdote. In the process of revealing her care for the campers and her camaraderie with the counselors, she demonstrates an equally important trait: the ability to laugh at herself.

Essay by Sarah Lindsay

"I don't do throw-up."

My own words were coming back to haunt me as I heard one of my campers yell, "Ewww, Bridger threw up." I froze. I forced myself to turn around and look. I glanced quickly, then immediately looked away. I stopped breathing through my nose so I wouldn't be able to smell it. I was horrified.

The one thing that I hate most is throw-up. Looking at it causes me to gag. Earlier that week I had been talking to my friend, Molly, who was a counselor in Cabin 3. She was telling me how she had had to clean up her camper's vomit.

"I would *never* be able to do that," I said.

"Well I didn't have a choice," Molly replied.

"I just…I don't do throw-up," I retorted.

Working at Camp Seafarer on the "Crystal Coast" of North Carolina for the summer was like a dream to me. I had gone there as a camper, and my experiences there have influenced my life greatly. The counselors were so supportive, and it seemed like they never ran out of energy. I was excited to have the opportunity to affect someone's life the way my counselors had affected mine. Being a counselor, though, was more work than I had anticipated. I was always exhausted, and it was hard to keep giving 100 percent of myself twenty-four hours a day. In the end, however, it was worth staying up with a homesick camper or saying a longer goodnight to the shyest girl to help bring her out of her shell. It was just so much responsibility trying to keep twelve ten-year-olds safe, while trying to help them have a great summer. Now my responsibility was spreading to the one thing I dreaded most, cleaning up throw-up.

I looked around at Bridger who looked like she was either laughing or crying. I assumed she was crying since she had just gotten sick. Then I noticed my co-counselors, Jessie and Liz, standing around. I looked at them, waiting for them to take the initiative and start to clean up. But they didn't even move towards it. Then Jessie made a move.

"I'll take Bridger to the health center," she said.

Darn, I thought, *I should have volunteered to do that.* I glanced at Liz.

"Sarah, I'm busy. Why don't you clean it up?"

I couldn't believe it! I was stuck with doing the one thing I have always said I would never do. *All right, I can do this*, I said to myself.

> I looked around at Bridger who looked like she was either laughing or crying.

What to get first?...Paper towels! I went into the bathroom to find some, but we were out. *Okay, it's going to be okay. I'll just go to the cabin next door.* I got some paper towels from Cabin 9 and hurried back to my cabin. As I approached my enemy, the throw-up, I noticed a lot of girls were crowded around me laughing.

"This is not funny girls, Bridger's sick," I told them and they backed up, still giggling softly.

All right here goes nothing, I thought as I started to fling paper towels down on top of the vomit. I then squeezed my eyes shut and went in for the kill, picking up the mess. I picked up the paper towels as fast as I could and threw them into the trash can. I had done it! *I can handle this job; the late nights, exhausting days and all the puke that comes with it*, I celebrated. Then I noticed that now the whole cabin was laughing.

"Sarah!" Bridger exclaimed, "The throw-up was fake!"

I learned, that summer, that with responsibility comes great rewards, such as my campers' hysterical laughing over the fake throw-up. Every smile and every hug made the draining job worth it.

Sarah Lindsay attended Vanderbilt University.

43

"MILES AND MILES OF TRASH"

If the following essay were written about editing the school newspaper or playing a varsity sport, it would fall flat. But for a student with deep commitment to a genuinely unique activity, a factual description of what happened, and when, can create a unifying identity for an application. Jonathan Gaynes tells the story of his involvement with the Student Ecology Movement, and his accomplishments are so impressive that they speak for themselves. The essay succeeds because of the concrete actions he describes: calling principals, planning initiatives, organizing volunteers, speaking at a convention, etc. "My passion is saving the environment" would be an eye-roller in most essays, but Jonathan's previous accomplishments give him credibility that few students can match. In his words, "Writing has never come naturally to me. I worked through the essay with a wonderful college advisor, and got advice from my parents as well. It took me over five rewrites to eventually create the final version."

Essay by Jonathan Gaynes

The Georgia drought of 2007 set the stage. The water level at Lake Lanier was down at least 20 feet, and portions of land unexposed for years were completely visible. There were beer bottles, old soda cans, gas tanks, and even refrigerators; relics of our lives waiting for discovery by future archeologists. Interlaced among these artifacts were the true villains, mounds of plastic bags. They came in all sizes, shapes, and colors; from bite sized zip locks to large industrial garbage bags and everything in between, the place was trashed. But my true passion came from observations made in the middle of nowhere, our oceans. A sea captain described the horrific sites over the air on "This American Life." The five hotspots, each the size of Texas, are filled with plastic bags, basketballs, tires, and diapers all afloat in the middle of the ocean, as far as the eye can see.

Motivated by these two distinct issues, I felt compelled to take action. I created The Student Ecology Movement (SEM), a non-profit organization, dedicated to "protecting the world which we live in now to ensure a healthy planet for our children." I called directors and principals of schools around the metro Atlanta area and mobilized like-minded students, solicited donations, and created a plan to help make a difference at Lake Lanier. Together with a workforce of twenty-five teens and adults we cleaned over 700 pounds of trash from the bottom of Lake Lanier. This project was just the beginning of the many lake and river cleanups to follow.

Using these cleanups as a springboard, SEM gained recognition as an important local environmental organization with a story on FOX's local news, a front page feature in the Atlanta Journal Constitution's *Living Section*, and a showcase on a local radio station, WMLB. One thing led to another and soon I appeared as a guest speaker at the Sustainable Atlanta Round Table meeting and at the Atlanta's Bioneers Convention.

The ultimate display of activism came when SEM brought the international Park(ing) initiative to Atlanta. With ten SEM activists, we collaborated with the residents of Atlanta to transform parallel parking spots into temporary parks. For this project, SEM received donations of sod, blooming plants, and trees from local businesses and horticultural centers. The purpose of the project was to raise awareness about the lack of green space, and to show people how much pleasure a little green space can bring. I realized that events like this not only raised awareness, but spark necessary discussions in the community.

> I want to be that catalyst... that force which will encourage all people to take some form of action.

Simple river cleanups and Park(ing) days won't solve global warming, but hopefully will help spread the words of the sea captain who saw the miles and miles of trash. It is important for us to keep doing "the green thing" in order to preserve the world for our children's tomorrow. My passion is saving the environment, and I want to be that catalyst...that force which will encourage all people to take some form of action in saving our world.

Jonathan Gaynes attended American University.

44

"A BREATH OF FRESH AIR TO MY BRAIN"

Author Axel Olson illustrates an important principle for those writing about service to others: Keep the focus on how *you* benefit. Olson describes mowing the lawn for an 88-year-old neighbor, and while his interactions with her are part of the story, most of the essay is about how a rote activity gives him peace of mind. Just as the process of mowing allows him to reflect, writing about the process of mowing gives him space to share his musings with the reader. The conclusion keeps proper perspective on a mundane activity. He is not changing the elderly neighbor's life but simply giving her human company.

Essay by Axel Olson

Describe a place or environment where you are perfectly content. What do you do or experience there, and why is it meaningful to you?

One might think it strange for a teenager to be content behind a lawn mower in his neighbor's yard, but there is something unusually rewarding about tackling the jungle of grass I face every week behind Margaret Norris's house.

I find myself months into my senior year, and the stress from AP classes, daily sports practice, extracurricular activities, a social life, and household commitments is not even close to subsiding. No matter how much time I spend on these things, I can never truly settle in to a routine. After school I am off to cross-country practice, then band practice, and then home to work on an essay or a project. Sure I enjoy the chaos of exploring all of my interests, but at the end of the day the humdrum job of mowing my 88-year-old neighbor's lawn has become an experience I look forward to for escape and reflection.

About once a week I slip into some comfortable gym shorts and a T-shirt and roll the mower across the street to Margaret's house. She lived on my street before it was paved and constantly alive with joggers, bikers, and cars. Now she is the only one left in her family. I park the mower and ring the doorbell. It takes her a minute to get to the door. We always seem to engage in the same conversation; we talk about school, college plans, and the upcoming play I am in at my school. But each time I gain something new from it.

The hum of the electric mower fills my ears, which are usually busy listening to teachers, parents, or music. The monotony of sound and movement are a breath of fresh air to my brain, which is wiped clean of unnecessary worry. This is when my ideas begin to flow. In fact, I conceived the plot of my feature film behind the mower in Margaret Norris' backyard. Something about her old brick house practically created my characters for me, and last summer I filmed several scenes there.

> **The hum of the electric mower fills my ears, which are usually busy listening to teachers, parents, or music.**

I trace the edge of the lines of cut grass, making laps around the yard. In the back of my mind I am aware that I will be painting lines in AP Art the following morning and running laps in cross-country the next day, but those thoughts are fleeting. I look up to find Margaret standing by her back door with a bowl of kibbles in her hand. I cut the engine off and meet her halfway across the yard. She tells me about the stray cat that has decided to make that old house its home too—keeping her company.

Maybe that is my job, to give her human company. She has that interaction with me, those simple conversations, and maybe that is what keeps her going. For me it is more than a job. She gives me time to think and, more importantly, reminds me to do just the opposite. I cross the street and wash the grass from my hands.

Axel Olson attends School of the Art Institute of Chicago.

45

A DIFFERENT KIND OF CHRISTMAS

Author Mary Plumb tells a remarkable story. Instead of a traditional Christmas vacation, her family packs its bags and heads off to work in a Bolivian orphanage. Mary vividly portrays the joy she found there and skillfully contrasts it with the materialistic Christmas she left behind. It would have been easy for her to lapse into heavy moralizing, but Mary lets her experiences show everything that needs to be said. The essay is punctuated with vivid vocabulary—words like "grumbling," "pranced," and "gallantly"—that add texture to the narrative without making it seem thesaurusy.

Essay by Mary Plumb

> "I do it for the joy it brings 'cause I'm a joyful girl. 'Cause the
> world owes us nothing, we owe each other the world."
> —Ani DiFranco ("Joyful Girl")

In the fall of my junior year, my mother announced that she had signed us up for a mission trip to Bolivia for Christmas break. My first thought was, "That's impossible! But I wanted a new computer and some new clothes. How will we ever get all the gifts down there? Our suitcases will be too heavy!" I was careful not to say these selfish things out loud. We—my mother, my three older siblings, and I—would be working as volunteers at the Amistad Mission in Cochubamba, Bolivia, a city of over two million people that none of us had ever heard of. Were we really going to spend Christmas working in an orphanage in one of the poorest countries in the world? For weeks leading up to the trip, I worried about what I would do there.

The minute we arrived at Amistad (the Friendship Mission), my fears dissolved. The children must have heard the grumbling engine and grinding of the bus tires on the gravel road, for as the primitive bus turned the corner, I could see no fewer than fifty sets of luminous, brown eyes welcoming us. Immediately sprinting toward us, one little girl, Naomi, leapt into my arms and kissed my face before even saying, "Hola!" Never before have I felt so welcomed by anyone—and these were complete strangers! Excited by our arrival, the children directed us to the community center, really a basketball court, which had been decorated with a Nativity scene made of crumpled manila paper. Dressed in tomato-red traditional Bolivian skirts, the teenagers narrated the Christmas Pageant as the younger children performed. Small native children were dressed as Mary, Joseph, Jesus, the three Wise Men, and the shepherds. The smallest girls pranced in full white dresses with masks made of cotton balls to make them look like sheep. Having obviously rehearsed for a long time, they proudly serenaded us with Christmas carols in Spanish, their joyous enthusiasm unbridled.

One day, I noticed a boy named Marcelo with a strange-looking apparatus of red plastic, rubber bands, and metal covering his face. My first response was to feel sorry for him: surely he was ashamed of his deformity and the need to wear this weird gizmo. But he came strolling up to the community center without a worry in the world, and as I approached to comfort him, he unleashed a huge smile inviting me to come outside to play soccer with him and his friends. No one else seemed to notice or even care about the brace installed to fix Marcelo's cleft palate.

The mission residences included ten houses, "casas," each housing a "family" of eight children, with a "mamá" and "tía" as caretakers. One afternoon I was invited to Casa San Francisco to eat lunch with one of the "familias." As guest of honor, I sat at the head of the long table with ten children sitting along each side. Over the wailing of the babies and bickering of the teenagers, the "tías" attempted to say grace. Next, they passed out plates of rice, each with cooked carrots, peas and a small piece of flavorless chicken. As I was served my plate, three-year old Maria spilled her apple juice all over my food. The ensuing silence told me that they expected me to be upset. Knowing not enough food was left in the pot to replenish my plate,

Eduardo, the eldest boy, gallantly offered me his. When I refused, he switched the plates anyway. During my weeklong stay, I noticed acts of generosity and kindness both large and small. These people had few material possessions to give, but during my week there, I received gifts beyond the tangible and became very attached to all of the children at the Mission.

Working hard from sunup to sundown was not exactly my original idea of how to spend my coveted Christmas holiday, but the week I spent working side by side with my family remains one of the best experiences of my life. We arranged activities for the kids—arts and crafts, trips to the park, and sports games. On Christmas day, when we helped the Amistad children host a fun-filled party for families living in dire conditions just beyond the Mission fence, our guests were overjoyed. The faces of both parents and children lit up as I handed each of them one simple present; filled with an appreciation for such simple things, these children deserved so much more, yet they were happy with what they had.

> My first response was to feel sorry for him: surely he was ashamed of his deformity and the need to wear this weird gizmo.

Not until several weeks after our return did I realize, "Hey, I didn't get that computer I had wanted so much, nor the new jeans." At the same time, I realized that I might have missed it all had I not gone on our Bolivia trip. The gifts I received last December from the orphaned children of Amistad added not a single pound to the luggage I carried home, for the lasting gifts they gave me were those of joy, of friendship, of growing up.

Mary Plumb attended the University of Texas at Austin.

46

TO CAMP, THIS TIME AS A COUNSELOR

Author Dana Waskover's essay starts like one thousand other summer-camp essays. But her ordinary beginning sets the stage for an unexpected twist. When she goes back to camp as a counselor, she finds out that life is a lot less fun and a lot more work than she remembered. Instead of exhilaration, she finds disillusionment—and a much more interesting essay topic than if she had had a wonderful time. The essay sparkles in part because Dana lets the story unfold without too much foreshadowing, which allows the reader to experience the letdown with her.

Essay by Dana Leigh Waskover

The summer after eleventh grade represented a meaningful and eye opening experience for me. I spent the summer as a counselor at an overnight camp, Raquette Lake Girls Camp, where I had attended as a camper for four years.

This picturesque camp is located on beautiful Raquette Lake, one of the larger natural lakes in the Adirondack Mountains of New York State. Seeing the lake brought back fond memories of the endless hours of fun and play I had as a camper. I remembered my first year as a camper and the challenge of passing the very essential deep-water test. Participation in all activities on the lake depended on whether or not I passed the test, which I did successfully.

The summers at Raquette Lake were a time of relaxation and play, of carefree days and nights in a setting of camaraderie and much happiness.

So it was with great joy and excitement that I returned to Raquette Lake as a junior counselor. This was my first real job and I was thrilled to be back at camp. Enthusiasm for the camp experience heightened when I arrived several days before the campers. I learned that I would be assigned to live in a bunk for fourteen nine-year-old girls and that I would be spending my days as a swim instructor and lifeguard at the lake waterfront. I looked forward to this experience.

When the campers arrived, I realized that I would have a substantially different experience than I had expected. After one day I came to the sobering realization that I was not a camper any longer. I was hired help. I was expected to work from early morning through bedtime. I was responsible for the total well-being of my campers. This included waking them in the morning, getting them washed and ready for activities, helping them follow a healthy diet, overcome their homesickness, and smooth out their relationships with friends. I was friend, mother, and disciplinarian to fourteen children.

> After one day I came to the sobering realization that I was not a camper any longer. I was hired help.

The lake, which had represented challenges and joy to me, became my workplace. I was stationed on the dock from after breakfast until dinnertime. My only break was for lunch, when I joined my campers and served them their food.

As a camper, if it were too cold or rainy, I would skip the lake activities and relax with my friends, all snuggled up in our bunk. As a counselor I could not do that. My summer as a counselor was one of the coldest and rainiest in camp history and I did not have the option to say that I did not want to stand on the dock because I was cold or wet. I endured the weather because I had made a commitment to the camp to work for the entire season.

The change in my status, from camper to counselor, being responsible for waterfront safety and the happiness of my campers, was both a sobering and maturing experience. I had to grow up. I had to take my responsibility seriously. All this responsibility, the hard days and long nights, did provide some satisfying relationships with my campers and other counselors, but the salary was not gratifying. I earned $750.00 for the entire summer's work.

In retrospect, my summer as a counselor was an awakening for me. I know that I have the perseverance to complete a task that I agree to do, no matter how arduous or uncomfortable it may be. I believe this strength will serve me well during my college years, as I work hard at my studies, face many challenges, and begin to identify a career that will bring me emotional, intellectual, and financial rewards. Somehow, I feel that Raquette Lake helped me evolve from child to adult. Just in time for college.

Dana Leigh Waskover attended the University of Tampa.

Racial or Cultural Differences

I f there is one kind of essay topic guaranteed to succeed, this is it. Colleges value diversity, and a student from a background different from the norm, especially a student who is willing to write about that fact, will add to the richness of campus life. We should hasten to note that essays on racial or cultural differences are not the exclusive province of minority students, as Essay 58 demonstrates. The biggest advantage to essays in this category is that they hit close to home. If you're writing about your race or cultural identity, you're writing about yourself.

47

CHATTING IT UP WITH A BAOBAB TREE

For exotic appeal, it is hard to top the following essay from author Prince Agbo. Prince is of African descent but grew up in France and French Guiana, and he uses the device of a palm tree talking to a baobab tree to represent the tensions in his multicultural identity. (Baobabs, native to Africa, are massive trees with trunks up to sixty feet in diameter.) Any writer can use personification; simply choose two objects to represent facets of a personality, sides of an issue, etc., pretend they are people, and let them go at it. The device generally works best when, as in Prince's essay, the objects have a common tie (such as both being trees) that makes the conversation plausible.

"Who Am I?" by Prince Agbo

As I am filing all those college applications, the question keeps coming back to me. Who am I? Where do I come from? Where am I heading?

Am I African? Am I French? Am I Caribbean? Or…soon an American college student?

As I reflect on my African roots, my French and Caribbean upbringings, and now, my new life in America, I could compare myself with a palm tree, being laughed at by an African baobab.

I will always remain deeply rooted in my African ground. Actually I am a palm tree here—a very hard to knock down palm tree. My neighbor is a friendly Baobab. He is my companion on this red ground. He is so tall and so powerful I sometimes get jealous. He is impressive, also. Who am I? Well, he may be tall, powerful, impressive, strong…whatever; at least I, the palm tree, did also grow up in France, unlike Baobab who will never see the French sun. Baobab does not like me thinking that way. He gets mad at me. Anyway, as he says, he absolutely does not need the French sun. His is the brightest, the yellowest, and the warmest sun on earth: the African sun!

Baobab does not like my reasoning. Neither what I say, nor the calm I say it with.

The African sun has those qualities, for sure. But, dear Baobab, I also know about them. Indeed, it is the African sun that, a long time ago, made my first seed grow. It is also this African sun that gave me that strong color, and the red of my sap. Dear Baobab, I have experienced the virtues of the African sun. But I have also experienced the virtues of travel. Though I remain the same palm tree.

Baobab does not appreciate my comment. Blowing, bowing, his devil eye confirms his saying: the French sun would never make me as tall as him. He is right. I am not that tall, certainly not as tall as he is. But my branches are wide, so wide that I can embrace different cultures from all over the world. Plus, dear Baobab, may I mention that your flowers lack some vitality...some brightness? I keep on considering your flowers, and they definitely cannot compete with mine: mine are brightly, joyfully colored; they actually come from French Guiana, to be precise. I am the only palm tree with rainbow flowers welcoming so many butterflies.

Baobab does not like my reasoning. Neither what I say, nor the calm I say it with.

"Who do you think you are?" he asks me, screaming.

I am me. I am always the same. Wherever I go, whatever I go through. Today, my flowers are covered with Vermont snow. Tomorrow, who knows...? For sure I am small, but I am rich, rich with those different weathers I go through, with those new experiences that each season and each trip brings me. Baobab stares at me; he looks confused. Then he bows until he reaches my height and, delicately, he uses his height to protect me from the snowfall. What's next? Baobab is curious.

Well, dear Baobab, for now I am still a bit sleepy, but soon will come spring and my flowers will blossom, paving the way for a new adventure: America!

Prince Agbo attended Cornell University (NY).

48

TWO BIRDS WITH ONE ESSAY

Though technically about an activity, this essay speaks most eloquently about the applicant's ethnic identity and his dedication to it. There is both passion and precision in his description, and like many good essays about ethnicity, Romit Bhattacharya uses it to dispel stereotypes (e.g., "speaking Indian") while showing, not telling, the importance to him of his Indian identity. The fact that the activity described in the essay occurs at 11:24 p.m. makes it all the more real. This version was the author's fourth try at an activities essay. "I continued to write essays until I felt that what I wrote corresponded with what I truly felt," says Bhattacharya. "I truly felt a sense of frustration and exasperation, but also a deep commitment to the cause."

"Activities Essay" by Romit Bhattacharya

I'm tired and a little bit desperate. My clock angrily glares at me through its neon green dial. It's 11:24. The biology exam tomorrow will be murder. I resolutely pass over my textbook, and instead return to the screen where Pandit Jasraj stares back at me. I run through a quick checklist in my mind: I sent out the emails to the members, I typed up the biography for the program, I bought Styrofoam cups for refreshments. Homestretch. I tilt the graphic of the vocal maestro just enough to look funky next to the bold text, "Pandit Jasraj, Live In Concert!" O God, WHY am I doing this? All I want is some sleep.

Why am I the first person called to make flyers? Why do I even do it? It seems hopeless. Another event comes and goes in an auditorium we rent out for the night. Everyone listens to some music and discusses it over a samosa or two, but our goal is not furthered. India Center still does not have the funds it needs to buy itself an address, a place that all the varied and fragmented Indian communities can jointly call their "home." Here they will cease to be Bengalis, Marathis, Tamilians, Gujarathis, or Punjabis. They will not identify themselves as Hindu, Muslim, Buddhist, Sikh, Jain, Jewish, or Christian. Here the community will build its own little microcosm to fit into the majestic mosaic of New York.

My friends often ask me if I speak "Indian" at home. That would make it all so much easier, and sometimes I wish there were one such language. But then it is that very diversity which gives Indian culture its multilayered richness. And although it means working extra hours to rally the community together, to shake them up and remind them to vote, to wake them up to the truth of harmonizing all their regional tongues to sing in one unified voice, I am willing to put in that effort. I want that united Indian voice to speak to every name on the membership list, and reach out and address each one's concerns. I want that voice to resonate in public parades and diversity shows, as well as reach into the corridors of Washington so that change can be brought about effectively. I want to strengthen and support the trembling immigrant voices with a vigorous chorus of "The Star Spangled Banner."

> **My friends often ask me if I speak "Indian" at home. That would make it all so much easier.**

Yes, I am willing to make my flyers bright and flashy, and send my emails with capitalized entreaties, and look out on that auditorium to see if the seats are packed and the donation boxes are jammed full.

So I do not resent it when Mr. Ralph D'Souza calls me and asks me to pick up the famous Kathak dancer Rachnaji from the train station, or check the sound system on the stage. I put on my India Center volunteer badge, slip on a dark blue blazer, and go cheerfully on my way.

Romit Bhattacharya attended the University of Pennsylvania.

49

FIGHTING THE CULTURE OF HIP-HOP

Autobiographical essays are solid gold when the writer can talk about something other than the affluent suburban upbringing typical of most students at selective colleges. Author Danielle Brown writes about aspects of the African American community, and in the process, illustrates the challenges she has overcome. She complements her critique of the culture of hip-hop with her dedication to enduring role models within the African American community, which she illustrates with her anecdote about the young girl she is tutoring.

Essay by Danielle Brown

"Lynching was ritualistic public square violence, part of a sordid history of white criminality."—Hakim Hasan

Looking out of the car window onto Crenshaw Boulevard, I do not see an angry mob cloaked in white, dancing on one of the street corners. Nor do I see towering willows ornamented with dangling bodies. As I look out of my window I see young African American boys flaunting diamond earrings that make their earlobes droop; young men and women bumping the latest "Jay-Z" song while bringing their twenty-inch rim-spinning Escalades to a halt at the red light. In the past, African Americans had coped with several acts of hatred, particularly lynching. Today my community is facing a new dilemma—one that is self-inflicted and a killer among African American youth. The mortality rate caused by "hip-hop lynching" increases every day in my neighborhood. Illiteracy, materialism, degradation of women, and praise of drugs and sex are preached to youth through negative hip-hop music, which causes them to carry these immoral ideologies over to their everyday lives.

The immoral ideologies that are taking over my community verify society's blind following after incompetent leaders. As Carter G. Woodson once said, "If you allow a people to control the way you think, you do not have to assign them an inferior status, if necessary, they will seek it themselves." To escape these negative influences, I have joined College Bound, a program designed to prepare minority youth for college and leadership in their community.

> **As I look out of my window I see young African American boys flaunting diamond earrings that make their earlobes droop.**

As of now, I am participating in the Rites of Passage, a program through College Bound designed to prepare seniors for college and adulthood. Although I approve of College Bound's goals to reach out to minority youth and guide them to academic success, there are not enough programs available to help the growing number of troubled minority children.

The community in which I live has had a significant influence on my outlook on life. Turning away from the misleading hip-hop "role models" that many of my contemporaries admire, I look up to the individuals who actually made a difference in their communities; leaders such as Marian Wright Edelman, Malcolm X, and Carter G. Woodson. Although I have found means of escaping immoral ideologies that are invading my community, I have chosen not to become a refugee of my neighborhood, but to give back what I can.

Currently, I am tutoring for a junior high remedial English class at my school. With our instructed trips to the library, I have gone beyond the expected vocabulary reviews and grammar sessions, stretching my abilities as a tutor to also assist as a mentor.

As we all know, in every rosebush there are thorns. From the moment I stepped into the paper-strewn English class, I knew the boisterous creator of this tumult would be difficult to work with. Although Veronica's aggressive and unruly temperament in the classroom intimidated her peers, this wild chimpanzee morphed into a tranquil panda while studying in the library. It was while I was helping Veronica with her Martin Luther King Jr. project that I learned something shocking. Despite his mass popularity and having read his biography, Veronica knew nothing about Dr. King. Straying away from the project, I went into depth about how important it is for young African Americans to know their history and those that shaped it. Although I eventually gave her some basic facts about Dr. King, I used Veronica's carefree attitude towards her project to indicate to her that she was not doing well in school not because of an inability to achieve but her unwillingness to succeed.

By working with younger children and influencing them to go beyond what hip-hop music preaches to them and to work further than the limits they set for themselves, I feel that I am able to affect the outcome of many lives that would have easily been sucked into the downward spiral brought on by negative messages given through hip-hop music. Volunteering for a summer camp at Pan Pacific Park in the past was a truly rewarding experience because of the effect I had on the youth in my neighborhood. My volunteering and current tutoring experiences have encouraged me to continue working with youth in my neighborhood, and I plan to continue to reach out to the youth in the community I will reside in throughout my college life. At my future college I intend to major in archaeology and minor in English.

Danielle Brown attended Pitzer College.

50

WHEN TWO WORLDS COLLIDE

Anybody whose parents were immigrants can relate to—or write an essay about—living in two worlds. With the premium that colleges place on diversity, such essays generally hit the mark. In this essay, the author uses a phone conversation to introduce the reader to the way her American and Korean lives intersect. She adds depth by giving the reader a peek inside the Korean culture, at least with respect to the importance of speaking good Korean. "The trick is to be both while being one," she says, a pithy way of describing the challenge of living in two worlds at once.

Essay by Anonymous

"Hello 엄마! No. I'm at the movies. 극장! 조금있으면가." Translation: "Mom! No. I'm at the movies. The movies! I'll be home soon." If I'm with my friends, someone will ask: "What was that?" And I answer, "I was speaking in Korean to my mom." This answer is never enough, as I have learned. Only after a few rounds of saying odd phrases for their amusement is everyone's curiosity satisfied. "How do you say _____?" they say. I answer patiently in Korean. I am bilingual. Most of my friends have witnessed my trait in action many times. I speak English at school, and mostly Korean at home, but when the two are intertwined, the English and Korean are hard to separate. My internal Korean and the English, that has perhaps become internal now, blend smoothly. The blending of both languages occurs quite often and quite naturally, in and out of the house.

The problems arise when these two worlds start to fight with each other. One fights the other for more attention, and both struggle to pull me in and own me completely. Then these two different worlds can be quite confusing, especially when I blurt something out at the spur of the moment and it comes out in the wrong language. I might roll my eyes and with a sigh say, "Duh," to my parents when they don't really understand the connotation. Or I might yell, "안 돼!" (No!) while arguing with my friends. The fine line shrinks even thinner. Balancing is the challenge. When you are immersed in two completely separate worlds simultaneously, it is not a dichotomy or an absolute division. The trick is to be both while being one. The two entities are completely different but never alone. That is who I am. I have had to master this skill because I am bilingual and because I am a Korean living in America.

> I speak English at school, and mostly Korean at home, but when the two are intertwined, the English and Korean are hard to separate.

In the Korean realm, those who do not speak Korean can be rejected, ridiculed, or even ostracized. There is an unspoken expectation that a Korean must be able to speak his or her native language and still speak English. Although bad English is understandable, bad Korean is humiliating. Pronunciation, intonation, and grammar must be flawless. If it's not perfect, you are labeled a sell out or a "Twinkie," one who has yellow skin but feels white on the inside. So essentially, you are excluded from both. My friend Joel is the ultimate "Twinkie." Sadly for him, he speaks no Korean and his English is bad too; it has a tinge of an accent that shouldn't be there. Joel struggles with being "too American" or "too Korean" or not enough of both. He knows as well as I do that proficiency in both languages is very important: English is essential to live life in America, yet Korean is essential to retain our culture. That day when Joel asked me how I "found myself," I told him: "It's a blending of the two without compromising either, and I really think I've found the perfect balance. I'm in the best place that I could ever be: in both."

The author attended Duke University.

51

"I WANTED TO BE TRUTHFUL"

A great essay doesn't need to be glitzy. This one begins with a simple-but-effective rhetorical question and ends with a repetition of the same question. In between, the essay consists mainly of a retelling of life experiences, but the directness of the prose makes the story interesting and even poignant. The author's use of the third person in the first part of the essay is a subtle way of signaling her shyness to reveal such intimate details—a touch that adds both charm and sincerity. The paragraph that begins with "Looking at my application" reveals the likes and dislikes of a typical teenager and thereby shows (rather than tells) that she has risen above her challenging circumstances.

Essay by Nicole Clarke

So there's a girl. You've read her application, but do you really know her? You know that she works hard and that she dreams of going to Princeton, but does that count as knowing her? I'll tell you a bit about her. Then, you decide.

She was born on the small Caribbean island of Trinidad. Bright-eyed and smiling, she came to America with her mother, having no idea of the hard times she would have to face. She lives with her mother, and her father has never played a significant role in her life.

This girl has had hard times, especially on the home level. Her relationship with her mother has deteriorated to the point where it is non-existent. She has had to make decisions about the "big stuff" on her own. She has had to deal with the financial troubles of a low-class single parent family, the drama that is a prerequisite to being a teenager, and the lack of sleep that is sure to hit after pulling too many all-nighters.

*****

Surprise, surprise, I am this girl. But don't worry; my life has by no means been all bad. I play an active role at school serving as both National Honor Society and Senior Class president. I spend my summers at math and science programs, and this year I've spent my free time working on an independent research project, and yes, to me these activities are fun!

This past summer I spent six weeks in Socorro, New Mexico, studying astronomy, physics, calculus, and computer programming at the New Mexico Institute of Mining and Technology. Aside from its academic benefits, the Summer Science Program or SSP also gave me room to grow as a person. Forging new friendships and developing certain characteristics that will stay with me throughout the rest of my life, this summer for me was when I "grew up."

People for years have been throwing terms like "mature" and "responsible" at me, but only now do I truly understand the breadth of these words. I am responsible for my own actions, my successes and my accomplishments, my failures and my mistakes, my hopes and my dreams, and the path by which I choose to reach them.

Looking at my application there are many things you won't know about me. I hate ice cream. I love meteor showers. I don't understand basketball. I cherish rainy nights. And, I believe in true love! I know one pair of socks can be worn more than once, although four times is pushing it. I absolutely adore bowling shoes, comfort and cuteness all packed into a "rental." I swear by true friends; they are angels in disguise. Sweatshirts should be an unchangeable part of the worldwide uniform. And snow days rock!

> I know one pair of socks can be worn more than once, although four times is pushing it.

So my life has not been easy. But, as I continue on this path to what lies ahead, I believe—and invite you to do the same—that life will be what you make of it. You cry sometimes, you laugh sometimes, and many times you'll be ready to give up, but you will reap the rewards of your hard work and looking back, your personal growth will make it all worth it.

So tell me, do you know me now?

Nicole Clarke attended Princeton University.

52

REFLECTING ON THE FACE IN THE MIRROR

Most people can remember a reflective moment when they stopped to look at their face in the mirror. Why not write about it? Author Katie Hua describes such a moment as she pondered her disappointment at being ineligible for National Merit Finalist recognition due to her immigration status. The essay includes several elements of good storytelling: an anecdotal beginning, a flashback, and then a sound (*Whoosh*) that brings her back to the present. "My advice is to give yourself tons of time on the essay," says Hua. "The essay is supposed to show admissions people who you really are, and if you are frustrated and pressed for time, it probably won't reveal the real you."

Essay by Katie Hua

I stood still, facing the giant bathroom mirror. *Whoosh*. The bathroom door swung open, and a group of girls came in, chatting and laughing. I stared into the mirror. A blonde, clearly more than a head taller than I, strolled past, reaching for the paper towel dispenser. Another stocky redhead briskly walked into the stall right behind me. The two different hair colors contrasted sharply with my own under the fluorescent lights. We were all wearing the same cardigan sweater, the same blue plaid skirt, and the same brown leather shoes. My uniform was impeccable, as I had been interviewed by a newspaper not fifteen minutes before. The girl that stared back at me from the mirror was short and skinny. She had a long face with dark brown eyes, black hair, and a big forehead. She was a red belt in Tae Kwon Do; she was a co-captain of Robotics; she was the founder of the school's American Mathematical Competition team. But she was also an international student.

"When can I stop being an international student?" I asked myself exasperatedly. My memory flashed to the interview. A reporter came in and asked me some questions for the local newspaper after I had just been announced as a National Merit Semifinalist. I remembered how she asked me what it felt like to be a semifinalist. I said I was surprised and excited. I smiled a lot and said the things a good student was supposed to say, but what I neglected to mention was that I did not qualify to be a finalist because I lacked the proper immigration documents.

But I did not lack anything else. Were my other qualifications not good enough?

In the back of my head I remembered my first step onto the land of the United States at the age of twelve. I remembered how thrilled I was to be able to listen and finally understand a casual conversation in English; I remembered my American counterparts' excitement when they learned how to say some basic expressions in Chinese; I remembered how we traded stories of growing up on opposite sides of the globe. We laughed at each other's strange accents and customs; we learned from each other's experiences.

> "When can I stop being an international student?" I asked myself exasperatedly.

My mind wandered farther and farther back down memory lane to China as I stood still. It was as if I could still see my cousins and myself through the mirror, running around wildly while our blindfolded grandfather, with his hands grabbing the air and his back stooped, tried to catch us. Memories of grandpa brought warmth into my heart. I smiled, knowing that a part of him has been passed down to me; and, though he was no longer of this world, he would see through my dark-brown eyes and feel through my youthful hands.

Whoosh. The door swung open again, and the two girls walked out, still talking and laughing. I took a deep breath and decided that it was time for me to go. I ambled out and saw a beautiful sunny autumn afternoon through the window. One of my friends ran up to me, patted my shoulder, and cheerfully said, "C'mon, let's go do some homework and chat outside." "Sure," I said as I grinned back. "Hey! Let's see who can get there first!" She ran past me playfully, leaving behind her a trail of laughter. "Wait!" I yelled after her as

I hurried to catch up: "Don't forget we still need to figure out that one calc problem!"

When I finally sat down on the cool green grass and squinted at the radiant sun, my heart was content. "I don't lack anything," I thought. "I don't need any man-made rules to qualify me. This is me. The complete me is right here, right now, basking under the glory of the sun. And that is good enough."

Katie Hua attended Princeton University.

53

AN EQUATION FOR UNDERSTANDING

Several clever twists help make author Antoinette Mack's essay stand out. Her first device is relatively simple: a mathematical equation for stereotypes. Readers who are so inclined could devise a similar equation to address a topic of their choice, though Antoinette's essay has particular impact because of the issue of diversity. But Antoinette has another turn in store, a second equation that suggests maybe she was hasty in her initial thinking. Whether or not she was, Antoinette shows herself to be an unusually self-aware young woman. "I had many meetings with my college advisor and talked to my mom a lot in order to zero in on my main point," says Antoinette. "I kept asking myself, 'What is the essential element I want the reader to know about me'?"

Essay by Antoinette Mack

I have always been a very rational and logical thinker. This is why I enjoy almost all math and science courses. So here's an equation for you: $\dfrac{assumptions^2}{ignorance} + differences = ?.$

The easiest way for me to solve any problem is to put it in a form that will make it easier to understand and solve. For this particular problem I will give you a personal experience that incorporates all of the above variables and we'll find out together what the answer to this equation is and just maybe how to solve it.

It was a regular Friday afternoon in December when I experienced an act of prejudice towards me. It wasn't the first, but I was old enough to evaluate this situation on my own. I was at a basketball game with my best friend when an older woman began talking to us. She told us who her grandson was (he was on the opposing team) and that she was visiting for the holidays all the way from Iowa. When the conversation came to a halt she asked us whether or not we were students at Peddie or with the visiting team. We informed her that we were indeed boarding students at Peddie. Her next statement was, "Isn't that great. This is a real expensive school. Do you two play sports?" We looked at each other with bewilderment, and responded in a light hearted manner, "Well we play for fun, but we aren't masters at any sport." That led her to ask, "Well are you on financial aid?" Needless to say, we were speechless.

Now let's look at the equation in regards with my experience. Two different kinds of assumptions? CHECK. Ignorance on her behalf? CHECK. Were we different? CHECK. Everything seems to fit, now let's break it down to understand more effectively. This woman assumed that since we were African American we had to play a sport, and when she found out that we didn't her next guess was immediately to assume we needed

So here's an equation for you:

$$\frac{assumptions^2}{ignorance} + differences = ?$$

financial aid. Where did these assumptions come from? This is where the second part of our equation comes in: ignorance. Her ignorance—not mean spiritedness, but ignorance—led her to believe certain things about a race of people. And ignorance comes from not knowing or understanding people's *differences*. Add everything up and what do you get: stereotypes.

Now looking back on this experience I have come to realize that there were some stereotypical actions on my behalf as well. Did I assume that the woman was assuming that I was poor because of my race? Yes. Was it my ignorance or blindness that made my mind go straight to racism and not think of any other possibilities? Yes. Was it the differences between us, older white woman and teenage black girl, that made me automatically point the finger at this woman? Replaying the sequence of events back in mind I would have to say, YES! This makes me think, stereotypes are everywhere. They don't solely exist within the majority. Everyone, even the minority, are capable of being stereotypical and judgmental.

Now, let's review, $\dfrac{assumptions^2}{ignorance} + differences = $ STEREOTYPES.

This is where I come in; I propose a new equation that will help fix the problems with stereotypes on any level. After some deep thought and inner monologue here is the new and improved equation:

$$\frac{actual\ facts}{education} + acceptance = ?.$$

If we replace our assumptions and preconceived notions with actual facts and truth, half of the problem with prejudice is already solved. Now add education into the mix, and we empower people to think for themselves and not listen to the heightened half-truths being told all over. Lastly, when there is acceptance of everyone's differences (because differences are inevitable), then and only then will we achieve: *understanding*. And understanding is what is needed for everything to prosper.

Taking a second look, I might have jumped the gun, because this older woman seemed harmless, she might have simply been coming from a curious place. I needed a little more understanding and maybe I could have been a little more sensitive. Or maybe she did mean it in the racist way, we'll never know. But this is what life's about, learning from your past decisions and using those experiences to shape your future choices. Without this incident, I might not have been forced to think about stereotypes and open my eyes to the fact that they really do exist.

Antoinette Mack attended Columbia University.

54

"TYLER THE OREO"

His unwanted nickname is gasp-inducing, but author Tyler M. Percell does not write about racial prejudice. He mentions it, and the reader knows it shapes his experience, but Tyler is too busy living to let it bring him down. The essay starts slowly with generalities that set a pattern of placing the slings and arrows he faces in a larger context. Some counselors might recommend that he begin with "Tyler the Oreo," but the muted opening helps him to keep the focus on him, his interests, and his determination to rise above stereotypes. The essay gains power with every paragraph, revealing a young man who "seeks his own path without worrying about the perception of others."

Essay By Tyler M. Percell

If I were to sum up my life in one line, I would use a quote from rapper Tyler the Creator: "I am a walking paradox." I choose this line because it speaks to me of contrasting pieces that shape my personality. At certain times in my life, people have pointed to these contradictions as problems that held me back; however, I have come to see them as boons that give me the confidence to take risks and also maintain a sense of independence.

The conflicted part of my journey started in middle school. This was a time where fitting in was not only the common thing to do, but it was also something that everyone treated as a job. No one wanted to be that kid who stood out or was not accepted into the social groups that formed around separate lunch tables. There was the black table, which was made of local kids who dressed and acted as if they had just come from a Jay-Z video shoot. There were the Indian kids who would effortlessly transition from English to Hindi and refer to each other as cousins. Across from the Indian table sat the stateside kids, who all lived next to each other on the East End of the island, and would spend many vacations together. Then there I was, alone.

I had come to Antilles in sixth grade from an elementary Montessori school where cliques did not exist. With that mind-set I did not see the importance of conforming to a certain group to feel accepted. Like the other local kids, I loved listening to rap music; however, instead of sagging my pants and speaking in a St. Thomean dialect, I preferred to wear polos and speak American English. People quickly picked up on this difference and within the first week of coming to Antilles, I was given the name, "Tyler the Oreo."

Some of my peers decided that although my skin color was black, deep down inside I was a white boy. No matter how hard I tried, that name stuck with me throughout middle school. Anytime I tried to talk or hang out with the other locals, someone would bring up Oreo jokes and make me feel like the odd one out. I continued to feel ostracized until I finally became close friends with Mohit, Muhammad, and Sameer, people who saw more than my heritage and background as a basis for our friendship. However, even then, I was made fun of for being the only black kid in a group of East Indian and Muslim boys.

> **Some of my peers decided that although my skin color was black, deep down inside I was a white boy.**

Reflecting on my transition to Antilles, even though I hated the stigma of "Tyler the Oreo," I now see how it has come to be an advantage. Being an "Oreo" gave me the freedom to do what I wanted, without worrying about how I would be perceived. As I have grown older, I have seen that because of this identity, I am able to put academics as my priority in school and become the top-performing male in my grade, while also maintaining friendships with people who could not care less about school because they know their futures are waiting for them in their parents' jewelry stores. I can sit in class and argue why Kanye West is the greatest artist of all time and in the same setting discuss what led me to spend my summer reading an anthology of F. Scott Fitzgerald's short stories. I can be the student body president, lead morning meetings twice a week in front of my entire high school, but still spend my free time cracking jokes with the "Three Stooges of Bollywood," the name by which my friends are commonly known.

Being the kid on the outside helped me grow into a young adult who seeks his own path without worrying about the perception of others. Acknowledging that I am composed of many contrasting characteristics gave me the independence to pursue things that I wanted and believed in. Now if someone were to call me "Tyler the Oreo," instead of shying away or fighting off the name, I pause and joke, "You're right, and just like the cookie, I'm everyone's favorite."

Tyler M. Percell attends Georgetown University.

55

"I COULDN'T IMAGINE WANTING TO DYE MY HAIR BLONDE"

Kids can be cruel, and students who come from minority backgrounds often have difficult stories to tell. Such is the case for author Christina Mendoza, who has the added twist of being part of a racially mixed family. Her essay tells the story of how she learned to take pride in being Mexican American. Christina does not identify one turning point or significant experience, and her essay is the better for it. Instead, she describes a process of evolution in which she gradually learns to take pride in her mixed-race background.

Essay by Christina Mendoza

"Ha ha! Christina is a dirty Mexican!"

Growing up in a small, conservative community, it's easy to be shoved into your own category if you don't look or act like everyone else. My hair and eyes, instead of being blonde and blue like all of my Czech classmates, were chocolate and espresso. My last name had a "z" in it, and my grandmother called me "mija." By the time I was in grade school, the teasing began, and I was hurt and confused. Didn't all grandmothers call their grandchildren "mija"? Why did everyone except for me have blue eyes? And why was I being called "dirty Mexican" when I was cleaner than the boy who made the remark?

After an afternoon of teasing and tormenting from my classmates, I asked these questions to my mother, between sobs. By this time, she had become extremely good at giving me the "you're unique and beautiful" speech, but it was hard for her to truly empathize with me because neither she nor my father knew how I felt. She was a Caucasian who grew up in California; he was a Mexican American who grew up as the majority in San Antonio. I was the product of the two—the "half-breed" daughter who was raised in the small town of Seymour, population 2,800.

My other family members didn't seem to have any trouble fitting in. My father's ethnicity is well-respected. He is the only doctor within a fifty-mile radius who can speak Spanish. My sister was the beauty queen of our town—her sleek, glossy hair and olive complexion were the envy of every girl. My little brother received the recessive genes (fair skin, blue eyes), so he looks like everyone else in Seymour. I felt I was stuck somewhere in the middle of my siblings, stuck in the middle of two cultures, and not accepted by either.

> **My assailant said in a mocking tone, "I wish I could be a smart Mexican."**

Time does have a way of healing things. I didn't just wake up one morning and think, "I'm proud to be Hispanic," but as I have matured, I have learned not to be ashamed of my ethnicity. Instead of hiding who I really am, I have embraced my Mexican heritage and have become proud of it. Finding out about the many opportunities that are available to students of Hispanic descent has motivated me even more to delve deeper into my culture.

Looking back, I couldn't imagine wanting to dye my hair blonde to feel better about myself. The blonde girls are unique in their own way, but diversity makes the world go round. I absolutely love being different and not walking the same path as everyone else. The last racist comment I received was after I was named a National Hispanic Scholar. My assailant said in a mocking tone, "I wish I could be a smart Mexican." Feeling sorry for his cultural ignorance, I smiled and replied, "Yeah, I bet you do."

Christina Mendoza attended Yale University.

56

WHEN ENGLISH BLURS WITH ORIYA

Good essays often begin with a close-up view of a concrete detail before pulling back to show the big picture. Many authors start with a snippet of conversation between two people. Sibjeet Mahapatra begins with a close-up of his bookshelf and follows the reader's eye until it reaches his grandfather, the primary subject of his essay. Mahapatra divides the essay into three segments—as any writer could—to highlight major transitions. After beginning with the bookshelf, he uses dialogue in the middle segment to emphasize his excitement at receiving the gift of his grandfather's book. Note the sentence of factual description between the quotations from his grandfather. Big chunks of dialogue are generally less effective than shorter ones interspersed with narration that keeps the story moving forward.

"Musings of Bygone Days" by Sibjeet Mahapatra

There's a slender volume on the top shelf of my bookcase, nestled snugly in between *Midnight's Children* and *The Sun Also Rises*. Given a cursory glance, there's nothing extraordinary about this book—a stylized peacock in green, orange, and black is the sole embellishment on a plain white dust jacket. A title and author are printed on top of the image: *Musings of Bygone Days*, by Hari Hara Das.

If you were to tug the book from its spot on the shelf, meaning to flip idly through the crisp, still-white pages, you would learn two new things about it. The first is that apart from the title, this book is not written in English. The contents are typeset in a peculiar language, full of swooping, curvaceous characters that intertwine sinuously on each page.

You would also see a dedication, located prominently on the inside cover. It's in black ink, written in a bold, flourishing hand. *"Presented with love to my dearest Sibjeet. Hari Hara Das, 28 July, 2003."*

Hari Hara Das is my maternal grandfather. He has written over fifteen books—five novels and novellas, four short story anthologies, several collections of poetry. My mother tells me that for twenty-eight years, he taught university students how to wield a pen with grace, and power, and restraint. He is an author in every sense of the word.

Every novel, story, and poem my grandfather has written is in Oriya. It's an Indo-Aryan language, rooted in Sanskrit, comprised of swooping, curvaceous characters that intertwine sinuously on each page.

I can't read a word of it.

My mother tried to teach me—throughout elementary school, not a summer went by in which she didn't try to entice me to sit down with a ragged Oriya preschool primer. But I was younger then, and didn't think that learning a strange alphabet was important enough to keep me from the street hockey games that were going on without me as I chafed under my mother's lessons.

*****

When I was twelve years old, my grandfather gave me *Musings of Bygone Days* on the last day of one of our biannual trips to India. We had stayed in his house for only a week, and though I was happy to spend time with him, I was more eager to play badminton and tease stray cats and plan pranks on my grandmother, abetted by similarly impish cousins.

> **Every novel, story, and poem my grandfather has written is in Oriya... I can't read a word of it.**

The morning of my departure, he pulled me aside and handed me the book. It wasn't wrapped, and I was thrilled to see his name on the cover.

"Is this one of the books *you* wrote, Grandfather?" I blurted excitedly.

"Indeed it is," he replied in his booming, professorial voice. "It's a collection of poetry."

Eagerly, I flipped through the first few pages—and stopped.

Crestfallen, I turned to him, and had the grace to look embarrassed. "Grandfather, this is in Oriya. I can't read it."

I began to hand it back to him, but he smiled and shook his head. "That's not the point at all. Someday, I hope you will be able to read this. Until then, please keep it, and fill in the words yourself."

*****

So I keep the book on the top shelf of my bookcase. Take it down, from time to time. Trace the characters with my fingers, marveling at their smoothness, wondering what they might say. I like to think I'll find out someday.

In the meantime, I tell my own stories, pen my own poems, compose essays and articles and critiques, just as he did for his entire life.

I layer my words over his, and the English blurs with Oriya when I write.

Sibjeet Mahapatra attended Yale University.

57

FINDING INSPIRATION IN FAMILY

There is nothing fancy about the following essay—it is simple, honest, and works beautifully. The anecdote that opens the story is an experience everyone has had: blackening the ethnicity oval. The author goes on to describe the lives of her mother and grandparents, and why their experience continues to inspire and motivate her. In writing about the IB program, she highlights her drive to excel and gives strong evidence that she can thrive in a highly competitive college. Says Danielle, "I had so many ideas all at once that it was way over five hundred words. I asked my mom to help me edit it and cut it down, and got guidance from my college counselor on how to make it more fluid."

Essay by Danielle Marie Needles

In the beginning of third grade, I took my first standardized test where I had to fill out my full name, address, my birthday, and to shade in the corresponding ovals. My teacher then said to fill in the oval that represents our ethnicity. One of the choices was "Hispanic/Latino." I paused for a moment. I knew that I was Mexican American; my grandparents emigrated from Mexico to El Paso, Texas, where my mom and her ten brothers and sisters grew up. However, when I came across this question about my ethnicity, I never fully realized what it meant to me. I filled in the oval labeled "Hispanic/Latino" and then smiled, for it was the first time that I could remember where it was going to be recognized that I was, in fact, Mexican.

Growing up in a middle class family, I never experienced the hardships that my grandparents (the Navarros) and my mom had to go through in their daily lives. My great-grandparents never went to school; my grandmother never received an education past third grade, while my grandfather never exceeded fourth grade, in their home in Chihuahua, Mexico. They emigrated to El Paso after they married, where my grandparents had to teach themselves English.

My mom and her siblings went to a predominantly white high school, where the only Mexicans she knew of were her extended family. My mom was very studious, always breaking the boundaries and exceeding expectations about how a Mexican girl in high school should be. Her counselors would tell her she should be taking homemaking classes which would help her out of high school, but she stuck with the most rigorous math courses and took four years of Russian. After she graduated, her dreams led her to a place outside of El Paso; my grandmother helped her secretly leave El Paso to Miami, Florida, for the hope of a better future. My mom ended up working at a law office and took night classes at Miami-Dade Community College. Her job gave her the chance to help her family financially, but it consumed all her time, leaving her studies behind. My mom became a very prominent and well-respected real estate settlement manager for twenty-five years at the firm, but to this day her only regret is not to have completed her education. For me the way to keep this story alive is through a strong education and by surpassing all stereotypes and keeping my faith.

> **I filled in the oval labeled "Hispanic/Latino" and then smiled.**

In my high school, 35 percent of the students are Hispanic. Since I've entered Washington-Lee, I've always been in the most advanced classes. During freshman year, I knew a lot of people with various ethnic backgrounds. At the end of my sophomore year, it was time to declare if one was to become an International Baccalaureate (IB) candidate. The majority of students who declared themselves as IB candidates were white, while a small minority were from various ethic groups.

During the end of my junior year and the beginning of my senior year, more ethnic students dropped out of the IB Program. Today, there are only a handful of students of ethnic backgrounds. The main reason why I've been pursuing the IB diploma was to challenge myself and that although I am Mexican, I am capable of beating the odds and trying to accomplish a task my mom's family was not given the opportunity to. In a way, I'm pursuing this diploma for my entire Navarro family, especially my mom.

I am thankful everyday for all that I have: a wonderful supportive family, the drive to pursue an IB diploma, and to be surrounded by a strong, dedicated group of friends. I know that the history and struggle of my mom and her family runs through my veins; although I don't have stories of personal experiences of growing up in poverty, or struggling through a time of racism, the best I can do is to tell my family's story by keeping it alive. It gives me hope and confidence to exceed through the boundaries by graduating high school and attending college—a task neither my mom, *mis tíos*, or my grandparents achieved. As a third-generation Mexican in my mom's family, what being Mexican American means to me is to embrace my past and to excel in the future.

Since that test in third grade, whenever I fill out my ethnicity on a standardized test, I fill in the "Hispanic/Latino" oval and I smile as I remember who I am and that I am proud to be Mexican American.

Danielle Marie Needles attended the University of Virginia.

58

COUNTRY GIRL, PRIVATE SCHOOL

The two worlds of author Jessica Lynn Parr come together in this engaging essay. She uses the first part to tell about the most exotic of the two, her tiny home town of Elgin, Texas. Images of small town life—from the local hardware store to the annual hay harvest—offer a sharp contrast to the more affluent culture of Jessica's private school. Another key to the essay is her ability to tell about both worlds without being judgmental of either, in the process demonstrating the sort of flexibility that is necessary to thrive in a new environment such as college.

Essay by Jessica Lynn Parr

"A time for warm hearts and hot guts." This is the slogan of the annual Hogeye Festival in the Hot Sausage Capital of the World: my hometown of Elgin, Texas. I have lived on Pistol Hill Ranch in Elgin, population c. 5,000, for all but the first two of my seventeen years. I have grown up on small-town morals, values, and ways of life. Elgin is a place where parents still teach their children to say "yes, ma'am" and "no, sir." Wiry old cowboys with weathered leather for skin take their coffee black at the City Cafe, and most men have two pairs of cowboy boots: one for working, and one for Sunday church. I can count on running into at least a handful of people I know upon each trip to the local H-E-B grocery store or the Elgin Post Office. Employees at Main Street Pharmacy and Ace Hardware have known me since I was a little girl too small to see over the counter. A familiar sight as I drive down Main Street is of men in Wrangler jeans, western shirts, cowboy hats, boots, and shiny rodeo belt buckles, leaning on their 4X4 trucks as they discuss all the important issues of slow but friendly small town life.

My parents and I live on about 140 acres of land where we raise cattle and farm hay. For as long as I can remember, ranch work has been a way of life for my family. Many summer days spent working in the hay fields and barns last until midnight or even later. My mom taught me to drive my Granny's maroon 1983 Buick Regal when I was only nine years old, so that I could take fresh ice water and box lunches out to my dad and the other workers on the farm. My parents both hold full-time jobs and yet they still manage to keep up with our ranch in their scarce spare time. I learned my earnest and diligent work ethic from their tireless examples. I remember the looks I got as a middle-schooler from the teenage boys working as hired hands on our ranch when I hopped out of the truck with my own pair of work gloves to help load the sixty-five pound square bales of hay. I have even had farmer's tan lines from driving our John Deere 4020 tractor all day long cutting and raking hay. I know the feeling of aching muscles and itchy bits of hay from head to toe after a long day laboring in the hot sun. I have grown up as Daddy's little cowgirl and ranch hand, and have learned invaluable lessons about agriculture, livestock, and the workings of a close-knit small-town community.

On the flip side of the coin, I have attended private school in Austin, the "big city" nearest to Elgin, since second grade. Top priority for my parents has always been that I obtain the best possible education, and thus they chose to place me in private school despite the daily hardship of commuting. My high school is at the complete opposite end of the socioeconomic

> **I know the feeling of aching muscles and itchy bits of hay from head to toe after a long day laboring in the hot sun.**

spectrum from Elgin. Many of my peers at St. Andrew's drive Mercedes-Benzs or BMWs instead of muddy 4X4 trucks and old rusted hand-me-down cars. I attend a school where 100 percent of our graduates enroll in four-year colleges, whereas in Elgin, a great many students work and attend a community college or trade school part-time after receiving their high school diplomas. Granted, there are several exceptions to either rule, however my point is to demonstrate how different these two worlds really are. I realize how privileged I am to attend my high school, and thus have always completely dedicated myself to taking full advantage of every opportunity. I commute a full hour each way to and from school, but have nevertheless participated in a fitness conditioning class that required I be at school by 6:15 every morning, musical rehearsals that kept me at school until ten o'clock on some nights, and demanding varsity sports schedules. My high school has given me a first-class education with infinite opportunities, and my exceptional environment has made it impossible for me to ever take these privileges for granted.

I have always been a little bit different because of my circumstances. My friends at school never tire of joking about the fact that I live on a farm with real cows. In Elgin, my friends have often teased me about being "too good" for their public school, or given me a hard time about spending half my life thirty-eight miles away in Austin. However, both sets of friends know me well enough to understand my dedication to education, and respect me for my unusual circumstances. I am fortunate to have such a broadened perspective as a result of my dual experiences. I recognize that my experiences are extraordinary, and I cherish the fact that I am able to enjoy the best of both worlds. Thanks to my unique background, I have an ability to adapt easily to new social and cultural climates. I bring my own distinct perspective to a situation because I have thrived simultaneously in two very different environments.

Jessica Lynn Parr attended Southern Methodist University.

A side from athletics, this category of essays is probably the toughest to pull off. Political issues don't usually lend themselves to personal reflections, and religion is hard to make concrete. That's not to say that it is impossible to write an outstanding essay about politics or religion. Sometimes, as in Essay 61, it helps to put yourself in someone else's shoes. Essays 59 and 63 succeed because the authors make the topic personal, while in Essay 62, the author describes a change in her personal views.

59

NO "CLARK KENT FEMINIST" HERE

This killer essay didn't even start out as a college essay. "I actually just wrote it for fun," says author Aviva Ariel. She takes a risk in writing about feminism, but rather than lapsing into generic political commentary, she sticks to talking about her own life. The result is a masterful essay that illustrates the power of vivid detail—for humor and simply for lively storytelling. "I don't think the topic is as important as the tone of the essay," says Aviva. "Two people can say the same thing, but you'll be attracted to the person whose personality shines through even when they say a simple 'hello.'"

Essay by Aviva Ariel

Sometime between waking up at the crack of dawn and fourth period I became a teenage werewolf. No, wait, I mean feminist.

It's as if I didn't know until someone pointed it out to me in English class, but it was more like an "Ooh, dude, I think you just stepped in some feminist," or a "Damn! You smell like feminist," or maybe even an "I think you spilled some feminism on your shirt, and it stains…"

I've been labeled many things throughout my life in Cleveland, Ohio, from preppy (but don't ever expect to see me in a collared shirt and khakis) to punk (maybe my new lip piercing and occasional green eyeliner add to this, but even for Cleveland, I'm about as punk as Marcia Brady) to slightly insane—I've even been told that I'm unique looking (why am I so sure it's not a compliment?) and maybe labeling me makes it easier to figure out who I am (hell—I don't even know!), but recently my whole class seems to have decided that I'm a bra-burning, men-hating Feminazi.

My English teacher, a minority-equalizing, feminist-loving, all around pro-everything-liberal kind of man, said that if a guy were to ever hold the door open for me, I would "punch his lights out."

I pictured myself through his eyes, toned and fuming hatred, simultaneously liberating the oppressed and crushing lanky teenage boys with my bare hands, their awkward limbs flinging in the air as I fought in honor of my fellow womyn.

Would I? I wondered. Maybe I would just thank him and walk through the door. Teenage boys displaying chivalry is not something I see every day, so I might pause. I might wonder, why this gesture of civility, right here, right now? But punch his lights out? I'm barely five feet tall—I aspire to meet the height requirements for amusement park rides, not to dominate all who cross my path.

But I should have seen it coming. After sharing with the group several weeks earlier that being whistled at in the hallways or told that I have a fine ass (or some other creative come-on) was about as flattering to me as being compared to Santa Claus (jolly, red, and round), it is only fitting—they finally discovered that I am the monster within their midst. It's as if I was biding my time at school until I could become a trophy wife for some successful businessman or an exotic dancer with breasts filled with more than my brain, and suddenly I've crushed their dreams by becoming this, this, this breathing, thinking, independent young woman!

I am not about to apologize for wanting to be seen as the love-child of Mary Wollstonecraft and Justin Timberlake (smart, sexy, and awesome on the dance floor). And even if it angers them to hear I think so, my guess is I will be more financially and personally successful than most of the boys I know.

> **I am not about to apologize for wanting to be seen as the lovechild of Mary Wollstonecraft and Justin Timberlake.**

I know I'm a feminist, but I am also just a teenage girl trying to survive junior year (because everyone knows being in high school is almost as enjoyable as four years of paper cuts). I could be a Clark Kent feminist—you know the ones; coy and giggly when the boys are around, fierce all-grrrl when she's alone with her posse. I could be the kind who keeps *Ms.* hidden inside a copy of *Seventeen* on the bedside table, or I could go all-out old-school in ripped jeans and combat boots—but that's not me, either. I want to be who I am, big or small, editor-in-chief or head cheerleader, point guard or math geek, and I want to make it so that when *my* daughter goes to high school and says she's a feminist, everyone in the school, from the kids smoking in the parking lot to the principal, just yawns and says, yeah, who isn't?

Aviva Ariel attended Skidmore College.

60

WRITING ABOUT RELIGION

There are many pitfalls to essays about religious faith. Since faith is in the mind (and therefore abstract), the challenge is to make faith come alive with concrete stories and anecdotes. The following essay begins as a story about singing and being on stage. Only in paragraph four does the author, Rachel Dubois, begin to explain why singing in her temple has special meaning. By the end, she is talking about *tikkun olam*, "healing the world," in a much more convincing way than she could have by beginning the essay with a testament to her faith. Says Rachel, "Writing about my religious/cultural background was the easiest topic I could have chosen because it was something that was inherently me."

Essay by Rachel Dubois

As I step up to the pulpit, I feel a familiar sense of calm come over me, the calm I always experience before singing to my congregation. Scanning the audience, I look out at the parents and grandparents, making eye contact with those I recognize and those I do not. I begin to sing with my youth choir behind me, and take a deep breath in preparation for my solo. I can feel the eyes of the congregation locked onto me, waiting, and then my voice soars out over the expectant faces.

When I finish singing, I see rapt expressions and tears. Even though I know they would be touched regardless of how I sound, every time I sing at a service, I am overwhelmed by the amount of warmth that meets my participation.

"Beautiful. Absolutely beautiful." I turn to see my cantor beaming at me, and I smile back. As I walk out of my synagogue, I am stopped repeatedly by wrinkly little women who grin unabashedly at me and well-wishers who say how much it means to them to see and hear young people at their Friday night service. The amount of praise I receive is almost embarrassing and feels somewhat undeserved, but it gives me joy and gratification that I can't find anywhere but here. Where else could you get a sticky, lipstick-smeared kiss from a complete stranger, and feel like it was the most heartfelt gesture in the world?

I have spent countless hours singing and performing, but there is a tangible difference between performing in a concert with my school choir and singing for my temple community. Whenever I contribute to my synagogue, I know that people appreciate my effort, whatever the results. To be able to participate without being judged gives me full rein to enjoy the experience. For this reason, belonging to a close-knit Jewish community has always been a vital part of my life. Over the years, I became more involved, moving from attending Sunday school classes to teaching younger students and helping to found my temple youth group. I joined the temple choir, chanted Torah on major holidays, and wrote for the temple bulletin. The more I undertook, the more I wanted to be active in my community. Gradually, my religion turned into a force that has grounded me and kept me centered throughout high school. An anchor point in my life, it has provided me with a rare sense of connection to my own identity and to the needs of those around me.

The summer I turned fifteen, I attended Kutz, a Jewish leadership camp, and was exposed to a vibrant and energetic group of teenagers. The passion that permeated the camp was infectious, and that summer, I realized that I wanted to devote my life to leading and nurturing a Jewish community. Abandoning my plans to become a doctor, which I had formed in kindergarten, I decided to pursue the goal of becoming a cantor. A cantor, similar to a rabbi, is a member of the Jewish clergy who leads a large portion of the song and prayer during a service. In pursuit of this ambition, I became the Religious and Cultural Vice President of my temple youth group, writing and leading services for teens at every youth event. This past summer, I journeyed to Israel on NFTY's L'Dor v'Dor program to examine my roots and solidify my goal of becoming a

> **I truly feel like I am participating in *tikkun olam*, or healing the world.**

cantor. Seeing my ancestral homeland was the final step; I felt a visceral connection to all aspects of Judaism.

What my community has offered me, I want to give to others. To be able to bond with a diverse congregation, create a spiritual moment for those many years my senior or my peers, and inspire all of them through song and prayer is an incomparable sensation. I truly feel like I am participating in *tikkun olam*, or healing the world. Not many people have had their career planned out since age fifteen, but to me, being a cantor was the only path that combined my passions with my identity. I know that nothing else in life could give me the spiritual joy and fulfillment that I crave, while having a positive effect on others.

Leaving the temple parking lot, I am perfectly content. Just as on every other Friday night, I smile an inward smile and think to myself, "Yeah, this really is what I want to do with my life. Good choice."

The only choice.

Rachel Dubois attended Yale University.

61

LIFE LESSONS AT DUNKIN DONUTS

Most applicants to selective colleges grow up in affluent households, and among those who do, it is refreshing to see an applicant who appreciates the other side of life. The author shows himself to be a keen observer of his working class colleagues at Dunkin Donuts. He empathizes with them, learns lessons from them, and connects those lessons to his plans for the future. Most telling, the author connects his observations of these workers to his views on capitalism and social responsibility. This evidence of his open-mindedness is more powerful than a slew of testimonials from teacher-recommenders. "The best advice I can give is to take your time when choosing a topic, and make sure it's important to you in your heart," says the author.

Essay by R. D.

My summer job at Dunkin Donuts has taught me many things. After scooping more than 800 ice creams and making more than 1,200 cups of coffee, I've become an expert at serving all our specialties really fast. The commuters running to catch their trains and the little league teams coming in for a treat after a game can count on me and my colleagues to fill their order quickly. But beyond the details of serving customers and maintaining the store, I've realized some very important truths about working people and hard economic realities. Maybe "America Runs on Dunkin" but Dunkin runs on the energy of low-paid, hardworking people.

For example, my supervisor Alfredo, an immigrant from Mexico, works two shifts at two different Dunkin Donut stores. Although his English is limited, he showed great patience when training me and demonstrated tolerance and understanding whenever I made a mistake. Alfredo treats me with kindness and respect even though he is aware that my life is more comfortable and carefree than his. Alfredo tells me he works so hard to take care of his young daughter, and in the short time that I've known him, I have gained so much respect for his work ethic and his values. Many people fail to appreciate the hard work and effort that people like Alfredo exhibit for such inadequate pay.

My co-worker and new friend, Jackie, works 80 hours a week to support her 16-month-old daughter. Jackie's only 20 years old, and has many expenses including rent, car payments, and a babysitter. Jackie counts on her overtime salary to make ends meet. I really admire Jackie because she's under so much pressure at home, and at work; yet she demonstrates optimism and keeps moving forward. I feel a little sheepish when I ask Jackie to let me leave work early to study for exams, because my stress seems so minor compared to all of her daily pressures. This experience has made me realize how lucky I am to be prioritizing my academic record because I am fortunate enough to be planning to attend college.

> Maybe "America Runs on Dunkin" but Dunkin runs on the energy of low-paid, hardworking people.

Right next door to Dunkin Donuts is a family owned bagel store, "Bagel Emporium." Every once in a while, the two owners come into our store and put a soccer game on our big screen TV. They are friendly to all of us even though, clearly, the Dunkin Donuts has taken away a lot of their business. This makes me understand why so many communities fight big name stores like WalMart because locally run business can't really compete with these giants. I've gained a total respect for working people and now I will always leave big tips wherever I can. I will also shop at a local establishments rather than a chain, despite the fact that I work for one now.

I hope that by studying business in college I can learn more about business and its social responsibility. I understand that capitalism provides a wonderful opportunity for businesses, yet I now have more questions about the injustices that can occur in the pursuit of profits. I vehemently believe that the lessons I've learned this summer have influenced my character and values, and will help me develop a better sense of business ethics as I pursue my career.

R. D. attended Bryant University.

62

THE DEVIL SLITHERING

Religion is not high on our list of recommended topics—unless you've got an angle like Melanie Naranjo's. Most religion essays talk about belief, which leads into the realm of abstraction. This essay describes Melanie's experiences. The fact that her beliefs follow from them is significant, but secondary. Without *telling*, she *shows* the diversity that she would bring to a selective college. No less important, she demonstrates the intellectual courage to rethink her views, a sure sign that she will also benefit from life at a selective college. In Melanie's description of how she "kicked the air," we can almost see the dangling legs of a little girl. "I went through multiple drafts, changing the introduction, rearranging the order of events, and weeding out any passive phrases or unnecessary words, in order to make the story as concise as possible," she says.

Essay by Melanie Naranjo

Some nights we took the route along the Hudson River. My mom drove past the boisterous New York lights and down a few, potholed roads. She pulled to a stop in front of a small, gray building that crouched between a blinking medley of *bodegas*. The building's roof capped cracked cement walls and Pablo, a prominent preacher, stood at the doors to greet us. When a man's voice vibrated through a microphone, my mom rushed me towards the gathering room. Before we took our seats, she dropped a five dollar bill into the wooden collector's box, smiling at the nod of approval from the preacher on our left.

It was a plain room, easily confused for a hotel lobby with its bare, cream walls. Its only distinguishing feature was a glass-framed bookcase holding the Kingdom Hall's many biblical volumes. During my daily preparations, I often used *Mi Libro de Historias Biblicas*. My annotated copy trembled on my lap as I kicked the air, impatient. As a six year old, I was always eager to show off my new reading skills. When the speaker's words finally hitched up into a question, worm-like fingers wriggled wildly into the air. At the preacher's call, I answered, *"El futuro rei de la tierra,"* then beamed when my mom squeezed my hand, proud.

Jesus, Jehovah's son and *"the earth's future king."* It's strange to think I once believed those words. I memorized everything without question, including my mom's stories of Satan hiding in Catholic churches, which explained why my Catholic friends never attended mass. My mom told me of threatening, pointed arches stabbing the air and hundreds of candles casting taunting shadows against decaying stone walls. But most terrifying of all were her depictions of the statues: wide, unblinking eyes on ghostly pale faces, constantly watching and waiting. It was through these eyes, she said, that the Devil slithered out.

I saw no serpents in their water-clear eyes, but felt myself drawn by their outstretched arms.

The images pierced me so deeply as a child that, just last year, I found myself unnerved as I walked towards my first *cathédrale* along *la rue Saint-Mélaine*; I feared that my mom's words might not have been as false as I had come to believe. Inside, wooden doors carved with delicate, twisting patterns opened to carefully painted murals lining *le déambulatoire* at the east end. A dazzling explosion of light filtered through the *vîtres* all around me, a kaleidoscope of religious tales. The statues along the wall gazed serenely into the air. I saw no serpents in their water-clear eyes, but felt myself drawn by their outstretched arms. I cupped two smoothly chiseled hands, frozen in prayer. Somewhere to my right I heard a mother's soft murmurs of praise. *"Très bien, ma bichette. Très bien."* The words mingled with the sound of rustling footsteps, ricocheting like a thousand marbles let loose against the walls. I stepped out of this architectural masterpiece and away from my religious past. I set out to see more.

Melanie Naranjo attended Harvard University.

63

WHEN YOU CARE ABOUT THE WORLD

Essays about international affairs can be dicey, but the rare student who genuinely cares about what happens in, say, Sudan, can pull it off. Madelyn Sullivan does so by connecting her first voting experience, which happened within weeks of when she wrote, with an article she read about human-rights atrocities in Sudan. The essay works because of her powerful idealism. At the polling place, her "heart beat slightly fast" and her hands "shook unsteadily." The article about the Sudan violence left her "brimming with tears." When Madelyn writes that she herself hopes to prevent tomorrow's Holocaust, most readers will believe her.

Essay by Madelyn Sullivan

I voted on November 2nd. As an eighteen-year-old woman in America, I am legally allowed to exercise my right to vote. Although my heart beat slightly fast, and my hands shook unsteadily at the polling booth, upon arriving home from my first voting experience, I was filled with a sense of accomplishment and relief. I sat on the couch that night, when I picked up a *TIME* magazine and began to read an article on Sudan by Massimo Calabresi.

The vast nation of Sudan is divided by both religion and culture, but mainly ethnicity: Arabs and Africans. While all citizens of Sudan are African, the nomadic tribes of Sudan are referred to as Arabs, while the sedentary tribes are called Africans.

The images I saw of the battling Arabs and Africans were stark and the stories I read were more horrific. The Janjaweed, "devils on horseback," is an Arabic group of local tribes funded by the Sudanese government to crush the radical Sudan Liberation Army. The group began attacking civilians, claiming that they were aiding insurgents. Janjaweed ride or fly into African villages, firing guns on men and children alike. They rape the women, leave most children, and kill all the men. These are of course, very loose rules. One woman described a Janjaweed rampage: "A fighter unwrapped a swaddling cloth and rolled a newborn baby onto the dirt. The baby was a girl, so they left her. Then the Janjaweed spotted a one-year-old boy and decided he was a future enemy. In front of a group of onlookers, a man tossed the boy into the air as another took aim and shot him dead."

Suddenly voting didn't seem as important as it had fifteen minutes earlier. Suddenly I didn't want to go to school the next day, but fly to Africa and give all my hot lunches to a starving family at a refugee camp. What surprised me the most, however, was a common theme throughout the article about the lack of world response. We cannot let another Rwanda or Holocaust occur while we are alive. Genocide is supposed to be a thing of the past. It is a story we read about in books or a special we watch on the history channel. Let Sudan be the one time that the world learned and said "never again" and meant it.

> A fighter unwrapped a swaddling cloth and rolled a newborn baby onto the dirt. The baby was a girl, so they left her.

As I sat on the couch, brimming with tears and watching the muted images of election results, I felt a desperate sense of despair. I had to remind myself that I am able to affect what happens in my life.

I voted on Tuesday. I am a woman. I am eighteen. And I had a choice. I am lucky, and I have the obligation to help people without my same rights. On Tuesday, what I voted for will not only affect my local and national community, but also the world. I am indebted to the citizens of countries like Sudan to vote for them, to give a voice to the people who cannot speak above the gunfire and violence that reigns in their country.

I realized then that my trip to the ballot box was perhaps not so futile and that I would indeed attend school the next day, no matter how great my desire to flee the country and save the world as a self-proclaimed knight-errant. I reminded myself that although I am an adult with adult responsibilities, I am still a senior in high school with plans to go to college. I can only hope that the best possible use of my time right now is to attend school to better educate myself. I can only hope that what I learn today will give me the courage and knowledge to stop tomorrow's Holocaust.

Madelyn Sullivan attended Bowdoin College.

A Significant Experience

W e've warned you about trying too hard to find one of these. Even if you really have had an earth-shaking experience, it's what comes afterward that should be the meat of your essay. One of our student authors, in Essay 67, writes about outdoor experiences that boosted her self-confidence. Essay 65 offers another variation; it describes a life lived in the aftermath of divorce, but events immediately surrounding the divorce are never discussed. The cardinal rule is not to let description of the facts crowd out your reflections on the significance of those facts.

64

A DEBATER COMES OF AGE

"I always knew I wanted to write about debate," says author Danny DeBois. His writing process illustrates a fundamental truth about the

Common App. Though "topic of your choice" is not technically one of the options, the five prompts are so malleable that most applicants should be able to choose their topics and even write their essays without much thought about them. Though Danny chose to write in response to prompt #4 (below), he could just as easily have used prompt #1 ("a story central to your identity"), #2 ("a time when you experienced failure"), or #5 ("an accomplishment marking transition to adulthood"). Says Danny, "My biggest piece of advice for writing personal statements is to swallow your pride and accept the help of others."

"Challenges Accepted and Voices Revised" by Danny DeBois

Describe a place or environment where you are perfectly content. What do you do or experience there, and why is it meaningful to you?

The timer emits three deafening beeps. My preparation time is up, and I gather my materials. My throat dries up; my palms sweat; my yellow legal pad quivers in my hands. Voices inside my head bombard me like anxious reporters shouting at a press conference. "What if your responses are dumb?" "This activity's too hard for you." "You're going to make a fool of yourself." I'm about to give my first speech at the beginning-of-the-year debate tournament for high school freshmen, and I struggle to find my voice, praying it doesn't crack.

Some people think only the insane hear voices in their heads. My theory is that we all have them, and they shape how we act. When I was starting high school, those voices inhibited me. I could never just sit down at a different table in the cafeteria and make friends; what would those people think of me? Yet for reasons I couldn't quite explain, I ended up branching out to a new group of people: my high school's debate team.

Debate turned out to be what I needed. Over time, it exposed me to feelings I hadn't previously known. At one of my first tournaments, I watched an opponent hunched over a mountain of papers, furiously preparing responses to my case with his gang of teammates and coaches. The voices in my head returned: "You're going to lose." "He's being programmed by thirty people much smarter than you." But when we finally started debating, I felt a new tingling—not nerves, but anger. "I can't lose to someone who just outnumbers my arguments." Instead of doubting myself, I began doubting him. I looked straight at the judges as if to tell them, "Challenge accepted."

That was the moment I became perfectly content in the world of debate. Unlike the high school cafeteria—a place of rampant, arbitrary judgment—the debate environment offers a unique intellectual challenge that lets me prove myself rather than relying on first impressions. There, I have the confidence to start a discussion on my own terms, and I get to decide which arguments to make. When I make a speech, I feed off everyone in the room: the judges nodding at my arguments, my teammates smiling at me, even my opponents glaring in my direction. Because of debate, I can speak in front of any audience, and can go into any round thinking I have a shot of winning.

> Some people think only the insane hear voices in their heads. My theory is that we all have them, and they shape how we act.

As a result, the voices that once tormented me now say something new. Once, while riding on a packed Amtrak train on the way to a major national tournament, I spent over an hour practicing rebuttal speeches. The middle-aged men with iPads and stern-looking women in black power suits around me fumed silently, probably wondering, "Why won't this kid just shut up?" Although I lowered my volume, I kept going, thinking, "Those people are in a different world, and I have a tournament to win." For once, my social inhibitions didn't control me.

Fast-forward two and a half years from that first debate round. The timer emits three deafening beeps. My preparation time is up, and I gather my materials. I take a sip of water to keep my throat moist; I crack my knuckles; I hold my piece of cardstock firmly in my hands. I look up at the audience filling the rows of lecture hall seats, staring down at me. In the silence, I clear my throat and hear the voices one last time: "All the work I've done has prepared me for this." "I can beat this case." "I've done this hundreds of times." I'm about to give my first speech in the last round of a national tournament, and I'm finally ready to use my voice.

Danny DeBois attends Harvard University.

65

A SHORT WALK, A SPECTACULAR ESSAY

One stroke of genius is all that author Juliette Mandel needed to make this essay sparkle. The walk, punctuated by the 256 steps, becomes the occasion for reminiscing about her life. Each new milestone, marked by a specific number of steps, brings her back to the fact that she is walking between her parents' homes. Brilliant. Of course, the other part of the equation is that she poignantly renders the conflict, pain, and disorientation that come with divorce. The 256 steps are both a physical and metaphorical distance that separate Juliette's two worlds.

"256 Steps" by Juliette Mandel

It's 256 steps from my front door to my front door; a journey I make every other day that sparks reveries of reminiscing over the days when my parents were one. So close are the two houses that shelter me and yet so far apart are my two parents.

Twelve steps up the road, I see the crack in the pavement and I remember the first time I rode a tricycle—a hot pink contraption with a white wicker basket. My mom helped me up on to the seat while my dad adjusted the pedals. Slowly, I began to pedal, faster and faster. Soon I was riding without the security of my parents. Yet within seconds I reached a bumpy part of the road and was propelled into the air. I distinctly remember the way my parents ran towards me, together, and when they reached me…I felt safe. My mom carried me while my dad made funny jokes to hush my crying. I laughed so hard I couldn't even feel the stinging pain in my knee. All I could think about was how happy I was with my parents.

Ninety-eight steps and as I round the corner, a car comes speeding past me blasting loud music. I dive into another memory, as the voice of Evanescence transforms into the voice of Cyndi Lauper. 2350 Broadway, apartment 716, my dad and Cyndi were in the midst of a "recording session." I ran around the room, playing with my airplane wagon while my mom sat separately, busy in conversation on the telephone. Mom told me to be serious for a moment while Dad and I continued to jump up and down, mimicking a "famous rock star" for Cyndi. Something had changed. My parents stopped kissing in public. They spent less time together. My parents had always been on the same wavelength, but because I had what my grandmother called an "old soul," I sensed intuitively that they were drifting apart. I was a stranger inside my own home—I was confused: my parents no longer seemed inseparable. In fact, they seemed so far apart, I could hardly remember when they'd ever been together.

After 187 steps, I feel tired and alone. I see a couple bickering in their yard, and I can't help but sink into my past. The fighting seems all too familiar. The screaming, the slamming doors, the vulgar language all envelop me. I had to change. I had to adapt to my new situation. My parents were fighting again, the word *separation* floated throughout the house, drifting in and out of every room stinging my ears. I became a chameleon, morphing from one parent to the next. I celebrated Christmas with my mom, Chanukah with my dad. I ate pasta with tomato sauce with my mom and mac and cheese with my dad. DIVORCE. They decided to go to court—the question of custody made me nervous. Monday: Dad. Tuesday: Mom. Wednesday: Dad until 9, then Mom. Thursday and Friday: Mom. Weekends: even more confusing. And holidays: alternate depending on even or odd year. My body split in two, mitosis rendered me into two completely different people. Two houses, two rooms, two beds, two pillows, two ME's.

> I see a couple bickering in their yard, and I can't help but sink into my past.

237 steps, I'm almost there. It's time to think of an opening to put him in a good mood. I'm forty-five minutes late, I know. It was because Mom needed me. Think positive, what can I say to distract his attention from infuriation? How about his girlfriend, or maybe a compliment regarding the house. Hundreds of opening lines whirl around inside my head. A whirlpool of words; I try to organize my thoughts so that they flow like the words in a sweet song. Time to

switch into "Dad Mode." No mentioning of Mom, no asking for money to buy shampoo or conditioner, no acting "rude," no complaining about the food served for dinner—I can do this.

256 steps, I've reached my front door and the transformation is complete. I'm ready. A five minute walk has sent me wandering through my past, zipping by the good times and the bad. I know they both love me, they just love different ME's. In only fifty-five hours and fifteen minutes, the short weekend will be over and I'll begin my journey back to my front door.

Juliette Mandel attended McGill University.

66

A LIFE-CHANGING EXPERIENCE? THIS ONE IS BELIEVABLE

This book has emphasized the pitfalls of manufacturing a phony "significant experience." We do not mean to deter those who may have a real one to write about. Author Marcus Lee vividly describes his remorse over killing a baby bird with a haunting story of youthful thoughtlessness. But his story describes not an all-at-once epiphany, but rather a gradually dawning awareness. Lee draws on the experience to offer insight into his conscience and why learning a lesson for himself was more meaningful than being punished by others.

"Baby Birdy" by Marcus K. Lee

It was the action of a single moment that eventually formed many of the values that I hold today and that will continue to define me. It's not like I planned it though. Neither did I think anything of it at the time. And now, though I wish it didn't have to happen, I don't exactly regret that it did. In a way it changed me—made me who I am today—and I wouldn't have it any other way.

In my childhood days, on holiday at the age of five or six, I remember finding a baby bird who was still struggling to fly, only ever succeeding in hovering low over the ground. I chased the bird in glee, and in my childish excitement, I attempted to step on it. I didn't feel anything wrong and still didn't even as I looked down at the bird that had committed itself to weathering out life's struggles, knowing that I had denied it that chance at life. But I never forgot that event. The impact was slow in coming; I only began to realize years later how truly disgusted I was at my action. I have spent a lot of time reflecting on that day ever since, and consequently, some of my strongest moral values emerged from that day.

Since then, I have developed into a lover of animals and the environment, helping spiders to escape the confinements of the house, discouraging my dad from harming even the snakes that venture into the house, and detouring from our kayaking path to pick up litter strewn in the sea during our International Award expedition. The most valuable thing I gained from this experience is the knowledge that it was my own personal realization that made me understand that my earlier way of living life was unacceptable. If someone had scolded me at the time, I probably would have felt some temporary guilt and then have shrugged it off thinking I had been punished sufficiently. But since I was the only witness to my action, the responsibility of judging my actions fell solely upon me.

For me, that one moment allowed me to change. It gave me that one push in the direction of self-reflection and self-development. It taught me that without first realizing something for myself, I could not hope to bring about a personal change. Just as someone else's understanding of my shortcomings is not my own understanding, the command of others for me to change is also nothing close to self-reflection and personally driven change. No amount of external coercion would have otherwise allowed me to see my mistakes.

> **It taught me that without first realizing something for myself, I could not hope to bring about a personal change.**

Often times this experience has allowed me to understand the stubbornness that many of us inherently have and use this knowledge to more effectively share my ideas or keep my mind open to new ideas and opinions in the light that it is easy to subconsciously reject thoughts that seem thrust upon us. I learnt that people don't change who they are upon a command. But just the act of silent realization can do so much more. And while acts like the one I did are never justifiable, they are only truly unforgivable when nothing is learnt from them.

Marcus K. Lee attended Princeton University.

67

A FRESH TAKE ON CAMPING

Many essays begin with an air of mystery that lasts for a sentence or two, but this one prolongs the uncertainty through a five-sentence first paragraph. Author Megan Topolewski drops a clue for each of the five senses, but only in the second paragraph does she spill the beans that her subject is a camping trip. Note as well that in cataloging what she "learns," Megan starts with the small stuff: how to pack ziplock bags, and the joys of eating off the ground. Starting with the mundane makes her more credible when she moves on to the big lessons.

Essay by Megan Topolewski

Please write, in some detail, about an experience, an achievement, a person, or a matter of particular significance to you.

Last year I got to taste life; the lukewarm water of revival flowing down my throat. I got to feel it, in the pumping of my heart, the layers of dry dust encrusted on my hands. I got to smell it; the magnified aroma of my body fused on my clothes. I got to hear it too; the melody of zippers. And I got to see it; the orange mountains and cliffs, and sand that I thought I was used to. But this time I didn't just drive by them or admire them from a pool side.

   I went shopping for hiking boots and pants that made me look like a miniature version of the tent I would be sleeping in for that week. We call it "Project Term" at my school, where we get to pick one of several trips to go on. I picked the most difficult, the one with the warning attached. The one without the bathrooms, the mirrors, the showers. I went into it so scared that I could not imagine a "me" that could have survived it. My big goal for myself was to do just that; to get through it. But I came out of it, indeed, as no one who I could have foreseen. I came back with clothes that needed to be washed twice, hair that had wildly regressed back into its natural curl, and the notion that the suburbs would no longer pass as satisfactory. I learned to eat spilled pasta off the ground, that it was fun and tasted just fine. I learned that there are more stars in the sky than I thought. I learned how to package my clothes air-tight, into ziplock bags. I woke each morning with every muscle muttering in complaint, but hiked a mountain that day anyway. I treasured my bruises and the new holes in my clothing. I felt what it was like to hold myself, dangling in front of a waterfall. I learned that my mountain bike at home has no idea of its luck in escaping the torturous trails out west. I know that it's best to take small baby steps to walk up a steep hill. I'm also learning that these things can be metaphors for life. The most important thing I came back with was a new belief in myself, where I had previously harbored doubts. I came back with ambition to learn about the world. Life, I'm ready for you.

> **I learned to eat spilled pasta off the ground, that it was fun and tasted just fine.**

Megan Topolewski attended the University of Wisconsin–Madison.

68

A FAKE SMILE WITH THAT ORANGE JUICE?

The essay that follows is a blueprint for how to transform ten seconds of small talk into a 542-word essay. Author Andrew Kim peels back layer after layer of his brief interaction with a flight attendant while showing remarkable self-awareness. "When this incident happened to me, I pulled down the table in front of me and immediately started writing. I knew I had to record my thoughts that moment to capture all the emotions involved," recalls Andrew. Only later did he see the potential for making this piece into a college essay. Would the essay be better with 100 more words to reach the limit of 650? Not a bit...

Essay by Andrew Kim

Some students have a background or story that is so central to their identity that they believe their application would be incomplete without it. If this sounds like you, then please share your story.

I woke from an unpleasant sleep. As with all sleep on airplanes, it was just to pass the time; very little rest lay in the upright position. I was used to it though. Long flights have become a part of my routine, and I've grown callous enough to ignore the discomfort.

But this flight was exceptionally bad. The screen in front of me wasn't working, so I couldn't check how much time remained in the flight. Along with that, my USB port wasn't working either, while my phone had a mere 38 percent battery left. Then I realized that I had missed my meal. Hunger settled in immediately. Once I noticed my hunger, I subsequently noticed all the discomforts: aching back, stiff neck, the nonexistent space between my knees and the seat in front of me. Shaking my legs awake, I decided to ask for some peanuts.

A flight attendant promptly brought three packages. I looked up to see that she also brought me a cup of orange juice. I marveled at her thoughtfulness. Her gesture made me forget the bodily pain, as if I were an old man regaining his youth. I eagerly looked up at her face to thank her, expecting a gentle smile.

But I saw an indifferent face, devoid of even a hint of verve and plagued with impatient desire for the end of the flight.

I felt a bitter disappointment, similar to that of love unrequited and of disillusionment about Santa Claus. What had been an extremely kind gesture a second ago was marred by the flight attendant's indifferent manner, one born of habitual acts, probably taught by a veteran cabin crew and blindly followed. I hurriedly took the cup, afraid that if I took any longer, the apathy would turn into irritation.

I ate the peanuts with an expressionless face.

At first, I was bothered. Then I thought about my own attitude. I realized my own conceit and was disgusted. With my fancy frequent flyer status, I had grown accustomed to expect smiles and excessive kindness. While it is their job, had I been more considerate, I wouldn't have thought her so outrageous. After all, she had been working in the upright position for hours, handing out smiles.

> **I felt a bitter disappointment, similar to that of love unrequited and of disillusionment about Santa Claus.**

Then I thought about my own reaction. I smiled and thanked her, though I was shocked inside; my grin was a conditioned reflex bearing no sincerity whatsoever. I've always valued sincerity, but this time, I was offended by her sincerity—indifference and exhaustion—and responded with insincerity. In that moment, my reaction betrayed that perhaps I desire the comfort of affection too. I would not have been bothered had she put on a superficial smile. I would have been too busy to even notice its superficiality. But in the discomfort of the upright position, I became an offender of the thing I have lamented for so long. I could not deny that I would have preferred an insincere smile to sincere indifference. I was ashamed, not only of my own hypocrisy, but also for condemning others for insincerity.

I finished the cup of orange juice. It had a faint bitterness, as if

I had brushed my teeth moments ago. I thought about asking for some more, but decided not to.

Andrew Kim attends Swarthmore College.

69

"I FELT LIKE AN ADULT IN MY FAMILY"

Many students will relate to the following essay by Margaret Elizabeth Connell, who describes the familiar rite of passage of learning to drink coffee. Margaret's flair for detail makes her a good storyteller, as in her opening description of grabbing her morning cup of coffee (but not drinking it until she arrives at school). Margaret draws in the reader for two full paragraphs before subtly sharing the main idea—that she wanted to drink coffee in order to feel grown up—almost as an aside. Margaret ultimately learns that she can be mature without the coffee, a final realization that has the reader nodding in agreement. "It took about three months to make my essay the way it is now," recalls Margaret. "I worked on it a lot during the summer before my senior year."

Essay by Margaret Elizabeth Connell

At seven thirty, every morning, I race down the stairs, as fast as my drowsy body permits me, and take a detour through the kitchen on my way to the door. I pick up my filled to-go cup, with the same urgency and accuracy of a relay racer reaching for the baton. The purple isolated container has been graciously filled by my mom with piping hot coffee brewed by my father earlier that morning. I don't dare try a drop of the scorching drink until I pull into the school parking lot. Once arriving at school, I finally sip on the black coffee, no cream, no sugar, armed and ready to face the long day.

My dad drinks coffee all hours of the day. When he's home, there's always a comforting, fresh pot in the kitchen that fills the whole house with a warm, cozy ambience. And my mom refuses to start the day without a warm latte. She concocts one every morning with different creamers and sugar. Ever since I was young, I had watched my parents drink coffee and I enviously dreamed about being old enough to enjoy a cup. My elder cousins grew older and began drinking coffee. In the mornings, they now could stand in the kitchen and lean nonchalantly against the counters, chatting with the adults. From my seat at the kitchen table I watched jealously and glanced pitifully to my glass of cold orange juice.

My family and I were in the airport early in the morning destined for Denver, Colorado, when my parents wanted a second cup of caffeine, so we went to the terminal's Cup O' Joe café. My brother, David, and I were always given hot chocolate as our default hot beverage, but that day, in an effort to assert my age, I asked for a cup of coffee. My parents, laughing in disbelief, scanned the menu and ordered me a cup half filled with coffee, but then leveled off with the familiar hot chocolate. The steamy liquid concoction eliminated my distaste for coffee! I could consume this new drink without trying to conceal my disgusted face from my parents. By my sophomore year I had become the champion, after weaning myself off the chocolate milk, I could digest a cup of hot black coffee with ease and grace. And I made sure my entire family was aware of my new talent by downing cups of coffee every morning.

> That day, in an effort to assert my age, I asked for a cup of coffee.

I loved the new privileges I gained as a coffee consumer in my family. I could participate in conversations about politics or family gossip during breakfast as I casually leaned against the counter and gawked at truths that were revealed. I felt like an adult in my family; my opinions could be heard, my actions could be trusted, and my independence began to expand.

But David allowed me to see the true reason for my new independence—I was actually becoming an adult. I had trained myself for years to become immune to coffee's bitter taste, but I didn't need to. My brother tried coffee and didn't like it, so he never drank it. And to my dismay, he was still earning the same increments of freedoms that I had once gained when I was his age. Coffee had nothing to do with it. I now only drink coffee when I want it. And I can stand in the kitchen and talk with the adults no matter what the temperature of my beverage is.

Margaret Elizabeth Connell attended Virginia Tech.

Humor

The world is full of people who laugh at their own jokes. Making other people laugh is harder. The best humor essays are spectacular; the ones that fail are embarrassing. Since being funny on paper is much more difficult than cracking a joke with your friends, only excellent writers should make the attempt. Be aware that there is often a humor generation gap, and get an adult to make sure that what is funny to you will also be funny to the older person who reads your application. The essays in this section show various approaches, from sustained parody on a single theme to free-floating, hit-and-run mockery of various subjects.

70
ESSAY AS MONOLOGUE

Says author Laura Cobb, "It all just hit me really quickly one Saturday. I had gotten my National Merit application, and the question about what set me apart had been rolling around in my head for a few days. A light bulb went off in my head; I repeated the line a few times, and then I sprinted as fast as I could to my computer." From there, it was less than an hour before Laura had completed most of her essay. For anyone with aspirations of being funny, the best way is often to get on a roll like Laura does in this essay. The key is to make them laugh while doing a stream of consciousness that highlights interesting and important things about yourself.

Essay by Laura Cobb

In your own words, describe your personal characteristics, accomplishments, primary interests, plans, and goals. What sets you apart?

I won my school's Pickleball tournament in tenth grade. How many National Merit Semi-Finalists can say that?

What? That's not enough to set me apart in the massive pile of applications? Well, maybe I hold the world record for most snow cones eaten in the summer of 2004, or the record for most piggy back rides given as a camp counselor. I'll have to double check on those. Academically, I'm valedictorian of my class. My sixth grade graduating class, that is. I gave a speech and everything.

Well, perhaps my work with autistic children would set me apart. Has anyone else mentioned being stabbed in the eye with a plastic zebra? (Fear not, my eyesight fully recovered a few minutes later.) Aside from that incident, the experience I had volunteering in a special education classroom has motivated me to pursue autism studies at a graduate and post-graduate level. I want to solve autism's puzzles. I want to research, to discover, and to cure. I want to make my mark in one of science's most fascinating and mysterious fields.

I only failed my driving test once.

I've won awards for placing seventh nationally in the Grand Concours National French Exam, but I'm also building my Spanish vocabulary by watching soap operas on Telemundo. "*¿Como puedes llegarme, Consuelo?*" See? That's academic initiative.

How about wanting to change the world? I've been active in my school's chapter of Amnesty International, I petitioned local government to support amendment of the Fair Labor Standards Act to protect youth workers, and my peers know never to challenge me in a debate over gay rights.

Also, two of my best friends have webbed toes. I don't know whether or not that means I get along best with people who are part duck, but it's an interesting coincidence.

Maybe, in order to stand out, I should focus on awards and other honors. I won the Brown University Book Award, and I also won the "Streaker" award for a particularly unattractive tan line at a recent camp. Plus, I was inducted into the National Honor Society around the time someone titled me the "least aggravating person in the world."

In the end, I could describe dozens of things that would suggest unique motivation, interests, or personality traits. However, I think the best representation of myself cannot be restricted to five hundred typed words. Perhaps I've scribbled in more correct bubbles on my standardized tests than some, but I think my biggest accomplishment is the confidence I've built in my entire person. I haven't spent my

Has anyone else mentioned being stabbed in the eye with a plastic zebra?

entire life trying to be a student at an elite university, I've spent it trying to be the best, most well-rounded person I can be. I hope, in the long run, that this is what will truly set me apart.

Laura Cobb attended Washington University in St. Louis.

71

REVENGE OF THE ALPHABETICALLY CHALLENGED

After a lifetime of being last, Stephanie Yeldell turns the tables. She has a virtually infinite store of experiences to call upon, from getting the last (rickety) desk to being the last to get a diploma. The reader can't help but feel a twinge of outrage on her behalf, but Stephanie does not wallow in self-pity. Instead, she shares her determination to "live life loudly." In her words, "I actually modeled my essay after a rant I had had with a friend of mine over dinner. When I sat down to write, it just came to me to turn that into an essay."

"…and Stephanie Yeldell" by Stephanie Yeldell

"…And finally, Stephanie Yeldell," is a phrase that I hear more than one could ever possibly imagine. One might ask "Why, Stephanie? Why is this?" The answer is simple: Our world seems to deem it entirely necessary to list individuals in alphabetical order, and by last name. For those who are alphabetically challenged, this form of listing individuals, that seems to be unbelievably prevalent, is every single shade of irritating one could possibly experience. It's annoying. In class, I get the bent, rickety, and estranged desk that has been rejected to the very back corner of the room. My locker is always last in the row, usually next to a doorway, trash can, stairwell, or a dirty couch that is constantly littered with random people. I am the last on every list. I am the last to receive anything, like parking stickers, important papers, letters from school, permission slips, report cards, school pictures, tests, and exam schedules. I sit next to teachers on class trips and will be announced last when it comes

> I actually modeled my essay after a rant I had had with a friend of mine over dinner.

to participation in chorus, A Cappella, and theatre. I was the last to walk across the stage for National Honor Society, and I will be the last to graduate in my class. In short: fate has it that I am last.

The art of dealing with being last is an act that I have nearly perfected after eighteen years of trial and error. The solution I have come up with: live life loudly. By this, I do not mean vocally (though I tend to be), but I mean loudly in respect to presence, and character. I find that if I can pour all of my being into whatever I am doing, it shows. I try to milk every moment for all that it may contain. I speak with all the passion words I possess and sing every note I can hit with relish. I want my presence to be received the second I walk into a classroom as well as it is when I walk into light on stage. On stage, I am more than an actor. In any role, no matter how small, I am a story teller. I can affect people. I can entertain them. I can open their eyes. I can take them to places they have never even dreamed of imagining. I can bring them more joy and more sorrow than perceived possible. I have an impact, no matter how small; despite the fact that my name will be listed last on the play bill. This impact, this connection, is monumental. It is these loud desires that run through my alphabetically challenged veins, and drive me to embody such a loud charisma and character.

Stephanie Yeldell attended Providence Day School in Charlotte, North Carolina.

72

EMILY DICKINSON, JIMMY BUFFETT, AND A CHEAP BOTTLE OF SHAMPOO

Multifaceted people sometimes write multifaceted essays. Though there is always danger in having a blurry focus, an essay that encompasses a number of topics can work if the purpose is to show the various sides of an author's personality. Alysa Hannon's essay, below, is packed with details. She says that her personality includes "an accumulation of quirks and nuances," and the same can be said for her essay. As is so often the case, the proof is in the details, which reveal her wide-ranging knowledge. Says Hannon, "I don't think it matters whether you write about your trip to Uganda or your first comic book: just so long as what is written is a glimpse into what it would be like to sit in a room with you."

Essay by Alysa Hannon

Contrary to what you may think, buying a bottle of shampoo is a complex and tedious process. First, I chose the five most outwardly appealing bottles, conscious that my seventeen-year-old female mind is being manipulated by blatantly false phrases like "made with real herbs so your hair will stay shiny for up to eight and a half hours." After repeatedly inhaling the essentially same fragrance from each bottle, mulling over which label and aroma has won my four dollars and seventeen cents, the Marxist impulse within me, instilled by my unfathomably cheap father, compels my reluctant hand to pick up the sixth, cheapest bottle which was eliminated in round one. I've described this process so that, to some small degree, you may understand how difficult it is for such an indecisive, meticulous person like me to choose a topic for what has been unconsciously labeled by my teachers, advisors, parents, and friends as the most important essay I will ever write. In my quest for the perfect subject, I have realized that my three-faced personality does not ameliorate the situation.

(I'm relatively sure that both illuminating my indecision and disclosing my undiagnosed multiple personality disorder did not rank high on my college advisor's "Tips for Writing Your College Essay.") To speak bluntly, I assume three personas; no one is less truthful than the others and each has a parallel essay topic with which I toyed.

The most visible facet of me is Ms. "I have a 4.27 GPA." She is a perpetually working student, a basketball starter, and a good Catholic schoolgirl at heart. Those who see me as my résumé consider my quest for a perfect paper topic asinine. From their perspectives, my subject was strategically chosen when I submitted my down payment for my community service trip to Africa last spring break. Despite the indelible mark my Malawian excursion left upon my perceptions, I have an intrinsic, unexplainable aversion to turning that experience into a Hallmark postcard.

Having discarded my African journey as a viable essay topic, I was persuaded by a small but disproportionately influential constituency to narrate the convoluted soap opera, melodrama also called my life. Because I am a relatively private person, I have disclosed my story to only a few travelers I have encountered along my way. My family and I have mastered the art of duality. As a child, I could emerge from a household teeming with turmoil and tension and saunter into my first period class with a ribbon in my hair and a gentle smile sketched across my face. Despite how important my college admission is to me, I don't think it

> **It is my instinctive compulsion to say a silent Hail Mary upon hearing the drone of sirens.**

appropriate, helpful or wholly insightful to recount the convoluted, unorthodox string of events that have taken place from second grade to the present. I continue to be shaped by my upbringing; however, I have made certain that I am much more than a familial sob story.

The final facet of my character is the most vague but most dynamic and to me, most telling. It is simply the accumulation of the quirks and nuances of who I have become over the course of seventeen years. It is I, the Bruce Springsteen admirer, the Jimmy Buffett parrothead, and the eternal hummer of those skillfully written hymns I can never seem to remove from my subconscious all day Sunday. It is my instinctive compulsion to say a silent Hail Mary upon hearing the drone of sirens and a quiet "God Bless You" after even the most remote sneeze. It is the way in which the words of Emily Dickinson can transport me into a realm of thought and reflection after an interminable day of tests and deadlines. It is the spine-chilling anticipation with which I long for November when I can start playing Nat King Cole's "Chestnuts Roasting on an Open Fire," and the eternal ability of a star-studded sky to leave me awestricken and contentedly trivial. It is I, the last girl to leave the locker room after every basketball game, intentionally taking a little extra time so that she can walk through the now dimly lit, empty gym, which always seems sacred. And the topic that sprung from the most basic instinct of this girl was a very simple story, one that seems to evoke suppressed chuckles when told. Two nights ago after returning from a field trip to the Metropolitan Museum of Art, I sat at my desk at around 10:30 p.m., in an attempt to shorten the seemingly unending list of tasks I had to complete by the next morning. An experienced studier, I could easily envision the order in which my assignments should have been undertaken: AP European History test, college applications, Bible reading quiz, math homework, etc. At the very end of the list remained an optional assignment for my AP Art History class, which entailed writing a poem after visiting the Egyptian temple of Dendur earlier that day. Despite the tests I would inevitably take the next morning or the applications due the next afternoon, I sat for thirty minutes and let my hand poetically glide across the blank sheet of paper before me, completely aware of my inefficient use of time, but unable to feign concern. To a stranger, my decision to narrate the manner in which I approached my homework may seem ludicrous; however, to me it is a fable of freedom. Two years ago, even two weeks ago, I would have felt the innate urge to write a poem instead of studying for an imminent test; but being the responsible student I am, I would have suppressed that Thoreauvian compulsion as I memorized the six wives of Henry the eighth.

In forty years, I suppose that my laundry list of credentials will have been many times amended and my collection of stories to tell, tragedies and comedies, will be gorged. But I hope, given the opportunity, I will always choose to write the poem.

Alysa Hannon attended Georgetown University.

73

THE APPLICANT HAS NO CLOTHES

For the few applicants who can be consistently funny in an essay, the following one will offer plenty of ideas. Author Daniel Fredrick is an actor who shows that he is also a pretty fair writer. He turns the application/audition process into a parody, and in the process shows unusual self-awareness. Was the admissions process frightening enough to drive him into the college of business? Not hardly, but it obviously gave him plenty of material to consider for a different career: stand-up comedy.

Essay by Daniel Fredrick

Do you ever have those dreams where you've arrived at school and suddenly realize you've forgotten to wear pants? Well, for most high school seniors that dream becomes a reality, at least figuratively. We must bare our souls, not to best friends, or family, but to complete strangers who may not even want to hear about it and may even flat-out reject us. What twisted institution would ever subject young adults in the formative stages of emotional growth to this experience? Oh, right. College.

During the sixth, seventh, and eighth grade, my family lived in New York City, where public high school is not the best option for a serious secondary school education. This means that students must apply to high schools all over the city, in much the same way they will proceed four years later in the college search. At the time, I considered how fortunate I was to be able to get some experience in this realm before I had to do it "for real." I had no idea how wrong I was and how ill prepared I would feel. I eased into the college process with a nonchalance belying the gravity of the situation. I figured that I would never actually *go to college*. This was all just an elaborate joke. I'd stay suspended in high school in perpetuity. Isn't that what the *Happy Days* kids did?

After views to the contrary were repeated enough times by teachers, parents, and friends, it dawned on me that maybe I really would have to go to college. And so it began. As a student who plans to pursue a degree in acting, not only did I have to write essays, visit colleges, and participate in interviews designed to yank out the weeds, I also had to audition. It is disconcerting enough to be told by a college that they don't feel you are right for them, but to also be told that you just aren't talented enough? It is a prospect frightening enough to drive me into the school of business (well, maybe not quite). So I dutifully prepared my two contrasting monologues, one contemporary and one classical, totaling no more than two minutes in length each, and prepared to go to school with no pants.

> I figured that I would never actually *go to college.* This was all just an elaborate joke.

As of this moment, I've auditioned for two of my four prospective schools and although I've been accepted to three, the decision of each theatre department will be the deciding factor. Writing this essay has suddenly made me realize the gross unfairness of the college process, and inspired me to try to balance out the issue. From now on, every college rep, department head, and theatre professor I meet, I'll simply request that in the interest of fairness, they remove their pants.

Daniel Fredrick attended Texas Christian University.

74

YELLOW TIGHTS AND PIN-CURLS

Author Courtney Cook's essay is so good that we hesitate to print it. Do not try writing an essay like this at home. But Courtney's essay has important lessons to teach. In addition to showing her incredible zest for life, it is chock full of specific places and things. After an impressive recounting of what she has "tried once," Courtney describes her role performing in "The Fantasticks." But she has no great epiphany and offers no lesson to be learned. The play has memorable moments but is not a peak experience. Real life is like that, and so are real essays. "I wrote the original essay for English class," recalls Courtney. "When typing up the first draft, all the words came naturally to me since it was me; I could barely type fast enough."

"Try Everything Once" by Courtney Cook

"Try everything once." That's my family's motto, and, as mottos go, it's a pretty good one. Because of it I have played rugby, survived an incredibly painful season of track, taught Sunday school, repaired roofs and drainpipes (Appalachia Service Project), tried kite boarding, been hang gliding, moved to Costa Rica for six months, biked for two weeks in Colorado and Utah, wore a Queen Amidala costume to school, eaten raccoon, guinea pig, and iguana meat, swum with sharks, lived and worked on an Amish Farm for a week, and enjoyed many, many other memorable experiences.

As you can probably guess, this fun-filled family motto has gotten me into some really interesting/embarrassing situations. For example, the one I'm in right now. I am presently crammed into a box with Rose (a high school senior and my partner for the play), and wearing the most embarrassing costume in the universe. Okay, let me explain the situation a tad more slowly; I'm in the school musical, *The Fantasticks*. Like I said, my family motto is "Try everything once," and as I have never done a play before...well, you understand. I was spurred into doing the musical through the actions of my brother. In the beginning of the year, he performed in a musical and, not wanting to be upstaged (no pun intended), I also decided to participate in a play. (My brother and I have somewhat turned the motto into a contest. I'm winning.)

Mr. Belich, my costume, the microphone, and doing hair and makeup all combined to make the play both an extraordinary and somewhat humiliating experience. Mr. Belich is Brookfield Academy's drama and music professor, and he is incredible at his job. However, he is always stressed out and yelling. Therefore, I prefer to spend as little time with him as possible.

> I am presently crammed into a box...and wearing the most embarrassing costume in the universe.

My costume, as I said earlier, was totally degrading, canary yellow tights, a red/orange button-up shirt that is both completely torn up and has the stereotypical bulging Shakespearian shoulders, purple doublet (also torn and puffy), equestrian riding boots, and a set of Shakespearian bloated purple shorts. Even more embarrassing is my makeup. I really don't like makeup in general, so suddenly getting my face covered in about three inches of the stuff was not an enjoyable experience for me. Also, as Joey (our brilliant technician) and I both determined, my hair is evil. Mr. Belich insists I put it up in pin-curls (and if you don't know what pin-curls are, lucky you), and whenever Joey tried to weave a microphone through my hair, major problems and pain tended to ensue.

The musical took up a lot of my free time and, overall, I can't say that I enjoyed it as much as the other activities that I could have done instead. Thus, it is unlikely I will ever try it again. However, I'm glad I was in a play at least once. My family motto is "Try everything once," and to me, that's one of the best things you can do with your life, try everything once.

Courtney Cook attended Ohio Wesleyan University.

75

SHE'S A PERRIER DRINKER, AND PROUD OF IT

If the whole college-essay thing seems a little contrived, feel free to make a joke out of it. Just make sure you have the writing skills to do the job. Author Angèle Larroque delivers a wicked parody by using her taste for Perrier to showcase her offbeat sense of humor. She invents screwball reasons why she loves Perrier, creates tongue-in-cheek categories of Perrier drinkers, and suggests that her devotion to Perrier shows her ambition. But is her love of Perrier enough to get Angèle into college? Read on and see for yourself.

"The Beverage That Changed My Life" by Angèle Larroque

I love Perrier water with the depths of my soul. I cannot get enough of the cool, fizzy bubbles rolling on my tongue. The crisp taste is pure bliss for the palate. The bitter aftertaste is the best part of the Perrier experience.

Maybe I love Perrier because I am French to the core. I have a complicated name that is difficult to pronounce, the metabolism of a hummingbird, and I own quite a few black clothes. I also drink bitter coffee and eat baguettes and I am sometimes rude to strangers. *Je suis francaise*, hence, I have inherited the Perrier gene. Perrier is not just a beverage; it is a way of life.

There are two kinds of Perrier drinkers. There are those who are snobby and sophisticated who take small snooty sips from a glass while at a swanky café, and there are the free-spirited drinkers. I am the latter. I am one of the c'est la vie, I-have-class-but-appreciate-chaos, fine-art-loving, passionate drinkers. We drink Perrier with almost every meal and carry it around in small bottles during the school day. Unlike the snooty Perrier drinkers, you cannot pretend to be one of us. Either you are born with the Perrier gene or you are not. I hate to admit the fact that when I was young, I hated the taste of Perrier. But what set me apart from other preteen Perrier haters was that I wanted to love Perrier and inevitably would one day. I then subjected myself to years of training the palate in order to love the taste. This shows that I am ambitious. I saw something I wanted and with hard work and dedication, I drank so much Perrier that I developed a love for it. I am a Perrier lover and can never escape it.

I am one of the c'est la vie, I-have-class-but-appreciate-chaos, fine-art-loving, passionate drinkers.

As I was writing this essay, my table companion and classmate told me something amusing.

"You know what you're going to be when you're older?" he asked. "You're going to be one of those skinny French girls in a Parisian café, chain smoking and laughing at all the American tourists!"

I can't wait.

Angèle Larroque attended Parsons School of Design.

76

DO YOU BITE YOUR NAILS? WANT TO WRITE ABOUT IT?

For a topic that literally everybody can write about, all you need to do is look at your hands. That's what Samantha Levy asked readers to do when she wrote the following essay. Samantha bites her nails—a fact that she is not proud of—but nail-biting gave her all the fodder she needed for a terrific essay. Nail-biting? An unconventional topic to say the least, but she pulls it off. The essay shows, among other things, her attention to detail, her ability to confront her insecurities, and her aspirations for the future.

Essay by Samantha Levy

Take a moment and look at your hands: their shape, texture, size, and delicacy. These parts of your body are one of the most important creations. They are the scribes of every document; the builders of homes, offices, and shelters; and what comforts many during a frightening experience. But, for me, my hands have yet to display any external similarities to the role they were created to fulfill.

One of the functions our hands are supposed to perform is a firm handshake. It shows character, attention—qualities that represent a good person. My handshake, although firm, embarrassingly reveals the pitiful remnants of my fingernails, outwardly signaling a nervous habit. And, at the end of each day, I must look in the mirror and recognize that I am a nail biter, an occupation I'm certainly ready to retire.

Unfortunately, and trust me I've searched, there are no official support groups for nail biters. All nail biters are left in seclusion to nibble away at what remains of their fingernails and their self-esteem. During these isolated moments, as I bite my nails or cuticles, I think of individuals with aesthetically pleasing nails in fear that they will look down upon me for the way I torture my fingers.

Likewise, I oftentimes find myself observing other people's hands. For instance, when dining at Greensboro's local Chinese buffet, Panda Inn, I continually notice that most of the female employees take great care maintaining their nails: they ensure that they never reach far beyond the fingertips, nor do they paint them a strange color. I've also found that these same qualities are present with the cashiers at the grocery store, and even most of my peers.

> **All nail biters are left in seclusion to nibble away at what remains of their fingernails and their self-esteem.**

It would seem that all I desire is to give up nail biting. However, in my heart, what I'd really like to do is find happiness in the accomplishments my hands achieve rather than focus on their appearance.

For even my hands possess beauty. They have delivered muffins to elderly in the hospital, typed continuously to finish newspaper articles within a deadline, and were very useful in pointing out each syllable while teaching my younger brother to read. Though superficially they are unappealing, my hands have led me to success throughout my life. Undoubtedly, I do wish that I had long, French manicured nails. But hopefully, I will grow to regard such physical features as simply superficial.

I am certain that the university I attend will help me strengthen my education and nurture my character and confidence to the degree that I would no longer perceive myself according to the physical condition of my nails. Instead, I will present myself to the world as Samantha Levy, a young woman who learned among the brightest, explored with the courageous, and took on the world hands first.

Samantha Levy attended the University of North Carolina at Chapel Hill.

77

WRITING ABOUT UNDERWEAR

If you want to write your essay about underwear—or a similarly inane topic—be our guest. Just be sure you know where you're going. Author Briana Mahoney uses underwear to set up a flight of fancy that showcases her skill as a writer. Why does Colgate ask a question like this? Not because they care about what you would bring, but because they want to know what you can embroider from musings about what will be (in most cases) an ordinary item. Briana uses the underwear to get to her madcap story, then loops back to explain that, yes, the story really did have to do with underwear and Colgate.

Essay by Briana Mahoney

What is one thing you would bring with you to Colgate and why?

Underwear. Say it to a kindergarten class, and they'll giggle endlessly. Write it in a college essay and…well, I guess I'll find out. But specifically I'm talking about long underwear; cozy, toasty, stretchy long underwear. I've never been much of a cold weather person, but give me a pair of long underwear and I'm "good to go."

I've only been skiing once in my life, but I remember it as one of my most exhilarating experiences. My first run down the mountain, my knees felt a bit weak and I was having trouble steering myself from side to side. With my family watching, I desperately tried to stay upright. Suddenly, I was blazing down the slope with my skis perfectly parallel as parents urgently tried to shuffle their children out of my way. With snow flying out in a wake behind me, my eyes locked in on the lodge dead ahead. Fearing for my life, and for those of the people carelessly milling about in front of the lodge doors, I finally caught on to proper skiing technique—in one direction, at least. With arms and ski poles flailing, I careened to my left, zooming past the horrified faces of the seasoned professionals waiting for the ski lift. Now completely off the slope and still flying across the level ground, I knew the end was near…then I spotted it—the fence. During my last moments of dignity (if any such moments had existed on this trip), I closed my eyes, braced myself, and slammed into the wood. As I recovered from the shock, I burst into giggles and thought to myself, "Let's do that again!"

> **As I recovered from the shock, I burst into giggles and thought to myself, "Let's do that again!"**

Now, the important thing to remember here is not that I have virtually no skills on the slopes or that I might endanger the safety of your children. No, the thing to remember is that I was wearing, at that glorious moment, a pair of long underwear. And so, you see, if I'm accepted to and attend Colgate, the first item I'll throw into my turquoise duffel will be my long underwear. Because if my run on the slopes comes anywhere near the thrills and chills of Colgate, I'm going to need a little warmth and some extra padding.

Briana Mahoney attended Furman University.

78

WHY DOGS ARE BETTER THAN CHILDREN

Animals are a fertile subject for tongue-in-cheek essays, and author Emily Perryman gets on a roll talking about the difference between a screaming toddler and an adorable puppy. There is no over-arching theme or meaning in the essay, but the ability to show a wry sense of humor and a flair for writing is more than good enough. When you're an admissions officer gazing at applications piled up to your navel, a little comic relief is much appreciated.

Essay by Emily Perryman

It's odd how a random thought can pop into your head and completely change the way you view something. Well, I realized today that I do not want children. This revelation came to me while walking into the grocery store. An exasperated young mother was trying to comfort her child. The little girl was throwing the ultimate temper tantrum, one worthy of an Academy award. She was stubbornly sitting on the ground, flailing her arms, kicking her feet, and was screaming at such a high pitch that it made me cringe. As I passed this sight, the mother looked at me, gave me a faint smile, and muttered, "kids…" under her breath. She then proceeded to carry her child to the car, kicking and screaming the whole way. I laughed and didn't think about it for very long.

When I was leaving the store, I was half expecting to see the mother still trying to get her child situated in the car seat, but I was denied that privilege. Instead, my attention was focused on an adorable Labrador puppy that was entertaining its owner while his wife was inside. It was doing such a great job of entertaining his owner that several other shoppers had stopped to enjoy the show, too. Well, this puppy was the epitome of an unproportional animal. Its lanky legs and huge paws were no match for the puppy's "pleasantly plump" body. It kept tripping over its feet while trying to catch its tail, even though its tail was not much more than a stub. When it would fall down, its belly would cushion the fall, but if the dog tried to roll over, his stomach prevented him from rolling all the way over. The puppy's owner would then pick it up and the whole cycle would start again.

That's when it hit me. Why in the world would anyone want a screaming, fussy child that grows up to be a screaming, fussy teenager when you can have a cute, playful dog that grows up to be your cute, playful best friend? As I proceeded to think about this on my drive home, I mentally compared and contrasted the two. Dogs don't complain if they are taken somewhere they don't like. In fact, dogs feel more than honored to get in the car even if it's just to the store on the corner. Children complain if they don't want to go somewhere and if it conflicts with their favorite TV show. Dogs are more than happy to eat *anything* you cook even if it's just flat out bad. Children say that their food is too spicy, too hot, too cold, not sweet enough, not pizza, too healthy, and too boring since homemade meals don't normally come with a prize. Dogs think that you are perfect, no matter how many times you might accidentally leave them outside. Children think that parents are weird and are anything but cool or perfect. The final thing was the one that sold me: the fact that the cost to raise children is on the rise since the education, housing, and medical costs are becoming more expensive, whereas the cost to have a dog remains constant.

> Why in the world would anyone want a screaming, fussy child that grows up to be a screaming, fussy teenager?

In the end, having a dog seems to be the better investment. They don't scream, kick, throw temper tantrums, and definitely don't complain about the cooking. Besides, when the dog turns eighteen, he's not calculating just how quickly he can get out of the house. He's just thinking about how much he wants to curl in bed with you to get his nightly belly rub.

Emily Perryman attended Southern Methodist University.

Family and Relationships

T he usual problem with writing about a person you admire is that the essay becomes about the person you admire— and not about you. The following essays all succeed in describing a teacher, friend, or family member(s) while also saying plenty about the author. As a group, the student authors show keen powers of observation—of how their relationships have evolved, and of what those relationships have meant to them. Particularly inventive is Essay 79, which begins with the aroma of French perfume in a sock drawer.

79

A WHIFF OF FRENCH PERFUME

Scents can leave a lasting imprint on our minds—a fact that Dori Chandler uses to her advantage in the essay below. She doesn't waste her breath telling about the importance that memories of a foreign visitor hold for her. The memory of French perfume in her sock drawer says it all. At only 261 words, this essay will put a smile on the face of any admissions officer staring at a pile of applications on a cold winter's night. The bookend reference to the perfume in the last sentence helps the essay end with a flourish.

Essay by Dori Chandler

I identify Laetitia by the tights scented with French perfume in my sock drawer, her ten-pound black boots, which still live in my closet, and her beautiful laugh I hear over the phone every so often. Laetitia lived with us as an exchange student the year my youngest sister was born. She was the first and only big sister I have ever had. Laetitia got my room and I moved in with my sister. From my eight-year-old perspective, she towered over me; she was tall and beautiful, a French masterpiece. Laetitia taught me so much over the year she lived with us and has continued to do so till today. During Chanukah, as we lit the Menorah she began to cry—remembering her father who had recently passed away. She was the first "adult" I saw cry. Laetitia taught me what a baguette, chocolate mousse, and crepes were, and how amazing it was to listen to her converse in French over the phone. When Laetitia left, I moved back into my old room but there was a void; my family felt it too. So, four years later we visited Laetitia in France. Her family was so welcoming and generous, even if we didn't always understand each other. Later, we went again for her wedding, a French Jewish Sephardic wedding. Her culture and language may be vastly different from my own, yet the love and care we have for each other is the same. I believe her scent in my top sock drawer will linger forever.

> When Laetitia left, I moved back into my old room but there was a void; my family felt it too.

Dori Chandler attended the University of North Carolina at Chapel Hill.

80

FAMILY LIFE AS ESSAY FODDER

Tufts University does not cut anybody a break with this difficult question. Rather than addressing the more generic issue of how your environment has shaped you, this question wants to know how your environment has shaped your goals. One possibility would be to talk about career interests, but for liberal arts students, the primary option is to reflect on how you want to live. This essay is a textbook illustration of how concrete detail—from the weedy garden to the jilted women—can create a vivid and interesting story. The idealism at the end has credibility largely because of the thoroughness of the description in the beginning and middle.

Essay by Marie Crowder

Describe the environment in which you grew up and how it has shaped your personal goals.

I grew up in a brick house on Nottingham Drive, a place with old furniture and young faces, with small rooms that never seemed to be empty. I grew up with my pointy nose buried in books, wearing stretch pants and bows and listening to my father's new songs on the guitar. I sat at a dinner table as girlish voices made fun of that pointy nose along with my big ears, and I finally learned to laugh about them. I grew up with a big-nosed father who always had a joke on his tongue and a mother who always had an answer. I heard that as long as I worked hard enough, I could do anything.

I grew up eating fresh tomatoes from my grandpa's garden and later saw that same garden overrun with weeds. I grew up during summers at the lake, with cousins who couldn't read until fourth grade and could break every object in sight. I watched at a distance as relatives struggled through life, searching for paths to independence. I heard stories from the adults' fold-out table, of women abandoned by the men whom they had depended on. Somewhere amongst those stories, I made up my mind not to make their same mistakes.

I grew up with a determination to make something of myself, to stand apart from the crowd. I listened to seemingly endless stories about the Depression and wars and old friends. I wondered if I would ever get a chance to tell my stories. I wondered what type of stories I would have to tell.

> I heard stories from the adults' fold-out table, of women abandoned by the men whom they had depended on.

I began to understand that I have a choice. I can choose the stories that I want to tell. I can choose whether or not I repeat others' mistakes. And I can choose what I make of myself. As to how I make these choices, I'm sure that all I have to do is remember the stories from when I grew up.

Marie Crowder attended the University of North Carolina at Chapel Hill.

81

"SOMETIMES WE TALK ABOUT JUST HOW AWESOME THE CUTTLEFISH IS"

For any applicant without a topic, the family dinner is a tried-and-true possibility. And few applicants have done it better than Sara Seymour, whose essay is a clinic on how to use dialogue and concrete detail to tell a good story. "Everyone eats dinner, but it's not important to everyone," relates Sara. "For me, it's part of who I am, and that's why I wrote about it." Though the essay seems to flow effortlessly, Sara wrote the first draft in fall of eleventh grade and put it through numerous revisions. When her dialogue sounded false, she went back to the dinner table and listened.

Essay by Sara Seymour

Describe a place or environment where you are perfectly content. What do you do or experience there, and why it is meaningful to you?

"Alright, Snapple Cap Question of the Day: What percentage of people in the world are left-handed?" asks my dad.

"Twelve," I guess.

"Three," guesses my brother.

"Nine," guesses my mom.

"Sara wins. The answer is eleven," says my dad. This is classic. My dad drinks Snapple every day with lunch, and every day he turns the fact from the cap into a question. He first aims the question at his coworkers at lunch, and then he tests our knowledge at dinner.

"Did you know that a disproportionate number of presidents have been left-handed?" offers my brother.

"Yeah, it's actually really interesting. I was reading this book, and there is a high correlation between psychological disorders and presidency," I add.

"It sort of makes sense when you think about it," explains my dad. "That job is incredibly stressful. I mean, any leadership position requires unique qualities."

Thus begins the next hour of banter and eating.

When I was younger I thought everybody had dinners like ours. It wasn't until the kids on our block used to ask me how it took so long for me to get back to playing tag with them in the summer that I realized it wasn't necessarily normal.

"What do you guys even talk about for that long?"

The better question would be, what don't we talk about? Sometimes we debate whether we like Hector or Achilles better. Sometimes we discuss how the Trolley Problem explains why socialized medicine might not be so acceptable to some people. Sometimes we laugh about how my brother impressed a bunch of graduate students because he actually chose to listen when I was talking about how the brain functions. Sometimes we talk about just how awesome the cuttlefish is.

"Did you know that a disproportionate number of presidents have been left-handed?" offers my brother.

When my brother found out that in my junior year I was taking AP Biology he smacked his hand against his forehead and said, "Oh, no. The bio lectures are going to be coming back, aren't they?"

I looked up from spearing my broccoli and smiled. Of course my nightly "lectures" would be coming back! How could they expect me not to share the most recent discoveries in the battle to fight AIDS?

"You know you love hearing about white blood cells and the immune system. What are you moaning about?" I teased.

Charlie shrugged and went back to pushing his food around with his fork. If he actually found it so bothersome, I doubt he would ask as many questions as he does.

In my eighth grade comment, my English teacher said, "You can tell she comes from a family that has dinner table conversations." I don't know that I appreciated what that meant then. Of all the things my family has given me, by far the most valuable is the practice of being a thoughtful person with a frequent opportunity to bounce my ideas off other thoughtful people. It doesn't have to be an argument necessarily. Sometimes it is, but usually, we listen, we respond, we are respectful.

My family and I have debated back and forth at the dinner table every night for as long as I can remember, connecting seemingly unrelated topics, exploring all the facets of life. My dinner table is a place where I am always content. These conversations are something that I truly love. Even the Snapple Cap facts.

Sara Seymour attends Yale University.

82

SIDELINING SIBLING RIVALRY

Most younger siblings could write a variation of author Luke Taylor's essay. But most older brothers are not class valedictorian and star running back of the football team. Younger brother Luke describes the struggle to find his way with good humor and lots of specifics about the other brother's accomplishments. But after Luke describes coming to the realization that his older brother is not perfect, the essay enters a more nuanced phase. Note Luke's skill at maintaining a balance between light and serious subject matter. Luke had to work hard to make the essay seems so effortless. "It was a long, tedious process to bring my essay from an ordinary essay full of errors to a polished essay ready to send off to colleges," he says.

"Oh, Brother" by Luke Taylor

Toddlers with buzz-cuts. Shirts tucked in. Shorts pulled high. Matching outfits chosen by Mommy. From the beginning, my brother and I have been incessantly competing with and compared to each other. Although Bryce is nearly two years older, adults frequently thought we were twins because we were about the same height and almost identical as young boys. While I no longer have to worry about people mistaking the two of us physically, I am still ensnared by the inescapable expectations and unbelievable pressure of being Bryce Taylor's younger brother.

Our competition, which consisted of underwater breath-holding contests and one-on-one basketball games, was once among the most memorable and pleasant aspects of my childhood. But as we matured and began replacing our pretend school sessions with AP classes and our play-room football contests with Friday night varsity games, the self-imposed struggle within my soul to match my brother's achievements began to escalate at an unhealthy rate.

Bryce was as close to a Greek god as anyone could be in high school. As starting running back on the football team, Bryce was one of the strongest weight-lifters on the team, one of the only players to start on varsity all four years of high school, and one of the key contributors on our school's first State Championship team his junior year. When he passed down his #10 jersey to me upon his graduation, it symbolized the demand for me to live up to his seemingly unattainable success as an athlete.

In the classroom, Bryce set an even higher standard than on the football field. Graduating as valedictorian of his class (I'm only salutatorian), scoring perfect 5's on all but one of his seven AP exams (I had only two 5's and one 3 after my junior year), and becoming a National Merit Finalist (I'm Commended), Bryce not only set a high bar, he set it as high as it could possibly go.

However, at graduation, I did notice his speech was dry and he looked uncomfortable speaking in front of an audience. Then it hit me—that boy is not perfect! He would rather be alone reading a book than surrounded by friends. Bryce refused to attend his senior float building (a social event for class bonding) until his classmates literally dragged him to the site. I am completely different, a "people person" who cannot spend enough time with friends and feels at ease when addressing a crowd.

Formerly, I viewed my brother's success as a burden on me to perform at an equally high level, which only led to unnecessary disappointment, stress, and anger. But after realizing the stupidity and futility of comparing myself to Bryce, I was finally able to celebrate his achievements and concentrate on making the most of my gifts without caring how they measure up to those of my brother. I learned to be comfortable with who I am. I meet my own expectations.

Bryce's dream to study at a prestigious university (Yale) was outside my scope a few years ago. He enlarged my reality, challenged me to transcend my comfort zone, and taught me to suppress my delusions of inadequacy. Because Bryce dared to aim for the unreachable and aspired to do great things, he set the ultimate example for me and taught me never to set a limit on myself or on my own dreams.

My brother's accomplishments now serve as a stimulus for me

to do everything with passion and excellence, not as my definitive criterion for achievement. What many of my friends think is a curse—being Bryce Taylor's little brother—is actually an incomparable blessing. It has pushed me to soar above the mediocrity and apathy holding many teenagers back and to become a focused and relentless individual. The competitive spirit engendered within me as an over-achiever's brother forced me to excel when I didn't feel like it or thought I couldn't do it. In my case, sibling rivalry was not detrimental but served as a constructive force in my life.

> **I learned to be comfortable with who I am. I meet my own expectations.**

I find it ironic that after all these years of looking up to my brother, he now must look up to me because I am a few inches taller. Oh, and by the way, my pants were never pulled up as high as Bryce's—I've always had more style.

Luke Taylor attended Vanderbilt University.

83

A SISTER WITH DOWN SYNDROME

Though its title includes her sister's name, author Claire Wyatt's essay is really about her perception of her sister and how it changes. She uses the first paragraph to describe the evolving relationship in exceptionally concrete terms. The two sisters have become somewhat distant, at least in Claire's mind, until an interesting and slightly mysterious moment when their roles reverse. The last six lines are noteworthy both for what they reveal, and for what they leave for the reader to deduce.

"A Lesson from Katie" by Claire Wyatt

I was never really upset about it. I never resented my parents for it. I didn't ever feel unlucky because of it. My sister had Down Syndrome, and that was that. Sure, I found it a little odd that while most of my friends' big sisters secretly applied lipstick on the walk to school, mine collected worms, which she would make into jewelry. But except for the occasionally painful quarrel (one of which left a bite mark on my right shoulder) my sister and I got along. The only problem was, after a while it became difficult for me to think of Katie as my sister, a person whose flesh and blood were identical to mine. There were just too many things that separated us, and soon I became the older sister, the leader and decision maker. In grade school, I noticed that the gap between us was growing larger. I outgrew monkey bars, but Katie didn't. I stopped climbing trees, but Katie wouldn't. I learned to write poetry, but Katie couldn't. I stopped roller-skating and began diving; I stopped trick-or-treating and began dieting. I'm not sure if Katie ever understood why, and to be honest, I'm not sure if I understood either. By high school the gap between us had gotten huge, and I remember feeling more like Katie's parent than her sister. But then, one strange and snowy night, something beautiful happened.

It was the winter of my junior year. The sky was black and empty, and its breath ached inside warm lungs. Life, it seemed, had either burrowed itself underground for warmth or had gone south for the winter like my Uncle Sherman, who can't stand the cold.

By high school the gap between us had gotten huge, and I remember feeling more like Katie's parent than her sister.

The trees were bare and lonely, and every once in a while they would point to a dimly lit, second-story window where my silhouette lay motionless on a bed. I was in one of those moods, those strange moods, where the world suddenly appears to be under water. Its sights and sounds majestically blur together, like some sort of half-dream. I felt uneasy and unfamiliar with myself and with everything around me. It's one of those states that comes occasionally in adolescence probably because of hormones, anxiety, and greasy foods all reacting with each other inside of our bodies. All I could do was lie on my bed. After I had counted something like three hundred of the tiny little dots on my ceiling, my sister entered my room. "What now, Katie?" I barked at her in my head, unable to make words come out of my mouth. I was anticipating her to begin her nightly ritual of describing, in exact detail, the events of her day: the food she's eaten, the friends she's talked to, the boys she might marry. But I stayed silent. I glanced in her direction to see if she was still there, and she was. She approached the foot of my bed and gently adjusted my feet to make room for herself. She sat down and stared at me for what must have been a long time. And then, as if she was aware of my inability to form words at that moment, she began to talk to me in sign language. (She had been learning it at school as part of some enrichment program.) I remembered only a few gestures that I had learned in elementary school, so she began teaching me. "School." "Mom." "Boy." "Bathroom." "Stupid." "Sister." "I love you." All of a sudden I realized that for the first time in nearly a decade, Katie was the older sister again. For the first time since we were kids, *she* was teaching *me*. And just like that, the gap disappeared. Just like that, we were sisters again. My emotionally masochistic fog quickly lifted and the world seemed clear to me again—clear but not perfect;

not perfect, but adequate. I realized then what I should have known all along: that my sister and I, despite significant differences, will always be sisters; that she's taught me much more than I have ever given her credit for. And I'll always be grateful to her for the night when she taught me to say, "Sister, I love you," in the only language that I could comprehend.

Claire Wyatt attended the University of Kansas.

A Moral Dilemma

T read lightly when describing how you handled a moral dilemma. It is easy to come off sounding smug when you describe "Why I Did the Right Thing." The best of these essays describe a real dilemma that requires a real choice and which may not have come to a tidy conclusion. Essay 84 is a particularly effective example of how to take a moral position without sounding moralistic. All four essays in this section reveal the author as a person who genuinely cares about doing the right thing.

84

AFTER EIGHTY YEARS, RIGHTING A WRONG

Author Alex Milne's essay sparkles partly because the reader doesn't know where it is going. Winnie the Pooh sounds sweet and innocuous, but before we know it, she is talking about her grandfather's racist views and why he changed the pronunciation of the family name. The juxtaposition of her typical high school life with the unfortunate origin of the "Milney" (formerly "Miln") pronunciation leads to an obvious question: Does it really make a difference to a teenager living eighty years after the fact? The answer for Alex is a resounding yes, and her thoughtfulness in confronting the issue shows her intelligence and idealism.

Essay by Alexandra Milne

"I love Winnie the Pooh! Are you related to A. A. Milne?" I can't even count on two hands the number of times I have been asked that question. "No I'm not; our last names are different. Well sort of… Well, there's a story…It's complicated."

I arrived at my new school in second grade. Another small private school, but here no one knew me. No one knew my family, where I'd come from, what I was like, and no one knew my name. I'd introduce myself; "Hi, my name is Alex Milne, I'm new." I've been at the same school ever since, and the same people have been calling me the same thing, Alex Milne (pronounced Milney). The invisible "y" never bothered me until I learned about the family history of it. Originally, my family pronounced our name as "Miln," one syllable. There aren't supposed to be two ways to pronounce my name. My grandfather, George Milne, was born in 1907, and, like many of his peers, he was a racist until the day he died. When he entered the military, he met a man in his unit with the same name: George Milne. However, much to my grandfather's displeasure this man was black. My grandfather, under no circumstances, would have the same name as a black man, so he immediately changed the pronunciation of his family name from "Miln" to "Milney," and that is the way it has been pronounced in my family ever since. I have always been known as Alex "Milney"; that is the way it is pronounced not only by my family but also by my friends and teachers. Many people just call me "Milney"—a nickname to distinguish between the four Alexes in my grade alone. When people call me by my last name, the emphasis on the change is magnified; I can't help but think of my grandfather. Sometimes the people in my school community, even teachers, whom I have known nearly my entire life, will ask which way it is pronounced. To avoid confusion, or having to retell the story for the millionth time, I tell them that it doesn't matter. I can do this because I can accommodate both mind-sets, a sort of cognitive dissonance: I can accept the family name while I internally disagree with the origins behind it.

Now I realize the severity of my grandfather's decision. The fact that he would take the extreme step of changing his given name to avoid comparison to another person he deemed inferior seems to me not only childish and foolish and trivial, but also immensely offensive. This change that he made really has had a large impact on me, enough so that I toy with whether or not to affirmatively revert my name back to the original pronunciation. It's hard to do, but I think it is worth the effort to be able to express my opinions. I understand that family history, especially family history I'd rather not own up to, is not unique to my family. Whether good or bad, every person has family history, and the hard part is dealing with the weight of it. However, in confronting our history we are allowed to build our own beliefs and create our own. My grandfather had personal values that left intangible marks on my family history, but I, Alex Milne, whether pronounced with a hard "E" or a silent "E," have taken the responsibility to forge my own beliefs and write a new history—one that includes George Milne—much to my grandfather's dismay.

> **Whether good or bad, every person has family history, and the hard part is dealing with the weight of it.**

Alexandra Milne attended Vassar College.

"*WRONG* FLASHED BRIGHT RED ACROSS MY MIND"

Sometimes a prompt poses a moral dilemma or asks for an opinion. In the essay below, written for Brandeis University's Writing Supplement, author Zoe Morgan-Weinman uses a personal story to explain why she believes Orthodox Jewish Law is unjust because only males can participate in a minyan (group) to say Kaddish (a prayer of mourning). She also shows that 250 words is plenty of space for a well-developed essay. "It was really helpful to tell a story rather than trying to explain my ideas on their own," she explains, "It also turned out that my essays were much better when I just sat down and wrote a whole piece as opposed to doing a lot of planning and overthinking."

Essay by Zoe Morgan-Weinman

Supreme Court Justice Louis D. Brandeis said, "If we desire respect for the law, we must first make the law respectable." Tell us about an unjust law (written or unwritten) that you believe should be broken (250 words or fewer).

A Scrabble tile skittered to the floor as Rabbi Zucker* walked in. It was a freezing Shabbat with everyone practicing their various observances: davening [reciting prayers], snowball fighting, inventing a new method of playing Scrabble. Rabbi Zucker called our attention: they needed a minyan to say Kaddish for Michael's grandpa. From a childhood of Sunday school and services at my reform synagogue, I knew that Kaddish was a mourner's prayer and a minyan meant ten people. I stood; Michael was my friend. "He'll appreciate that, Zoe," Rabbi Zucker said, then to the room, "I need ten more." I quietly reminded him that he only needed nine, which prompted the

---

*Name changed for privacy.

response that no, he needed ten *boys*. I backed away involuntarily; *WRONG* flashed bright red across my mind. I didn't count. My care and support for Michael and my desire to help didn't matter. If I had put on a pair of slacks, gone into that room, and sang in a deep voice, would I love him more? If the genetic lottery had tossed me a Y chromosome instead of one of my X's, would I have a better strategy of handing him a tissue when he cried? I understand that Jewish Law is ancient and thus often hard to comprehend. But being counted in a minyan is, to me, being considered human.

> I backed away involuntarily; *WRONG* flashed bright red across my mind.

I said Kaddish that night because human is all any of us can ever be and I believe G-d counted that minyan as eleven.

Zoe Morgan-Weinman graduated from Jewish Community High School of the Bay.

86

LYING AWAKE, REHASHING AN ARGUMENT

If you've ever laid awake at night replaying an argument in your head, we have an idea: write your college essay about it. That's what author Austin C. Pate did after staying up all night thinking about a tiff over race and political correctness. The essay is long, 881 words, and its success hinges on Austin's ability to let his thoughts unfold as he is telling the story. As he describes wrestling with what happened, he thinks it through with the reader at his shoulder. His reasoning ability makes for interesting twists and turns. The length of the essay is in sync with the topic; Austin is clearly a thoughtful young man who will follow the truth wherever it may lead.

Essay by Austin C. Pate

"The aim of argument, or of discussion, should not be victory, but progress."—Joseph Joubert

Much of what we learn, and most of our best thinking, is not because of what is spoon-fed to us, but rather as a result of interactions with other people, including active questioning of our surroundings, beliefs, and ideas. Sometimes the best of these opportunities go unexplored. During rehearsal for an American Conservatory Theater production I was in this fall, a fellow cast member offered to tell a joke, which she warned, might offend some people. After her disclaimer, and to the horror of the rest of the politically correct and socially aware cast, she recited what turned out to be a racially provocative quip. The result was a moment of disgusted silence, followed by a barrage of angry remarks. Embarrassed, but still defending her claim that she did not retell the joke out of prejudice or malice, I watched as she was verbally beaten down. Though it was initially hard for me to justify, I could see both the humor and the reasoning behind the joke. This caused me both shame and concern, but I still felt inclined to play devil's advocate among the group. The attempt was not as fruitful as I had hoped. The topic was too immense to argue on nerves alone, so after my quick questioning of the opinion we collectively had reached, I left it alone.

Unable to sleep that night, I ran over the argument again and again in my head, each time altering how I should have responded. Lying in bed I stumbled upon a painfully obvious and yet completely ignored parallel between our conversation and the context of the play we were all proudly performing. *School Girl Figure* is a dark comedy by author Wendy McCloud about the horrors of anorexia and the society that perpetuates such a disorder. Does the play not serve the same function as the joke told? What we—as a cast—were doing was taking a very serious topic and making light of it in an over-the-top, surreal manner. This made me realize that, contrary to how it may appear, politically incorrect jokes or storylines may not be created in order to ridicule the subject, but rather as social commentary. There are two sides to humor: it can be destructive when used at another's expense, or it can be constructive by bringing controversial humor to an otherwise ignored or taboo subject.

"It is different if you are making fun of yourself," others yelled at her. "But *you* are not allowed to joke." If someone suffering from anorexia were to come see our play, it may be painful or offensive; however, in a different crowd the words might have an eye-opening impact. Is it necessary for me to suffer from anorexia in order to comment about it and society's roll in its proliferation? When I laugh at an offensive joke, I am not doing so because I accept the generalization that is being made; I am laughing because of the ridiculousness of the existence of such a stereotype. People cope in vastly different ways. Some people choose to deal with heavy topics through serious conversation, and cannot see how it could possibly be made light of. Others deal even with tragedy through humor. Both are completely legitimate ways of coping. I don't think it is right to judge why one person might see humor in a given situation, or why another does not. To determine that all material that could be offensive to anyone cannot be joked about is dangerous. Censoring humor limits the tools that we as a society have to understand and examine our faults and shortcomings, and without it as our filter, we risk misunderstanding and handicap our possibility for change.

"Stereotypes just perpetuate ignorance," shouted one of the disgruntled cast members. I found it hard to disagree with this assessment. Under the wrong circumstances, in the wrong context, to the wrong person, the potential awareness that controversial comedy can create is nullified by inappropriate employment. I came to the conclusion that common sense trumps any good intentions, and while we cannot be responsible for our own feelings, we must try to be responsible for the feelings we invoke in others. Nevertheless, there is a clear danger in labeling a particular way of communicating as "wrong."

> "It is different if you are making fun of yourself," others yelled at her.

As the sun was turning the sky from pitch black to a deep blue, I realized two things: first, I had to forget about trying to get any sleep; and, second, I had been thinking, and the cast had been arguing, not just about the joke that had been told, but also about political correctness in general—specifically, the underlying tension we were all experiencing because of the nature of our play.

When we question our initial reactions, though our opinions may not change, we may better clarify our own feelings and gain insight into those of others. Had I not been bothered enough, I would not have lingered on the subject at all, and any subsequent thinking I did would not have occurred. Education is not only the acquisition of facts, but also the constant questioning and dialogue that brings us closer to some sort of understanding. School is just one catalyst; conversations, art, or arguments are all potential lessons that we sometimes neglect to utilize.

Austin C. Pate attended California Institute of the Arts.

87

OFFERED A FREE CAR, HE SAYS,"NO THANKS"

Author Charlie Shrader has a moral dilemma over an issue that most people would not give a second thought. Should he accept the gift of a car from the father of a friend? Charlie is able to write a 547-word essay about his uncertainty because he develops all the layers of the issue: his long-standing love of cars, his father's mixed feelings, his surge of euphoria upon receiving the car, and the ambivalence that he begins to feel after receiving the car. In one of his best lines, Charlie notes that the gift "caused both my mind and my driveway to become a little too crowded."

Essay by Charles Crichton Shrader

"So, you want this car or not?" Dr. Matt Petrilla asked again, in his simultaneously pushy yet polite manner.

This smart, stocky man, a medical doctor and the father of a friend, had thrown me into a sudden state of blissful surprise: less than a minute before, he had offered me a free car. We set a time for me to test-drive the car, and then he left me astonished and dazed.

Since my early childhood, when I begged my father to let me drive the golf cart at every opportunity, and when I developed a certain fascination with bumper cars, driving has always ranked high on my short list of life's great pleasures. Most of all, it affords the extreme satisfaction of independence, that glorious freedom for which the adolescent heart traditionally yearns. The idea of having my own car floored me.

That night, I told my father about the car. Until then, he had provided me with a car for regular use but not one I could call my own. "That just doesn't happen!" he exclaimed disbelievingly. He spoke in total favor of accepting the car, since he loathes denying what he calls his "thrifty Scottish side"; his mannerisms, however, were not entirely in synch with his words. In my overriding excitement, I did not see what exactly had disheartened him.

A few days later, Dr. Matt handed me the key to my new car: a forest green, Mazda 626 sedan, fitted with the most comfortable beige leather. Dr. Matt, who thrives on rebuilding wrecked cars and giving them to kids in the community out of sheer generosity, also proved his genius by converting it from automatic to manual transmission, since he knew how much I enjoyed the stick shift. On the way home, I quickly popped in my CD of Respighi's *Pines of Rome* and trembled in ecstasy as my car's powerful speakers pummeled my senses with the grand final movement, "The Pines of the Via Appia." I was in love.

Over the next three weeks however, despite my great contentment with the car itself, conflicting emotions beset me. Guilt bothered me most: "Why do I deserve this car? Shouldn't I give this car to someone who needs it more?" I often asked myself. I also felt guilt concerning my father's feelings, for now I understood his initial distress: he had worked diligently to provide an extra car for his family, and he knew how much it meant to me to be able to drive; I felt that I was almost disrespectful of my father by accepting this gift, though he would never mention it. The now-burdensome car caused both my mind and my driveway to become a little too crowded.

> **Guilt bothered me most: "Why do I deserve this car? Shouldn't I give this car to someone who needs it more?"**

I agonized over what to do, since returning such a stunning gift bordered on the unthinkable, but in the end I found clarity. I returned the car to Dr. Matt, who completely understood my dilemma. No decision had ever so thoroughly freed me. Dr. Matt now could give the car to another thrilled kid, and again I could appreciate my father's gift. Never in my life did I think I would turn down a free car, but in this case, nothing could have made better sense.

Charles Crichton Shrader attended Brown University.

Personal Growth

I t isn't easy to take your own measure, to honestly evaluate where you have come from and where you are heading. Perhaps you have overcome personal challenges (Essay 88), or have begun to see shades of gray in the world instead of black and white (Essay 90). One of our authors uses Western history as a metaphor for his life (Essay 93); another offers a more whimsical view of growing up (Essay 89). The best essays about personal growth succeed in showing a real transformation toward a more mature perspective on the world.

88

"DO YOU HAVE A CVS CARD?"

It isn't necessary to travel to Costa Rica to save the monkeys or work in an orphanage in Africa to have a good topic for your essay. Aspiring applicants can find rich material in the most mundane activities, like, for instance, working a cash register at CVS. The following essay from Paul Mains is a case in point. Mains has the self-confidence to poke fun at himself and his social anxiety, which he overcomes in due course thanks to his new job. His eye for detail is what makes this essay sing, as when he describes the teenager who attempts to buy cigarettes with food stamps, or when he reflects on how language persuades people to buy things. By the time he builds to the inevitable happy ending, readers have no trouble believing him.

"Retail Therapy: Overcoming Social Anxiety through Part-Time Employment at CVS" by Paul Mains

I am in retail hell. I stand behind the cash register, palms clammy, heart pounding, my mouth curled into an effortful and thoroughly unconvincing smile. I sport a pin that encourages customers to "Ask me what's FREE!" but its bold typeface and exuberant colors cannot disguise my fear of the dreaded general public. It's noon, and the store is abuzz with chaotic consumers, hurried housewives, and troublemaking teenagers. They terrify me. I blink and a line forms at my register. "Do you have a CVS card?" I ask timidly, my voice nervous and quavering. Yes, it seems like a simple enough question, but for a socially reclusive fifteen-year-old on his first day of the job, in even the simplest question lies seemingly infinite anxiety.

> I stand behind the cash register, palms clammy, heart pounding, my mouth curled into an effortful and thoroughly unconvincing smile.

An eight-hour shift lasts a decade. When it's over, I walk home, feeling worn-out, with a newfound hatred of consumerism. "It's money," I rationalize. After all, the whole reason I applied for the job was that my lack of monetary assets was becoming more desperate than my lack of social skills. I just did not expect that earning money would be so nerve-wracking.

It rapidly became clear to me that part of the job was being in the spotlight from time to time, whether I liked it or not. In just my first few days, I had to carefully explain to a short-tempered teenager that he could not use food stamps to buy cigarettes. Later, I had to convince a debit card user with an aptitude for colorful language that I was not co-conspiring with her bank to rob her of her money. It was exhausting. But after the third "Let me speak to your manager" in a single day, I noticed a peculiar absence of the anxiety I usually felt in such a situation, and it was then when I realized that I was gaining more from my CVS experience than just money.

Months went on, and an eight-hour shift seemed more like eight hours. Paychecks were rewarding, but I found myself more and more looking forward to the work itself rather than solely my weekly paychecks. Customer issues became routine and painless; small talk no longer caused extreme anxiety. No more did I feel as though I was fighting for survival against an angry mob: the "dreaded general public" that I once so feared wasn't so dreadful after all.

Encumbered less by social anxiety, I was able to observe more acutely the inner workings of the store, and I was surprised to find that a part-time job as a cashier could not only be somewhat enjoyable, but also decidedly stimulating. More closely examining the advertisements on the soft rock-playing, ever-repetitive CVS radio demonstrated to me ways in which language is manipulated in order to sell a product. (Who would question the legitimacy of a facial scrub made with "Arctic cloudberries"?) When studying the concept of register (linguistic change due to social stimuli) in my Linguistics class, I paid more attention to my interactions with customers and saw first-hand how different people use polite (or, for some, impolite) language to establish relations between themselves and others; over time, these observations helped me learn the proper intonations and inflections for a proper "How can I help you?". I used my limited knowledge of the Spanish language to communicate with a Hispanic woman who spoke no English (I may have sounded like a five-year-old, but we were ultimately able to understand each other).

Now, I look forward to my eight-hour shifts. Darting eyes and nervous laughter are things of the past. "Do you have a CVS card?" I ask with cool confidence and a textbook-perfect cashier smile. I invite bargain hunters to "Ask me what's FREE!" because I will tell them that this week, they can get a free toothbrush with the purchase of CVS brand mouthwash. Still, there are many times when

I'm the center of attention. Most recently, I had to stop an errant 150-pound vat of hazardous, photo waste chemicals from wreaking a path of destruction down an unfortunately-sloped parking lot. But the brightness of the spotlight no longer blinds me. And though an outsider may think that my bi-weekly paycheck is the sole reason why I work, that's not the case: while I do enjoy going to the bank and cashing a hard-earned check, my income is not what makes my job rewarding. It's the ability to hand the teller my deposit slip with an untrembling hand; the fearlessness with which I look her in the eye; and the anxiety-free smile that I give her when I wish her a nice day—these are the true rewards of my job.

Paul Mains attended Carleton College.

89

WHEN YOU'VE LOST YOUR MARBLES

Childhood memories can make for an endearing story, as long as you don't try to wring too much significance out of them. Author Juliana DuTremble tells a story about her childhood curiosity with flair and telling detail. The essay doesn't describe a life-changing transformation, but it is much better than most that strain for one. It ends with a light-hearted reference to the admissions process that simultaneously makes the point that Juliana wants to get in, but that she isn't so uptight that she can't poke a little fun at herself.

Essay by Juliana DuTremble

It was my fifth birthday. Imagine the joy that must pulse through the veins of a hungry homeless person who just happens to find a winning lottery ticket laying in the gutter. The look on that person's face would be much like the one I wore when tearing apart my present to reveal nothing more than a bag of marbles. The marbles fascinated me. They weren't just pretty pieces of painted glass smoothed into a nice round sparkling ball. There were worlds, whole universes even, contained within the intricate weavings within them. It made my little mind wander through uncharted mind quests, thinking that perhaps my house, my town, my world, was also contained within a marble cherished by another little girl.

One by one, my beloved marbles were swept under the carpets, consumed by the vacuum cleaner, or lost on the playground, until one day I had one marble left. It was a hot, humid day in the middle of June and my mother was outside making some new additions to her perennial flower bed. I'd been observing her work over the past few months and noticed a fairly simple pattern: she would dig a small hole, put in a tiny round object, and a few weeks later there would sprout a beautiful flower. Well, my naive brilliant self had a far better plan, and I at once set forth upon planting my glass ball in hopes of growing a "bed of marbles."

Ten years passed, and the marble garden had been long forgotten. Then one day, my mother was carrying out her annual gardening ritual, when suddenly a shimmering blue-green marble surfaced in the dirt. She hastily called me to her side, placed it in my hand, and instantly the flashback of my childhood endeavor played through my mind. Naturally, I kept the marble in a safe place—the safe place being a zippered pocket in my purse. It was as if I'd suddenly been showered in good fortune from the good-luck gods. At the time, I attributed much of my luck in making it to the county-wide spelling bee to my marble, as well as actually being admitted into the Maine School of Science and Math.

> **It was as if I'd suddenly been showered in good fortune from the good-luck gods.**

It is with great regret that I report the mysterious disappearance of this marble which I have cherished most of my life, as silly as it may be. I would love to finally discover where exactly my marble vanished to. It is a deep shade of indigo, and when you hold it up to the sun it shimmers in an iridescent green that will take your breath away. If you happen to discover my marble laying on a park bench, or upon a table at a yard sale, please, call my toll-free hotline at I-MISS-MY-MRBL. If at all possible, try to make it before I receive my decision letter from Cornell College—I might need a little luck.

Thanks.

Juliana DuTremble attended Cornell College (IA).

90

DOLPHINS, THE PRESIDENT, AND A SPUNKY SIX-YEAR-OLD

The following essay is more than merely a tale superbly told. At the beginning, author Anne Erickson is a six-year-old who sees the world in black and white; by the end, she is a sophisticated thinker who sees the world in shades of gray. The essay flows so well because of the follow-up information that gives texture to the stages of her life. As a six-year-old, she was pleased and then disillusioned, while as an older person she lived her ideals in Albuquerque. Says Anne, "Sitting down knowing that you're writing a big, scary college essay can make you sound wooden and formulaic. Instead, have fun writing about yourself. Later, you can work on all that college-essay-checklist stuff."

Essay by Anne Erickson

Potential to Contribute: Tell us about a talent, experience, contribution, or personal quality you will bring to the University of California.

In my six-year-old mind I see the president, sitting at his plush desk chair in a navy blue suit. He's examining an important document. Or better yet, he's in the middle of a crucial meeting with leaders from all over the world. His secretary enters. She looks worried. "We've received a letter of some importance," she says. His brow furrows as she hands him a small envelope addressed in sparkly pink pen. "Anne Erickson, age six, Oakland, California," he muses, examining the careful writing. He rips open the envelope to read my note. "My God, Louise, it's regarding dolphin-safe tuna. Call out the National Guard!" Louise would head over to that red telephone, dial a few numbers, and the powers of the U.S. government would be unleashed for the sake of my carefully articulated plea for the dolphins.

It was lucky that I learned to write just as my emerging sense of justice took hold—my letters gave me an outlet for my worries about the world. I remember the feeling of satisfaction it gave me to stick those letters in the mailbox. I was, after all, imparting crucial information: someday, when they were old and retired, the politicians would all thank me. "If it hadn't been for that little girl," they would say, "I'd never have known about those dolphins."

I was thrilled when I received my first presidential envelope in the mail, but soon became indignant to discover that the president sent me the same photocopy in response to each of my painstakingly crafted letters. I didn't give up, however. I simply broadened my target audience, pursuing my dream of a planet safe for animals through posters, clubs, subscriptions to Greenpeace newsletters, and the sheltering of a variety of odd creatures. The Norwegian ambassador renewed my faith in humanity when he sent me a handwritten note in response to my concerns about whaling.

As I've grown, so has my perspective on environmental issues. I still feel just as passionately about the need to save the dolphins, the whales, and all manner of animals, but my passion has been complicated by my slow realization that everything needs "saving"—even humans. A trip to South Africa when I was fourteen left me addicted to international travel, and I came away just as intrigued by that country's people and politics as by its monkeys and lions. Volunteer work in Panama and Honduras has shown me first-hand how difficult it is to strike a balance between human survival and environmental preservation: I'm still angry when I hear about "slash-and-burn" deforestation on TV, yet in the Panamanian village that was my home for two months, burning trees meant farmland, survival, and a way of life for my host family.

I am no longer the little girl with the one-track mind who wrote letters to the president.

My loyalties and passions have expanded as I learn more about the world. In both Panama and Honduras, I worked in schools with kids I adored, and learned to discuss politics and history in Spanish. This fall, I used that Spanish in Albuquerque, New Mexico, where I became an Election Day volunteer, getting my first taste of political action and becoming acquainted with volunteers from across the nation, not to mention the unforgettable residents of Albuquerque precincts 67 and 73.

I am no longer the little girl with the one-track mind who wrote letters to the president. Each time I discover something new about myself—my interest in politics, in public health, in teaching—life certainly becomes more frustrating and complex. But my passion for new experiences, and my tenacity and commitment to working for true justice in the world, has never wavered: it will follow me into college and beyond.

Anne Erickson attended Stanford University.

91

A NERDETTE GROWS UP

Author Sophia Sinsheimer's essay unfolds naturally, like one side of an interesting conversation. Her writing process began with the Common App prompts in the summer after eleventh grade, and even though her preferred topic (theater) did not "technically" fit any of them, it was easy enough to cast her experiences as a coming of age story for prompt #5. By the end of the summer, she had her first draft and plenty of time "to let the piece stew in my brain until I felt totally satisfied with it."

Essay by Sophia Sinsheimer

Discuss an accomplishment or event, formal or informal, that marked your transition from childhood to adulthood within your culture, community, or family.

I was always a chatty kid. From the time I was two, I had *Curious George* memorized and I would precociously recite it to my parents. I knew things! But the plight of my childhood, or at least, the plight as I saw it, was that I could talk and talk for hours, and for some strange reason, no one would ever listen. Or at least they wouldn't take me seriously. As a really little kid, I had a very high, squeaky voice, so whatever I said was somehow adorable—like those stereotypical cute kids in movies who think they're smarter than they really are. As I got out of preschool, my voice got less shrill, but all of a sudden people started to notice—I was a girl, and I was a flaming brainiac—Nerdette. My new dilemma became figuring out when to share my opinion, and when to stay silent, constantly fearing the opinion of my peers.

That's when I found theater. When I was seven, my parents sent me to Shakespeare camp, thinking it might be a good alternative to softball or gymnastics. I was cast blind into a scene from *Richard*

III, I had three lines, and it was one of the best summers of my life. Now Shakespeare, he was one precocious chatterbox! He invented words! He wrote plays about kings, fairies, fools, and made fun of them all! I may not have known what a pomp'ed ruffian was, but I fell in love with the way it sounded. Here was an art in which there was no wrong, no boundaries, and no peer group saying you look stupid for using a word like "marvelous" in everyday conversation. I was in love, I was on air, and all my precociousness was set loose, all my worries set free.

> **I may not have known what a pomp'ed ruffian was, but I fell in love with the way it sounded.**

Fast forward ten years. I had been in and out of the theater, in professional shows, school plays, even the oddball skit. I had trained nearly everywhere in the Bay Area. I had joined a choir, become its president, and then graduated on to private voice lessons. My junior year of high school, I was chosen to direct a one-act in our school's festival. It would become the greatest test of my life so far. I had a cast of six, in a controversial drama about a family in which everyone is gay except the youngest child, who comes out as straight. This was the ultimate test of my peers (even in San Francisco, they aren't as accepting as you would expect); I feared my cast would face retribution. My six actors were a completely odd group—only one or two had ever acted before, but they were all completely genuine performers. To watch them as they put themselves out there for my project, facing potential peer retribution/ridicule, I felt incredible gratitude. "Okay, guys, time for rehearsal. Quiet down." I honestly don't know what I was expecting, but each person turned to face me, silent in a lightning flash. I felt their trust and the faith in me as the leader. Each one was hanging on to my words as if I were someone important, I would chart the course, and everything would be okay. In that moment, I became an adult, as all these trusting eighteen year olds waited for my word. I was understood, my words were heard, my precociousness became an asset. Nerdette, for that split second, perhaps for the remainder of the rehearsal, became the queen. It didn't matter that I was a girl who had ideas, because there were finally people who needed them. It was the greatest gift, to pass on my training, my chutzpah, and my blessings to these peers of mine. That experience will nourish me, course through me, and coat me throughout everything I am and everything I do in my life.

Sophia Sinsheimer attends Northwestern University.

92

"THE GIRL WITH THE HUGE HAIR"

Author Andie MacDonald is a person comfortable in her own skin—and hair. Many students could use her essay as a model. She makes her hair into a metaphor, with its two layers representing two sides of her personality. It helps that she is funny, as when sharing that after waking up, she looks like she has "just been mauled overnight by a large bear." The essay's charm lies in the fact that she has embraced a trait that would make others self-conscious. Writes Andie, "I had started out writing some really serious essays about things I had done, but they were all coming out really cliché (which was frustrating) so I just started writing really random things. I have big hair and people always remember me as 'the girl with the big hair.'"

Essay by Andie MacDonald

I can't imagine wanting straight hair. People suggest it all the time, but I simply could never change my hair. It's a part of my identity, part of the reason people remember me. You see, it's not your ordinary hair—it's HUGE. And I'm not just talking curly; I'm talking mega frizzy and tangled. But no matter how difficult it is to manage, I would never get rid of it because my hair defines who I am.

> I had started out writing some really serious essays about things I had done, but they were all coming out really cliché.

The bottom layer is actually fairly straight and smooth. It's orderly, predictable and easy to manage, kind of like a part of me. I'm organized. Never mind that my room may be completely covered with piles of clothes. Still I can always find my favorite pink T-shirt or that last Harry Potter book. Maybe my room is the epitome of organized chaos. That bottom layer of hair is calm, not too frizzy, again, relaxed like me. I've always been one to chill, maybe watch a movie rather than stay out prowling till unprecedented hours of the morning.

The top layer of my hair is oh so different. It spikes like crazy; it puffs as if the laws of physics didn't apply to certain renegade strands. Actually it's crazy and unpredictable, kind of like another part of me. I've always had a creative, somewhat impulsive streak, whether it was inventing games to play with my brother or building a tower with ketchup-cups from McDonald's. I absolutely love to make things. When I was eight, one of my birthday presents was a huge box of tape and string of assorted types and colors. I was so blissfully happy with those simple, but magical "art supplies." I used it all within a few days making various tape contraptions which even blocked the stairs. I'm creative. I'm unpredictable, just like my hair. I like to try new things, to extend into new directions like that renegade curl refusing to lay flat.

Without a shower in the morning and copious amounts of gels and mousse, I look like I've just been mauled overnight by a large bear. But actually I'm ok with chaotic hair. It's me; it's wild, crazy, and unpredictable, and yet with care, creativity and effort, it can actually be tamed, organized. Trust me. People remember me because of my hair. That's exactly who I am. I'm me, Andie MacDonald, the girl with the HUGE HAIR.

Andie MacDonald attended Duke University.

93

"BEAUTIES WHICH PIERCE LIKE SWORDS"

Lack of a grandiose topic was no problem for Sean O'Keefe, who penned this essay to describe little more than the fact that he went into an intellectual slump in middle school. He compares his life to the course of Western civilization, telling his story with on-target references to Plato, St. Paul, C. S. Lewis, Dante, J. R. R. Tolkien, filmmaker Peter Jackson, and Malcolm X. The essay speaks eloquently about both the breadth of his reading and his mastery of the themes therein.

"How Reading Changed My Life"
by Sean O'Keefe

One overpowering image appears whenever I remember my middle school years: the Dark Ages in Europe. Was I suffering through isolation, oppression, or misery? Fortunately not, yet I was, as Plato would put it, in the gloom of my cave, bereft of the light of intellectual illumination.

I liken my early childhood, a time of radiant learning, to Greek and Roman antiquity. Whenever a particular topic (like dinosaurs, wildlife, or astronomy) seized my interest, I would read every wisp of related information I could find. In Classical Greek and Roman fashion, I laid the foundations of my future through my love of reading in my childhood. I stopped reading for pleasure, however, when I reached adolescence and became consumed with athletics. Like the Europeans after the fall of the Roman Empire, I vaguely sensed that something great still existed, dormant but waiting to be reborn.

As Dante's *The Divine Comedy* ignited the Italian Renaissance, J. R. R. Tolkien's *The Lord of the Rings* rekindled my dormant love of reading and ignited my life's Renaissance. Seeing Peter Jackson's first *LOTR* movie in ninth grade inspired me to tackle the book itself. Immediately, I was swept off into Tolkien's heroic tale. I discovered a story, inspired by the ancient world's greatest legends and myths, with profound relevance to the modern world though its timeless themes of friendship, courage, corruption, good and evil, war and peace, victory and defeat, love and hate, and hope and despair. I was moved by, as C. S. Lewis put it, "Beauties which pierce like swords." I felt like St. Paul when the Lord knocked him off his horse on the road to Damascus. For the first time, I realized that literature helps us discover how we want to live and where we want to go in the future.

During the seventeenth and eighteenth centuries, the philosophers of the Enlightenment brought about remarkable progress by re-evaluating Europe's previously accepted doctrines and traditions. Reading *The Autobiography of Malcolm X* incited my Enlightenment. The book demonstrated how personal growth comes from having honesty, compassion, and a capacity for sincere introspection. Malcolm X's story gave me, for the first time in my life, an open mind. I recognized how everyone, including me, will instinctively clutch onto preconceived beliefs and prejudices. Additionally, Malcolm X's remarkable regard for history taught me that without an understanding of the past, there is no wisdom to guide us in the future.

> I felt like St. Paul when the Lord knocked him off his horse on the road to Damascus.

The future is uncertain. We will face many great challenges in the twenty-first century: achieving peace and stability in the Middle East, defeating the ideology of Islamic Jihadism, and harnessing the energy of globalization to improve the human condition. Difficult choices must be made to meet these challenges, and I want to help make those decisions. My favorite stories have armed me with a love of reading and the sense of history and faith I need to face the future with enthusiasm. That is why I'm so excited to discover what the future will hold.

Sean O'Keefe attended the University of Chicago.

94

DOLLY PARTON, THEN AND NOW

It takes creativity to handle essay questions such as the following one from the University of Pennsylvania. The trick: don't spend too much time worrying about whether your preferred topic fits the question. What do they mean by a "first experience"? Author Allison Rapoport gives one answer with an inventive essay about seeing the world with a more mature eye. Says Allison, "An applicant should steer the essay to a topic about which they are passionate, and s/he should not be afraid to take some risks in doing so. It is not productive to spend time anticipating what the admissions staff 'wants' to see."

Essay by Allison Rapoport

First experiences can be defining. Cite a first experience that you have had and explain its impact on you.

I first became aware of the transformative power of music when I attended my first live concert. This was my first weeknight excursion with my father, the culmination of many episodes of desperate begging and pleading. *Dolly Parton.* The sound of her name alone was enough to get my pulse racing, my feet tapping. I knew every chord, every lyric, of every song. However, if Dolly had walked past me on the street I would not have recognized her. Up until this concert I had only experienced music through my 1960s era Realistic radio. It was neither an attractive nor a reliable piece of equipment: paint-splattered, with a broken antenna and a faulty speaker which gave way to a gritty, faltering sound. I had never been disappointed by it. This night would leave my expectations forever changed.

In person, Dolly's singing was crisp, processed, easier to digest, and presented with an intensity that my radio had somehow filtered out. I was captivated, absorbing every word and every visual cue from this highly engaging and amusing speaker. I grinned, and danced. I stood on my seat in my effort to hear better, to get a better view of the stage. I marveled at how lucky I was to be in the presence of such a beautiful and talented woman, whose sequins and smiles lit up the theatre in rapid succession.

I left the concert feeling utterly elated. I had discovered a new context in which to set my musical appreciation. This revelation would set me on a search for more moments where I could be similarly elevated, a search that continues to this day. With these memories in mind I once again sought out a Dolly Parton show this past October. My hope was to rekindle the emotions this experience had stirred in me as a child. What I saw in this revisit, however, was a complete reversal. From this vantage point I could see that the idol of

> I could see that the idol of my childhood was lip-syncing every word.

my childhood was lip-syncing every word. She merely pretended to play the instruments set before her, and the onstage banter that had once titillated me now seemed crude and unsophisticated. I did not dance, and I rarely smiled. As I began to second-guess my memory of my first concert, my attention drifted away from the stage. Then I spotted her—a younger girl standing in the front row. Eyes widened, she stood motionless, mesmerized by the scene before her. We experienced the same concert, but while she longed to be pulled in, I could not help but pull away.

My first concert instilled in me a wonderful sense of what the visual components of a live show can yield—a magical and enlightening experience that entertains without detracting from the music. I found myself unable to recreate the feelings it stirred in me. However, I do not regret my attempt to discover them anew, as I realized something important about the moments I inhabit. Even if I were given the opportunity to return to the exact place and time of the first Dolly Parton performance, I would still not feel completely the same as I once did. Experiences are shaped not only by the circumstances that surround them, but also by the perspectives that we bring. Perceptions change and evolve inevitably as the mind matures. This is a process that should not be lamented, but rather, embraced. It is what fueled my search for Dolly's music in the first place, and it motivates me to search for the next music, the next transformative experience that will resonate with my present state of mind. My first concert showed me that the search is worthwhile. My revisit demonstrated to me that the search will never end, nor should it.

Allison Rapoport attended the University of Pennsylvania.

Anyone who wants to write about a trip should keep in mind that thousands of other applicants are doing the same. Avoid the travelogue essay, which ploddingly recalls every place you saw and everything you did. Better to write about sitting still and listening, as did the author of Essay 95, or to write about how going abroad changed the way you see yourself (Essay 97). Write about misadventures with family if you like (Essay 98), or use a piece of literature as an ongoing metaphor for what you experienced (Essay 99). The main thing is to use the description of your travels as a jumping off place for reflection rather than as an end in itself.

95

ON A BAR STOOL IN THE VILLAGE OF HESSEN

Plenty of high school students take trips abroad, but not many are as savvy or adventuresome in learning about their new surroundings as author Walter Brummund. The essay has two highlights: the description of how he overcame resistance from the guidance counselor and others, and the interlude on the bar stool which shows his curiosity. The latter makes the generalities in the last paragraph much more believable. Walter also shows that it is possible to write a fine essay without a flashy opening paragraph.

Essay by Walter Brummund III

Evaluate a significant experience, achievement, risk you have taken, or ethical dilemma you have faced and its impact on you.

My junior year abroad in Germany was a very significant experience for me. At the beginning of my sophomore year of high school my family decided to take in a Japanese exchange student. Over the course of the year, Satoru became a part of our family and a dear friend. I had been thinking about going abroad even before we decided to host Sato, but by observing what a great experience his exchange year was for him, I was given the courage to go ahead and apply for a place in the Youth for Understanding year abroad program in Germany.

I faced some criticism for my decision to pursue a year abroad. My high school guidance counselor was worried that I would not be able to take the PSAT and try for a National Merit Scholarship. My parents did not want me to go because they did not want to lose one of my last years of living at home. I was discouraged by many people who thought a year abroad was something outside the norm that would jeopardize my academic career.

By going I decided to take that risk and am better off for it. Not only did I improve my German and live in a different culture, I was able to meet all kinds of people. During our Easter vacation my host family took me on a family retreat to a small village in Hessen. The first night was so beautiful and clear that I decided to take a walk around the village. I lived in a larger city in Germany, and wanted to experience what life was like for the inhabitants of the village. While walking around I stumbled across a small hotel. I went inside and took a seat at the bar. It was a Sunday night and there were only a few people there. I ordered something and just sat at the bar, looking through a magazine and listening to the conversation the middle-aged men sitting near me were having. They were discussing the politics of the local men's soccer club and the feasibility of organizing a competitive team. They talked for hours about it quite animatedly. By listening to this one conversation, I was able to capture the spirit of life in that village and felt that I could understand the people there. Moments such as these were the high points of my year.

> **I was discouraged by many people who thought a year abroad was something outside the norm.**

My year in Germany forced me to look at things in a different way as I was confronted with a different culture with different ideas. By experiencing new perspectives I was able to contrast my views with the views of others, and thus understand myself better. I got a better understanding of what is important to me and what defines my life. The most important thing I learned during my year abroad was that there is a lot to learn from your environment if you take the time to appreciate the perspectives of others.

Walter Brummund III attended the University of Wisconsin–Madison.

96

A TRIP TO FRANCE, AND AN ESSAY ABOUT GETTING THERE

The following essay has two parts: a description of author Catherine Davis and her tendency to be "part of a minority," and Catherine's quest to pay for a trip to France. The strand that holds it together: Catherine's determination to follow her own interests rather than those of others. The balance of the essay is serious, but she does a good job of showing her ironic sensibility. In the first clause of the last sentence, she skillfully echoes the opening of the essay by returning to the accomplishments of her brothers and sisters as a foil for her own.

Essay by Catherine Davis

I'm somewhat used to being a part of the minority. I've always been considered the "different" child of the family, the one not quite like the others. My three older brothers and sisters were all quiet, athletic, highly motivated scholars, excelling in subjects like math and science and being awarded MVP of the team. I was different.

I've never been a very shy person. Math has never been my best subject, I don't always do what I'm told, and I've never been named MVP of any sport.

In seventh grade, I became a part of another minority: the French class. Most of my friends decided to take Spanish, because it would "be more useful in the long run." I didn't care about the long run at that point; all I knew was French sounded beautiful and fluid and promising.

I wanted to learn the language flawlessly and be as creative with it as I could be with English. I continued French as I entered high school—year after year, word after word, grammar rule after rule. It was my top class, the one in which I felt most comfortable expressing myself.

Finally, last year, I received the chance for which I had been waiting. Our French teacher, Mrs. Besserer, had contacted an English teacher in Pau, France, and set up a foreign exchange program for that spring break. A small group of French students in the high school were invited to go to France for ten days in March. I was

I don't always do what I'm told, and I've never been named MVP of any sport.

completely euphoric, until I heard the news that it would cost over $2,000.00. For others, the money meant nothing, but my parents could not afford to pay for my trip. They advised me to forget what seemed to them a luxury.

I wanted to go to France more than anything, and I knew that I couldn't let this chance pass me by. So I decided not to play my favorite sport that winter. With the help of my French teacher and the dean of students, I secured two jobs tutoring fourteen- and sixteen-year-old students in French, biology, English, and science. I also took a job at a resale shop slaving long hours under the stern eye of Mrs. Collins, who taught me what indentured servitude must have been like.

By about a week before the trip, I had collected enough money to go, and my excitement was unsurpassable. In mid-March, Mrs. Besserer, three other students, and I flew eight hours straight to Paris.

I will never forget that experience. Not only did I see the Louvre and the Cathedrale of Notre Dame, but I was submerged into a culture completely unlike my own and completely fascinating. When we flew to Pau for the second half of the trip, I went to live with a girl named Emmanuelle, to whom I grew very close. She took me to her high school, where I gave an English talk about America to the students in her English class. We went shopping together, and we visited the famous Chateau of Pau.

I may not ever be the star of the basketball team like my sisters and brothers, but I've found my own little niche in this vast wall of opportunities, and I intend to dig even deeper into it for every year that passes.

Catherine Davis attended the University of Notre Dame.

97

IN COSTA RICA, SHE FINDS A NEW SELF-IMAGE

Author Abby Fried provides a textbook example of how to write about community service or foreign travel. It isn't about the helping, or the sight-seeing, but rather what you learn about yourself. For Abby, the revelation comes from being "physically content" in a place where physical appearances don't seem to matter as much. Her writing process is a model of how to approach the essay: "I sat down and wrote the entire thing in one sitting. Then I left it alone for about a week. Then every day I went back and made changes. My first draft was twice as long as it should have been, so I did a lot of editing."

Essay by Abigail Fried

The upbeat rhythm of merengue music electrified the air. My unaccustomed feet quickly adapted to the practiced steps of my dance partner. As the tempo of the music increased, my partner swept me across the floor in a rush of quick movements that I carried out with little skill, but with all my heart. As the song came to an end, I breathlessly thanked my partner and tried to explain what a fun time I had in my slightly broken Spanish. I noticed the sixteen other Americans, with whom I had traveled from the United States to Costa Rica, sitting together on one side of the room. A month earlier, seventeen Americans from all over the United States had anxiously pulled up next to this hall in Santa María, Costa Rica. We would be living in the town for a month, helping the "ticos" build a gymnasium, paint buildings, and do other jobs around the town. We were a group of teenagers, some more eager than others to start work the next day. I was among the more eager ones. I had participated in many community service projects at home and I looked forward to the work in Costa Rica, yet nothing could have prepared me for the fabulous jolt that would send me head-first into a new culture and a new life.

On the first day some of the men and boys engaged us in a soccer game. They quickly separated us into teams, although I realized they were a little confused as to which positions the four girls should play. They were simply not used to female athletes. However, once the game began, I recognized that we were a pleasant surprise. Having just recovered from an injury, I was far from being in great shape, but there was something about the atmosphere around me that was wonderfully energizing. Even as the rain started to fall, we continued, slipping and sliding through the mud. I, completely delighted, finished the game brown from head to foot. The men had accepted us into their community.

As the weeks progressed I won further respect with the females as well as the males in the community for my dedicated work and enthusiasm. My appearance mattered little; all they seemed to care about was getting to know me. This discovery was shocking. As a teenage girl, who for the past few years had been trying to fit her naturally athletic build to waif-like model ideals, I was accustomed to being assessed physically before any inquiry was made into my personality. I learned how differently these people think. During work hours they would often work with me, sweat dripping down our faces, cement crusted to our clothes, paint staining our skin, and having a great time. Evenings we danced, played games, and talked. I learned more from them about myself and what it means to be a person than I have ever learned elsewhere. I started to look at myself and see the aspects I liked instead of those I wanted to change. Being physically content left me free to concentrate on who I was. I found myself to be more expressive and energetic than I had ever been.

Even as the rain started to fall, we continued, slipping and sliding through the mud.

Santa María, for me, was a turning point in my life. The people there accepted me immediately. I didn't have to be anything. I just had to be myself. Now at home and at school, I feel confident that I no longer have to present what I think people want. I only need to present me, and they can find what they like in me. As I danced with my tico partner, my American friends merely sat and watched, not suspecting my newfound revelation. My Costa Rican experience transformed me from a passive observer, mired in superficial appearances, to an active, self-confident young woman prepared for my adult life.

Abigail Fried attended Boston College.

98

TWO PARENTS, FIVE SIBLINGS, AND ONE VERY CROWDED CAR

Author Clare Malone struck gold when she decided to write her essay about family vacations. She explains her choice this way: "I am only eighteen years old, I don't have any really unique life experiences, like living in a foreign county or traveling around the world in a sailboat, so I decided to write about my family." Good choice. Clare sets a light-hearted tone from the beginning with her tongue-in-cheek rhetorical question—"Sweatshop?"—in the second sentence. She uses a kids'-eye-view to gently mock her mother, always a good thing when done with affection. Anyone who ever got dragged along by mom or dad can relate to this fine essay.

Essay by Clare K. Malone

Sweltering heat, abhorrently close quarters, and short tempers. Sweatshop? No, such were the family vacations of my youth—countless hours in a poorly air-conditioned vehicle, seven traveling companions and a driver whose frustration often bordered on road rage. It has been said, however, that traumatic experiences forge strong relationships and teach us important life lessons. In fact, it is unavoidable not to learn a little bit about human nature when you are seated so close to another person that you can't tell where they end and you begin. Looking back, summer vacations have constituted some of the most vividly memorable times of my life. From my cramped place in the back seat, I developed a curiosity for knowledge, an appreciation for my lively family, and learned more card games than a career gambler.

My mother's ardent wish to immerse her children in the sights and history of the United States was the inspiration for our summer sojourns. She had the idea that we should visit all fifty states before she was through with us. Her ambition sucked the historical marrow right out of every possible tourist destination. We began with the thirteen original colonies and set out to embrace Americana. Along the way, each child was expected to keep a journal recounting his or her reflections of the trip. My mother was very gung-ho about these logs, and threatened that if we didn't write in our journal, we wouldn't be able to eat dinner. Consequentially, the majority of our writings dealt not with the sights we had seen, but instead discussed when we last ate, who got the window seat, and how many arguments had ensued. A large part of our sightseeing was spent on the road in our fire-engine red Suburban, a vehicle my mother lovingly refers to as her "seventh child." The hours in the car, though excruciating, taught me the importance of compromise and cooperation in human relations. Space was limited to say the least, and as the youngest, I had the smallest amount. I quickly learned that getting my way through means of force was not the answer, as everyone in my family had at least six inches and twenty pounds on me. In order to garner extra leg room or a pillow, I honed my powers of persuasion and came to realize the importance of a kind word or deed.

> During our first few journeys, sleeping at Knight's Inn was a novelty to say the least.

The first stop was Washington, D.C., an obvious destination for our inaugural trip. Countless exhibits at the Smithsonian, a visit to Ford's Theatre, and a tour of the White House were succinctly summed up in my journal: "It was a long day and I'm very sleepy now." D.C., of course, was only the beginning. While other kids did Disney World, we drove sixteen hours to Fort Ticonderoga to watch elderly men re-enact Revolutionary War battles. Then there was the period when my father, in a bizarre midlife crisis, decided that his calling was to commune with the whales of the Northeast. So, for a couple of Augusts we drove to Maine and Massachusetts in order to whale-watch in the icy waters of the north Atlantic. It was our family's answer to the traditional Caribbean cruise. Williamsburg, Virginia, was another favorite stop. Our family embraced the colonial feel of the town on varying levels. My parents were mesmerized by the process of eighteenth-century soap making, while, on the other hand, we kids headed straight for the gift shop. For the rest of the vacation, despite countless odd looks from strangers at rest stops, my sister refused to remove her treasured colonial coonskin cap from her head.

The best part of a trip always came at the end of the day when we got to rest. During our first few journeys, sleeping at Knight's Inn was a novelty to say the least. My mother recalls the first time my sister and I stayed in a motel; we literally screamed with excitement. Apparently the bathtub held a particular fascination for us. We insisted upon being photographed within it, as indoor plumbing was a new phenomenon. On later trips, my father found hotel costs for eight people to be overwhelming, and so we began camping as an alternative. Conquering the great outdoors with my family turned out to be quite the character-building activity, offering new, but not always pleasant experiences. One particular incident comes to mind that involved improper construction of a tent, a midsummer thunderstorm, and a rude awakening in the morning to find myself bathing face-down in rainwater. A few more fiascos convinced my parents we were not camping material, but I gathered a little more mettle and determination from our escapades (as well as an appreciation for hotel beds and maid service).

Our vacations have continued over many summers. We've seen the infamous Boston Harbor, tiny Rhode Island and her ocean views, Virginia's stately old plantation houses, and have been charmed by the warmth of Carolina beaches. Though I have grown older, my excitement and enjoyment of our summer ritual has never waned. Each passing year gives me a greater appreciation for the living history I have witnessed, those who surround me, and fills me with anticipation for what lies beyond the next bend in the road.

Clare K. Malone attended Georgetown University.

99

IN STEP WITH GULLIVER, TRAVELING THE WORLD

Lots of essays use analogies, but only for a line or a paragraph. Author Casey Mank's entire essay is built on an extended analogy. After (conveniently) reading *Gulliver's Travels* en route to Europe and Africa, Casey tells the story of the trip as a rejoinder to the book, describing how her experiences parallel those of Gulliver. Along the way, she finds numerous points of comparison to maintain the analogy. Imaginary as they were, *Gulliver's Travels* were nothing if not exotic. Casey's own exotic details, such as being chased by crowds of children screaming "azungu," are necessary to put her own travels on par with those of Gulliver.

Essay by Casey Elizabeth Mank

I had never been outside the continental United States when I decided to travel to Africa. By the time I returned to school from my two-week-long sophomore spring break, I had landed in England, Kenya, Malawi, and South Africa. Maybe more people would have started smaller with, say, a tame vacation venture to Mexico or Hawaii, but since I had always planned on visiting everywhere eventually, I figured, why not? Why not make sure traveling abroad for the first time lived up to the high standard of excitement set by my vivid imagination. During the decidedly un-fascinating thirty-six hours of flight time required, I kept myself occupied with books. One of these was *Gulliver's Travels* by Jonathan Swift. Although he is a fictional, middle-aged British man, and I am a female high school student of the twenty-first century, I immediately recognized the similarities between Gulliver and me. With hypocrisy, egotism, and bitingly satiric outlook aside, I felt that Gulliver's perspective on his unbelievably exotic adventure could be no more full of surprise or curiosity than mine. We both found ourselves away from the home and culture we had always known, thrown into exciting and sometimes frightening situations which ultimately changed our comparatively sheltered perspectives and broadened our previously narrow horizons.

Gulliver's first unlikely destination, Lilliput, is home to a highly civilized but miniature society. My own first stop outside the country was Gulliver's homeland, England. The accents, the double-decker red buses, my first glimpse of Buckingham Palace (complete with impassive guards), and, of course, almost constant rain, made me feel as though I had stepped into a tourist pamphlet about London, rather than into the city itself. I admit to being a slight Anglophile, and during my brief time in London, I found it impossible to fully grasp that I was finally there. I imagine Gulliver felt the same disbelief in Lilliput, where every aspect of the land resembled a dollhouse. He took detailed notes about the appearance and customs of Mildendo, the Metropolis of Lilliput. As I scribbled in my diary on the red-eye flight out of Heathrow, I too tried to preserve every detail of Piccadilly Circus and the British Museum so that my friends and family back home would be able to see the city just as I had.

> **Armed guards were assembled on the ground around our plane, their weapons clearly visible from the window.**

In Brobdingnag, Gulliver encounters giants, and escapes several near-death experiences. While I must admit that Gulliver's second stop was more dramatic than mine, I did have the first frightening experience of my journey at our second landing: Nairobi, Kenya. At the Nairobi airport, we were not permitted to leave the plane. Security officers came onboard and searched under our seats and in our bags. Armed guards were assembled on the ground around our plane, their weapons clearly visible from the window. I realized that, movies not included, I had never actually seen, let alone been close to, real people holding real guns and looking very ready to use them. Gulliver and I were both surrounded by unfamiliar and threatening forces that we had no way to control. Fortunately, in Swift's imaginary world, an eagle snatches Gulliver's box from the ground and flies away from the hostile country of Brobdingnag. As my plane took off, I felt only relief to be ending that particular brief and nerve-wracking episode in my adventure.

Even Gulliver's first experiences on the floating island of Laputa couldn't have been more astonishing than my own initial impressions of Africa. When I stepped off the plane in Malawi I was hit by a wall of humidity very different from the chilly March weather back home in Pennsylvania. We drove for hours on bumpy dirt roads, passing countless thatched huts and women on the roadside carrying water or firewood. I felt as if I had fallen into *National Geographic*! Everywhere I looked was something I had never seen before. As Gulliver expressed it, "The reader can hardly conceive my astonishment."

Africa became even more surprising as my trip went on, but I quickly learned to expect and look forward to cultural surprises and strange sights rather than facing them with apprehension. In less than two weeks there, I had danced with a witch doctor, seen a wild bull elephant, and been only a few feet from an irritated pod of hippos. I had been chased, on a daily basis, by crowds of children screaming "azungu," which means "white person." Suddenly I was the minority! I was just as much a mystery to them as they were to me. I had braces at the time, which was a constant source of fascination and amusement to our hosts. Small children would laugh and point, tugging on my clothes and pointing emphatically back and forth between my face and some

> I had been chased, on a daily basis, by crowds of children screaming "azungu," which means "white person."

nearby metallic object. When someone finally translated for me, I discovered that they had decided that my braces were earrings put in my teeth as a sign of wealth. Like Gulliver, I tried to learn as much of the language and culture as I could in such a short time, which resulted, just as it had for him, in many memorable confusions, and a few almost-conversations.

Gulliver's last and most important journey takes him to a rational, peaceful utopia governed by talking horses. In this country, men have been reduced to a wild state and are used as beasts of burden.

Faced with such a revolutionary social reality, Gulliver is forced to re-examine his own society and question the lifestyle he has always known. The aspect of my trip to Malawi which most deeply affected me was the volunteer work our group did during our stay. We were exposed to people who had lived through hardships never experienced in the United States. We spent most of our time working with a temporary home for infants and toddlers orphaned by AIDS. We also painted, taught, and made donations at local schools. The gratitude of doctors receiving our boxes of latex gloves, for lack of which they had been forced to postpone many operations, was incredible to see.

The two weeks went by so quickly! When it was time to leave, I was torn between excitement and regret. Going out to dinner with my parents on the evening of my return was as much of a culture shock as my first meal in Africa had been! I was surprised by the price of my food, and ashamed not to finish it all. Two weeks in Africa had forced me to see the world differently. Like Gulliver, I began to question the aspects of my own culture that I had never even noticed before. I felt some of his disillusionment, but I had seen so many fantastic things on my trip! The hardest part about coming home was answering the ridiculous question, "How was Africa?" How could I explain to someone who had never been there? Every waking moment had been absolutely fascinating. Like Gulliver, I had carefully documented all of my experiences and adventures in far off lands, and my Africa journal is still some of my favorite reading.

Casey Elizabeth Mank attended Muhlenberg College.

100

BEATING THE MY-TRIP-TO-EUROPE BLAHS

You know the down side about trip essays—too much trite babble about learning from other cultures, not enough real insight. But how many travelers go off the beaten path in a country where they don't speak the language? Unlike ordinary travel essays, this one shows real passion. The author, Sarah Mitchell, demonstrates her eye for detail in her description of Rome, even as she makes the interesting point that in order to really appreciate travel, it is necessary to get out of your comfort zone. Sarah is impressive because she actively seeks such experiences.

Essay by Sarah Mitchell

I am most comfortable when I am lost. Deliberately getting lost fuels my drive for discovery. On a trip to Italy the summer after my sophomore year, I discovered the pleasure of using public transportation to get to know the city of Rome. This ancient city can intimidate and overwhelm a person, leaving her confused about how to process new information. You can easily forget that the city is alive because you become so absorbed in the ancient Roman ruins and the extravagant Baroque churches. The city becomes surreal. Escaping from a tourist's view of Rome enables one to appreciate Rome for the beauty of the ordinary in addition to the extraordinary.

By taking buses deep into the city, where few tourists venture, my friend Andrew and I attempted to discover the real city of Rome. Not knowing our destination or our surroundings we got "lost" within the city. Riding buses to the end of the line can lead to unexpected sights and adventures. Walking down unknown streets, we saw an old woman, hobbling along, weighed down by her bag of groceries and the weight of time, slowly making her way home. Yet the wise smile on her face clearly showed that she did not need my sympathy. Further along, young lovers stood bickering, screaming and gesticulating. However, minutes later, when their anger subsided, the lovers walked hand in hand out of the alley, covertly stealing a kiss when no one should have been looking. Tottering along, a young child took shaky steps, fell down, and cried. The mother swooped down, delivered kisses and soft, calming words, and picked her baby back up to try again. Images

> **Riding buses to the end of the line can lead to unexpected sights and adventures.**

like these slip easily from one's notice when blinded by the tourist's dark glasses. These images broke down stereotypes and brought Italian culture to life in a completely new way.

My understanding of human nature increased greatly as a result of the discoveries that I made while "getting lost" in Italy. Vitality and passion for living are so apparent in all aspects of Italian culture. Every night during my week in Southern Italy, fireworks exploded and lit up the night sky for no apparent reason other than to celebrate for celebration's sake. I learned to live on my own time, rather than by the strict constraints of the time of watches and clocks. I could appreciate my surroundings so much more when I was not rushed and the fusion of the ordinary and the extraordinary filled me with a new sense of appreciation for life, human potential, and joy.

I believe that the ability to get lost separates the true traveler from the ordinary tourist. By being able to set aside my preconceived ideas, I truly experienced a new culture and did not just "visit" Italy. Although I hardly spoke a word of Italian, I was amazed by how much of a conversation I understood simply by observing body language and tone of voice. This experience really taught me about the similarities between human beings. As the culture became more real and more personal to me, I was able to see my own experiences reflected in the lives of the people around me. Whether you choose to be a traveler or a tourist goes much deeper than visiting far-off places. An individual can either choose to accept the view of the world presented to him or her, or be unafraid to seek the truth. I came to understand how much beauty the latter option holds, and how great a reward sacrificing comfort and letting go of fear can provide.

Sarah Mitchell attended Rice University.

101

THE MOST MEANINGFUL VACATION

We would hesitate to advise anyone to write a 934-word essay—like the one that follows—unless you have as much passion and skill as author Anne Ruleman. The length of this essay adds to the sense of wonder that Anne experiences in London and highlights the fact that she is in overdrive every minute. From her flight to London that finds her marveling "at the hugeness of the earth," to the flight back when she puts the finishing touches on her journal, she is intent on experiencing everything there is in London. Says Anne, "This essay describes one of the most significant events in my life, and writing it was an exploration of a portion of myself rather than a task."

Essay by Anne Ruleman

In June of this year, my parents and I took a weeklong trip to London. This trip was one my parents had been planning to take for years but had never had quite enough money before; it was to be our first real family vacation and my first time to go abroad. Such an event would, under normal circumstances, have inspired in us an unbearable level of excitement, but at the time the trip was scheduled, my grandmother was terminally ill with lung cancer and could die at any time. However, we decided to risk going anyway, and we took off from the Atlanta airport on a drizzly Monday afternoon, bemused and perhaps finding it hard to believe that it was really us, and that we were actually going to England. That night, with a quiet fascination, I watched the sun set over the Atlantic and rise again a few hours later, and I marveled at the hugeness of the earth.

When the plane touched down it was early in the morning, broad daylight. A haze of lines, shuttles, and buses took us from the Gatwick airport to our hotel in South Kensington, and a few hours after our arrival we stepped out onto the pavement to explore that area of the city.

I found that morning that I had entered a dreamland realized. I was a devoted Anglophile, and so London was the center of my world. From England's heart came nearly everything I held dear: the writers I loved and revered—Frances Hodgsen Burnett and Roald Dahl and J. K. Rowling, C. S. Lewis and J. R. R. Tolkien, Charles Dickens and Jane Austen—the great kings and queens of the past whose lives intrigued me so, the places I had no clear picture of but whose names, long ingrained in my mind, resounded with the quaint mystery and hidden power of an age-old melody— *Gloucester, Piccadilly, Charing Cross, Tottenham, Chancery, Blackfriars, Westminster*...I said them aloud to myself and felt something deep within me stir.

Over the course of the week, I explored what seemed like every part of London. I saw the White Tower left by the Normans and the little chapel under whose floor lay Anne Boleyn, her head in her arm, and Lady Jane Grey, Queen of England for nine days. I saw the crumbling fragments of the wall that surrounded Londinium, built by the Romans more than eleven hundred years earlier. I rode the Underground many times with an undying enthusiasm that only a small-town dweller could have for public transportation. I was moved almost to tears while wandering through Westminster Abbey, seeing the stained-glass windows that had been pieced back together with such courage and diligence after being smashed during the bombings of the Second World War. I walked across the Millennium Bridge and smelled the sweetly damp, faintly salty air of the River Thames. I strolled through Kensington Park, and the lush green of the grass and summer foliage was a thousand times more intense under the gray sky. I regarded with amazement the different people who inhabited the city—seldom had I seen in one place so many Indians, Muslims, Asians, and people whose ethnic origin was entirely lost to me, and I loved them all simply for their presence. I saw many, many beautiful things, and I also saw imperfection—the filth, garbage, crime, poverty, and ugliness found in any city—but it did nothing to dim my idea of the magnificence of London. I had been afraid that the reality would be disappointing, since my expectations were so high, but it was not. Seeing the city's darker side made its lighter side all the more radiant.

But above all things, what I found the most surprising was how at home I felt in England. I was a foreigner in a country I had never visited before, and yet I had a stronger sense of belonging there than I had ever had before in my life. It was as if I had returned home after a long vacation. This feeling first struck me the morning we arrived, and it increased as the week wore on. Though I was certain everyone could tell I was American, the more time I spent there, the less I saw myself as an American, an outsider in someone else's land. I became aware that the world did not consist of "me" and "them," that the world was more enormous and grand than I had ever before understood it to be, and that I was very much a part of it. This at-homeness with the world—the world that, in spite of its divisions, seemed to come together in that ancient city—moved me perhaps more deeply than anything I had ever felt before.

> I saw the White Tower left by the Normans and the little chapel under whose floor lay Anne Boleyn.

I kept a journal that week, from the time we left Atlanta to the time we left London. As we took off from Gatwick I watched the city pass beneath the plane, then the misty rolling fields that looked like a green patchwork quilt. I was writing about what I saw and thought when I suddenly recalled a particular phrase from a poem I had read in *The New Yorker* a couple of months previous—"There is another world/ And it is this world." The poem's title was "The Visiting," and the poet was Franz Wright. I remember reciting the poem to myself and looking out the window of the plane, just before finishing the journal. I quoted those lines from the poem and, in the last sentence, observed, "I never quite understood what it meant until now."

Anne Ruleman attended Earlham College.

102

A PUMA WHO GOT A LITTLE TOO PLAYFUL

Author Laurel Janeen Smith finds herself in a jam as she opens her essay. It begins as she is traveling with an older sister in Argentina. After sightseeing for several weeks, the two of them have stopped to volunteer at a wildlife refuge. (Her sister had previously worked there.) To make a long story short, Laurel gets up close and personal with Sonko the puma and, well, we'll let Laurel tell the rest. Says Laurel, "I never thought my life was in danger, just my face."

Essay by Laurel Janeen Smith

His teeth clenched over my delicate skull, and I felt hot blood drip down my cheeks as his claws slashed at my face. My legs crumbled beneath his heavy weight as both of us came crashing down the rocky hillside. I fought to thrust myself from beneath him, remembering the mangled stuffed animals surrounding his cage. Finally I managed to get to my feet, but unable to pry my head out of the puma's mouth, I calmly called up to my partner. "Victoria, could you please help me?" After a minute or two she reached us and looked down at Sonko batting me around like a new toy. She cursed at the familiar sight and helped free me from Sonko's grasp. Trying to regain some composure, I wiped the blood from my face with my mud-and-sweat-soaked shirt. I readily passed Sonko's cord to Victoria and cautiously walked in front of the puma. I continued, deeper into the jungle, with nothing but an empty water bottle, a chocolate bar, and a cucumber in hand.

Everyone has gone to the zoo and seen these gorgeous creatures. Their golden fur flows like water and their black eyes pierce through the distance. Behind bars they look almost surreal in their cages where the adoring public views them at their leisure. Every time I walked past an animal at the zoo I never thought twice about the life beyond the bars.

The daily routines that have caged my life for eleven years had started to wear on me. That's one of the stronger reasons I found myself in South America last summer at a wild animal refuge.

I fell in love with the place when I found a "chuchi-chuchi" (a wild teddy bear with a tail) sleeping on my straw mattress as I entered the hostel. I started working in the monkey park rehabilitating monkeys. After having monkeys climb on me, pull my hair, spit, puke, and pee on me all day, every day, for nearly a month, the idea of spending a day in the tranquil jungle with a puma sounded more than inviting. Victoria approached me in the early morning frantically questioning me whether or not the monkey park could spare anyone to walk Sonko, one of the more "playful" pumas. I quickly volunteered, and laughter flew from Victoria's mouth as she imagined me walking a puma twice my size. Finally though, she led me to the puma's cage with much gratitude.

The morning sun glimmered through the thick jungle trees. Every time I turned around and saw the eyes of the huge cat following my every move, I became filled with a new excitement. Victoria passed me the cord after a few hours and walked up ahead. Sonko followed. Walking a puma in the jungle seemed oddly natural, and I enjoyed listening to the dirt rustle beneath his huge paws; his smooth flowing stride astounded me. I reached for rocks and branches as I climbed the rough, steep trail. Suddenly Sonko stopped and looked down at me, then back towards Victoria. She was nowhere in sight. A menacing grin spread across his big pussycat face, and before I knew it, he had jumped on my head.

> I enjoyed listening to the dirt rustle beneath his huge paws; his smooth flowing stride astounded me.

After being attacked by the puma, I continued my day normally. I had just been mauled by a huge animal and had no time to sit down, nothing to drink, hardly anything to eat, and was in the middle of the jungle. None of this seemed slightly absurd; although, I did wish I had a knife to peel my cucumber. The truth is a puma jumping on my head wasn't abnormal. If people knew how often Sonko jumped on heads, they would probably laugh at my dramatic re-enactment. Nevertheless, I still enjoy telling about "the one time a puma jumped on my head."

Laurel Janeen Smith attended Ithaca College.

Why I Love
First Choice U.

At least once during your college search, you'll be called upon to declare undying devotion to a college or university. You don't need to tell them all that they're First Choice U., exactly, but if you make them think you want them, you'll increase the likelihood that they'll want you. Specifics are more important here than in any other essay. Cite particular programs, as in Essay 109, and don't cop out by saying that, for instance, you want to go to Columbia because of the excitement of New York City. (Join the cast of thousands.) You may ultimately decide to attend elsewhere, as did the author of Essay 103, but that doesn't mean you can't make it look good in your essay.

103

"LEARNING FROM A TEACHER WHO KNOWS ME WELL"

Author Chanda Patel has a blueprint for the "why us?" essay that will work for many applicants. As part of any campus visit, be sure to remember the names of anyone with whom you talk, especially if that person helps you form an impression of the college. Patel has the advantage of an in-depth conversation with a department head, and by merely telling the story with some insight of her own, she makes a convincing case that Swarthmore is the right college for her.

Essay by Chanda Patel

I come from a long line of no-nonsense scientists, from doctors to engineers to researchers. My apple, on the other hand, fell about a thousand yards away from the family tree. For as long as I can remember, I have loved art, both making it and viewing it.

I believe that an education from Swarthmore would help me achieve my goals as an artist. During my visit, I met Sydney Carpenter, the art department chair, who showed us around the entire art building and answered all of my questions. Although it was the last day for sophomore art students to declare their major (a very busy day for Mr. Carpenter), he spent over an hour talking to me. I was surprised and impressed by his consideration for a mere prospective student.

> I was surprised and impressed by his consideration for a mere prospective student.

As Mr. Carpenter showed us the five senior art majors' work, I saw first-hand the kind of individual attention that Swarthmore students get. I was amazed, not only by the artwork, but also by how well Mr. Carpenter knew each senior. He knew their assets and challenges as artists, plus their preferred media and the concepts they were exploring. Learning from a teacher who knows me well, both as a student and a person, is something I value at my current small high school. Because the art department at Swarthmore is equally close-knit, I believe I would fit in well.

While a career in the arts is my current goal, I still enjoy other disciplines and want to explore new ones at college. During my visit, I noticed an atmosphere at Swarthmore that was accepting of trying anything you want, even outside your major. The opportunity to study art as well as other subjects I love, such as Biology and the

Classics, sets Swarthmore apart from other schools. Between the traditional art program, small but diverse campus, and passionate faculty, Swarthmore is a place where I could thrive both as a student and especially an artist.

Chanda Patel attended Carnegie Mellon University.

104

A LITTLE HELP FROM DAVID LETTERMAN

If there is one kind of essay where a little overkill may be in order, it is the "why us?" essay. Even if they give you a tiny space, give them some meat. This essay does just that with a top-ten list. Along the way, author Rebecca Kastan shows her thorough research; she has visited the chamber of commerce website, knows about the football team's record, knows that cookies are served at the Schulman Center, etc. She also shows the second requisite quality: passion for the university.

Essay by Rebecca Kastan

Rebecca Kastan's Top Ten Reasons Why Vanderbilt Is Her #1 Choice (*David Letterman* Style):

10.

Weather: I have lived in Columbus, Ohio, my whole life. Although it has been the best place to grow up, I have to admit that weather is not our forté. Weather can have an effect on people's mood and outlook. I checked out what the Nashville Chamber of Commerce says about weather, and it sure sounds good to me!

9.

Football: In my house, knowing the game of football is not a luxury, it's a necessity. Not just because my dad is one of the biggest Buckeye fans you will ever know, but because my brother, Jake, is also the quarterback for his high school team. I have been his number one fan since day one, and if I didn't understand and love this game, I would not be able to participate in dinner conversations. While looking into the nuts and bolts of Vanderbilt football, I discovered an extremely challenging schedule. I also learned that the Commodores have won many awards for being the smartest bunch of guys in the conference. This team is improving each year, and I would love to be around to see them **win more games**.

8.

Cookies at the Schulman Center: My Judaism is a significant aspect of my life. Given my priorities, I will be spending much time at Hillel. It's nice to know that while I'm there, I can enjoy a yummy cookie.

> **It's nice to know that while I'm there, I can enjoy a yummy cookie.**

7.

Size: Vanderbilt University is the perfect size with 6,146 under-graduates and 4,566 graduates and professional students. The university is not too big, yet there will always be new students and faculty to meet. I also appreciate how the administration has set a goal of diversifying the student body.

6.

Nashville, the Music Capital: I am a fan of all music from hip-hop to country to jazz, and I learned on my visit to Nashville that it is the mecca of the music industry. During my college years at Vanderbilt University I know that the music culture will be something I would love to explore.

5.

Field Hockey and Lacrosse: These sports have had an incredible impact on my life. I have played seven years of field hockey and served as captain of the Junior Varsity and Varsity teams (two varsity letters and the "Hustle Your Buns" award). I have also played five years of lacrosse (two varsity letters and the "Most Improved Player" award). Playing team sports has been one of the most enjoyable experiences of my life. I also believe in the value of exercise and staying in shape. While my coach is encouraging me to try to walk on the lacrosse team, I know that I can continue to always play club or intramural athletics at Vanderbilt.

4.

Fun: Whether it's school, sports, or social activities I know I'm going to enjoy and love this school. I have heard nothing but tremendous things about Vanderbilt from previous graduates and students who still attend, and I have really had a great time when visiting. The "fun factor" is pretty important when you are eighteen years old.

3.

Extracurricular Learning Activities: Jewish tradition teaches that community responsibility is not an "extracurricular" activity—it is a requirement. In my family it is not a question of whether or not you do community service—it's just a question of where and how often. When I researched Vanderbilt's community service history there was a long list of different opportunities for me to get involved in as a student. I was excited to learn that Vanderbilt has a study abroad program at Hebrew University. If I were to study abroad, this might be a good match for me and my interests.

2.

Academic Opportunities: I have worked hard in high school, and I want to go to a college that offers me great opportunities for academic excellence. I know that in the future, when I am looking at jobs or graduate school, having Vanderbilt on my resume would be a terrific asset. I believe *this* university is the place where I will be able to surpass everyone's expectations as well as the ones I have for myself.

1.

Magic: Vanderbilt University just feels like the right place for me.

Rebecca Kastan attended Vanderbilt University.

105

IF IT QUACKS LIKE A DUCK...

Many try but few succeed in finding a clever way to express undying devotion to Future Alma Mater. Author Cody Phillips succeeds gloriously with the following fun-filled paean to Whitman College. Phillips manages to strut a little scientific knowledge—an *anas platyrhynchos* is a mallard—but he is mostly content to ride a whimsical wave. He plays on the fact that many people can hear words in the quacking of a duck (as in the old AFLAC commercials) and manages to work in nearly a dozen reasons why Whitman appeals to him. He saves the best for last; we'll wager that almost any college would have a tough time turning him down after this creative tour-de-force.

Essay by Cody Phillips

It was a cold day in February when I found myself in the most unusual of situations. I was happily reading the *Baseball Geek Bible* near a mountain lake when I was approached by one *anas platyrhynchos*. Curious, I looked up from my book just in time to see him bellow a 95-decibel QUACK! Its intensity shook me, and strangely, I could comprehend its meaning. He was saying "WHITMAN!" Confused by such an outburst, I bent over to ask the aquatic avian what he meant. Suddenly, I was rocked by an even louder QUACK! It was in this call that I knew the duck's plea. He had heard of the warm waters of Lakum Dukum surrounding Whitman and had dreamt of the day when he might fly to such a paradise. However he could not make the journey alone and needed my help. Looking at this curious mallard, I asked "Well, what's in it for me?" The duck's only response was to QUACK so loud that I was pushed to the edge of consciousness. In my semi-lucid state, the mallard flooded my mind with images of hiking trails winding through the beautiful Pacific Northwest; a student to teacher ratio of 9:1 allowing for engaging classes and debates; a library open 24/7 where the introspective can mull over Descartes' philosophy or tomorrow's lunch; a school which welcomes those that love to learn; 45 departmental majors for the undecided; an eco-aware campus; a varsity sports program for the athletically gifted and an intramural one for the athletically minded; an active student life; a rock wall to rival the Cliffs of Insanity; and a lot of modern art.

> I came to with images of Whitman swirling around my head.

I came to with images of Whitman swirling around my head. Scared and confused by this psychic duck, I quickly walked away, but soon realized that I had been tailed. This duck has been following me since February and I cannot shake him. I need to go to Whitman. He has started to quack threats at my family. Please help.

Cody Phillips attended Whitman College.

106

TAKING INTROSPECTION TO A NEW LEVEL

It is no coincidence that the first page of the application of St. John's College (MD & NM) is devoted to its essay questions. Applicants are asked to write up to four essays that total five to ten typed, double-spaced pages. St. John's is devoted to the study of the great books—think Plato or Euclid—and it wants students who are dedicated readers, writers, and thinkers. St. John's students take introspection seriously—hence the following essay by author Andrew Perry. It is longer than most essays and deeply self-revealing. It might not be a particularly good essay for someone applying to a business or engineering program, but for St. John's, it is perfect.

Essay by Andrew Perry

Explain in detail why you wish to attend St. John's College; please evaluate the strengths and weaknesses of your formal education to date.

I settled on St. John's a few months after I had finished applying to, visiting, being accepted by, and finally deciding not to attend three colleges. I had finished my senior year of high school by correspondence and a few classes taken credit-by-exam, so in truth my senior year was a year off. I wasn't enamored of the prospect of spending another year away from school and away from activity, but I couldn't in good conscience throw myself into a college I didn't care about. What had bothered me about the schools I had applied to was that all of them seemed to be opportunities to flounder, to waste time in a pre-adult, post-child no-man's land. And who could blame a teenager for floundering when faced with so many diverse choices, with very little experience to guide him. That isn't to say that I am a glutton for responsibility, the point is that there are less expensive ways of avoiding it. I decided not to go without a clear reason why I was going.

Another stumbling block was the lack of structure in so many programs. Take a few classes. Declare a major. Take more classes. Change your mind. Why should a person go to college, voluntarily to choose to continue their education? There may be as many answers as there are people who've asked the question. In my opinion, the answer is in order to come out on the other side a human being, with a more capable mind. Usually I shy away from these kinds of analyses because they tend to sound trite or over-idealized. It might be a handicap to stay away from those kinds of questions—at this rate, I may never be able to articulate why I do one thing rather than another. I prefer to keep those thoughts intuitive; I have the most luck that way. If it isn't right, I'll know it, though perhaps not why.

I can't know St. John's until I try it. My visit gave me an idea of what to expect, and I was fairly well sold when, in my tutor interview, Mr. Cook described the program as "education for the soul." It seems to me that there are many ways to educate a soul; as I write this, I am staying in a hostel in Oregon, and while the different travelers come and go, it occurs to me that one could grow a great deal just by moving from place to place. I, on the other hand, am more likely to hunker down in the first appealing coffeehouse, where I wrote these essays out on paper.

I can't say whether or not I'm an old child or a young adult, whether I'll be fulfilled or miserable, disillusioned or illusioned still in Santa Fe [the location of St. John's]. I have now spent too much time in inactivity, I have found a program that seems worthwhile, one that I think I won't be able to trick, one that I won't be able to cheat or sidestep. Maybe Plato will prove as useful as my car when it sat inert and heavy on jack stands in the driveway for a month, I can't say. What I can say is that I am interested, a rare phenomenon with higher education, and think that four years of reading and writing could prove to be worth the portion of my irresponsible youth.

> It occurs to me that one could grow a great deal just by moving from place to place.

As for high school and all that came before it, I can't rightly complain. I had it better than most; I took tiny classes in the same building from the time I was five until I was seventeen. The evaluation of my education is another area I'm hesitant to stay in for any length of time. Look at the numbers, but understand that I never thought I fully deserved any of them. This is not false modesty, I was lucky, I flew by the seat of my pants, I picked things up easily, and the only struggles I had were the deadlines that I'd let myself get ever more perilously close to, especially in my last years there.

I could have worked harder, I had the ability to accomplish more, but I didn't have the desire. My evaluation of my education is this, I learned a lot, but I could have learned much more. And now, I want to make up some of that lost ground.

St. John's seems like a place I could test myself in, maybe grow a little more, and dust off some of the disused parts of my mind. I sincerely wish I was more certain, but who is to say whether or not I'd just prefer to float around some more, do something else in a year or a day. For the time being, and time being basically free right now, St. John's still seems like a good choice.

Andrew Perry attended St. John's College.

107

A MASTERPIECE IN SEVENTY-EIGHT WORDS

Is it a coincidence that the shortest essay in this book just may be the best one? Think about it. Yale's admissions officers liked this essay so much that they mentioned it to the guidance counselor of author David Roosth. Says David, "My best advice for future students is to investigate the college very intensely and write about the little esoteric things that most would overlook. The best way to find those little idiosyncrasies is to ask the students who are on campus."

"Why Yale" by David Roosth

Upon a recent Yale visit, I conversed with a Yale senior in the admissions office about his experiences. He had only two complaints about the university: there were too many student protesters, and the university sands the roads instead of salting them in the winter. I love that Yale is a place where the students are motivated to change the world, and the faculty encourages them to act. Sanding saves the environment. What annoyed this Yale student impresses me.

> **What annoyed this Yale student impresses me.**

David Roosth attended Yale University.

108

"STRAINING TO SEE IF THAT BOY WILL RAISE HIS HAND"

Author Isabelle Teare's essay illustrates how a summer program at First Choice U. can pay dividends in the admissions process. While other students may struggle with "Why Georgetown?" she has first-hand knowledge and experience at the ready. It helps that Isabelle is a superb storyteller. She engages the reader with an emotion (frustration), explains relevant details of the scenario, then relates the story of her time there. In her last paragraph, she deftly bookends the essay with the solution to her opening dilemma.

Essay by Isabelle Teare

Please relate your interest in studying at Georgetown University to your goals. How do these thoughts relate to your chosen course of study?

I was getting frustrated. I knew I had a point and evidence, but I couldn't get him to agree. We were walking up the hill from New South Dorms, winding around Healy and toward the ICC auditorium. I was arguing the liberal side; walking with me was the most conservative boy I had ever met. We had been jousting the whole way, yet I couldn't get him to see why I was right. "Save your breath for the debate," he said.

We were at Georgetown for the Junior State of America program, and it was my turn to get up on stage. At home I had always been good at arguing with my parents, but this was different. I wasn't a teenager pushing for a later curfew. Instead, I was an advocate for a cause presenting my case before a jury of my peers.

I walked through the glass doors, but before I had a chance to clamber on stage the boy stopped me and said, "I will listen to both sides with an open mind, and if your speech changes my mind, I will vote for your resolution." It was a challenge. I smiled and walked on, ready to prove something.

That summer at Georgetown changed me. I was introduced to the smartest kids I had ever met, and they pushed me. No matter where I was, I was learning. On the bus, in Leo's eating lunch, on the way to class, in class, at the gym, lying on the grass—it was constant. It isn't enough to be smart yourself: you have to surround yourself with people who will inspire you, challenge you, question you, and make you think. That's what happened to me that summer, and I was hooked.

> When I went back home, to the island I love so much, I was acutely aware that something was missing.

When I went back home, to the island I love so much, I was acutely aware that something was missing. I couldn't figure it out. Everything was the same. Then it hit me that that was the problem: nothing had changed. No one had changed, no one had questioned themselves, and no one was inspired. I have loved my time on St. Thomas, but I can't wait to go to college for more of what I experienced that summer.

My first goal is that I want to learn. I want to stretch my mind to its limit, taking in as much as possible. I love art, history, literature, and debate, and know that I want to continue studying these subjects, as well as find others to pursue in college. Further, the Jesuit philosophy was once described to me as education for the head, the heart, and the hands: thinking about something, caring about it, and most importantly doing something about it. In addition to learning, caring and serving are also my goals.

Finally, Georgetown will allow me to achieve one other goal: to sail competitively in college. I have listened to my college counseling father guide other students through this process for years, forever saying, "Find the college that fits you." Georgetown fits me. It has the academics, philosophy, and sport for me, all in a location bursting with opportunities to learn, care, serve—and compete.

Georgetown was the first place I was truly challenged, so I want to continue my experience there. When I think back, I am standing behind the podium as the moderator asks for a vote: "In favor of the affirmative?" Hands begin to go up, but I am only looking for one. I am straining to see if that boy will raise his hand, anxious to see if I have done for him what so many of these people have done for me: hoping to see if I have inspired him, made him question his beliefs and change. My eyes scour the audience. Finally, there he is, with his hand raised in the air and a smile on his face.

Isabelle Teare attends Georgetown University.

109

GOING GA-GA OVER GW

Author Samantha Strauss's essay about why she wants to attend George Washington University contains no startling revelations, but it doesn't need to. An ordinary applicant would talk about wanting to study political science; Samantha knows she wants political communications, a more specialized major that few schools aside from GW offer. Her reference to "the SAC" (Student Activities Center) shows that she knows her way around GW lingo. Samantha ends with a flourish, cataloguing all her contacts with GW and making a smooth reference to the university's advertising slogan.

Essay by Samantha Strauss

Tell us in approximately five hundred words what motivated you to apply to GW and describe what contacts you have had with us. We have told you about the dynamic GW classroom, campus, and city experience; now tell us how you will make use of these resources in meeting your educational goals.

What motivated me to apply to GW is quite simple: it is the best school to study political communications, its location is amazing, and the people/campus fit me perfectly. Because of the long list of majors and class choices, I will have the opportunity to explore all of my interests ranging from political communications to the use of technology in the media to psychology. GW will enable me to reach my undergraduate educational goal of being a part of a rigorous, vibrant academic community, which will then prepare me to succeed in any field of interest I may choose in the future.

I am applying to GW as a political communications major. Where better to study that major than GW? From my experience working with California senators Dianne Feinstein and Barbara Boxer, I learned that the major issues are resolved in Washington and that if I want to be part of that process, then I need to be positioned in the center of the government at the school that will teach me the skills I need to succeed. GW is the perfect match.

Washington, D.C., has everything I want. With its beautiful landscaping in an urban setting and with three major colleges within fifteen minutes of each other, I am provided with the college life that I'm looking forward to. Additionally, with all the museums and archives, I can find information that will allow me to do high quality research. Also, being located in the center of the political atmosphere helps me move forward in my interest of politics and how to make changes in the world.

Then, there are the people. Every single person that I have talked with who has attended or is attending GW has taken the time to answer every one of my questions. All answers have been insightful, informative, and have driven me to understand that GW is the school for me. I already feel like a part of the GW community even though I am still in the application phase.

> **I already feel like a part of the GW community even though I am still in the application phase.**

Finally, the campus. It feels right to me, it is the perfect size, the dorms are unbelievable, the SAC has everything I need, and overall it felt like a good home away from home.

From my visit to the Foggy Bottom campus, to visiting chat rooms and phone conversations with current students, and the information sessions with college representatives, when I imagine where I see myself going to college, GW comes to mind. GW is more than a college for me; it's a once-in-a-lifetime experience that I truly don't want to miss. Just as GW's slogan is "Something Happens Here," I want to be a part of the "something."

Samantha Strauss attended George Washington University.

The Search for an Opening Line

If there is one part of the essay that applicants sweat over—and rightfully so—it is the opening. For a full discussion of how to begin your essay, turn to page 23.

The pages that follow reproduce the first seventy-five words, more or less, of each essay in this book, from Essay 1 through Essay 109. Browse the excerpts and see which ones pique your interest. Notice that many of them are straightforward—proof that it is not necessary to dream up a catchy opening in order to write an excellent essay.

But many of the openings do have flair. Check out the techniques that our authors have used and see if any of them might work for you. We're not suggesting that you lift particular topics or phrases, but rather than you pay attention to the literary devices our authors use. We do the same thing in our writing. For instance, at the beginning of chapter 3, we open with a flight of fancy that seems bizarre to the reader—until a voice wakes the narrator and reveals that the scene has been a dream. Did we invent that technique? Hardly. We could have lifted it from dozens of other books, and those authors in turn would have gotten the idea from books they had read.

The most tried-and-true way to open is with an anecdote. Below are many examples of anecdotal beginnings; particularly good ones include those from Essays 16, 29, 42, 48, and 87. Likewise, there are more than a few zingers from writers who can turn a catchy phrase; notable examples include the openings to Essays 10, 59, 70, 73, 76, and 98.

But these are just a few of many highlights. Take a look and see what resonates with you.

1

"I speak Spanish to God, Italian to women, French to men, and German to my horse."
—Charles V

I don't speak German. Horseless, and with two cats that understand only Russian, I never had the need. Besides, languages don't fall into neat categories for me as they did for Charles. But they do have a place in my life, and recently I have come to better understand just how important a place it is.

2

If I could have an entire year to do anything I pleased, I would spend it indulging myself in every book that years of required reading have prevented.

3

Now I was at the front of the classroom, using what little artistic coordination I had to draw a great big figure on the board: yes, those had to be eyes, an L-shaped nose, wrinkled eyebrows, a gaping "O" for a mouth. I added little stress lines on either corner of the cheeks, just to show how intent my hastily composed figure was on examining this *"Sylvan historian, who canst thus express a flowery tale more sweetly than our rhyme."*

4

I can say with certainty that there is nothing that has more of a positive effect on my life than Latin. Of course other things have grabbed my interest over the years, like poetry, math, singing, and women, but my true passion is for the Classics.

5

Call me eccentric, but I've always thought libraries are some of the noisiest places on earth. The patrons may be polite and scholarly as they go about their business, but the books themselves make quite a racket. They whisper and murmur on the shelves, promising adventure, knowledge, and the meaning of life to anyone perusing them.

6

The brain: an almost indecipherable (at least to me) mass of neurons. Some extend an infinitesimal distance in the brain while others run through the length of the body. Each neuron is constantly sending and gathering tiny electrochemical signals which travel along a nerve axon, shooting along at incredible speeds towards its destination.

7

I once asked a mantis shrimp this very question. I repeated it to him verbatim from the University of Chicago writing supplement, and after he recovered from the initial shock of learning that I had only three types of color receptors, he attempted to explain to me exactly what I was "missing." Although this particular mantis shrimp was bilingual, he eventually gave up on me, because there was no accurate way to describe in English the extended rainbow of the world around him. He concluded that our individual experiences of the world were fundamentally different and proceeded to scuttle away with an air of intellectual superiority.

8

After a pleasant early morning flight I had finally reached my destination. As I stepped out of the plane and toward the arrival gate I caught a gust of hot, dry desert air. I knew I was back in astronomy country, where over 80 percent of the nights are clear and the Milky Way's frothy band arches majestically across the black sky abyss.

9

"E2V2" was my own creation and I would drive it in BattleBotsIQ , a national robotics competition. I felt my body tense for the battle against the spinbot, Chromedome. Before the match, I had reviewed and decided my strategy against spinbots—attack it before it spins up and then keep hitting it.

10

When I was ten years old, I met Vince Lombardi. I saw him at the post office. He was sitting quietly with George Marshall and Humphrey Bogart. Vince cast a triumphant smile in my direction. His excitement was so contagious that I could not help smiling with him.

11

My coach always tells me that there is some reason why we, as debaters, can take four weeks out of our summer vacation, away from our friends and our families, to enclose ourselves in lecture halls and cramped dorm rooms to learn the depths and intricacies of debate. He has never told me what this reason is, but now that I'm beginning my senior year and I have attended three of these camps, I think I finally understand why.

12

I have always wanted to waltz through the foyer of the New York Public Library in the arms of Fred Astaire while Glenn Miller gently plays "Moonlight Serenade" on the balcony above. I wish I could gaze upon the White Cliffs of Dover at the side of Irene Dunne. Sadly, time has passed me by, and the closest that I will ever get to the likes of Fred Astaire, Myrna Loy, and Tommy Dorsey is through the music and films that they have left behind.

13

Wedged Clay.

Most people think that clay is clay, that mud is mud. Well as a matter of fact, this is simply not so. Wedged clay is rolled and twisted at a factory to remove air. This clay is much smoother and easier to work with than ordinary clay. It's the best invention since sliced bread for the potter.

14

The first magic trick I remember was something really simple. My uncle made a coin disappear and reappear behind my ear. It's a classic trick. He made a silk scarf disappear too. Simple things, but when I saw them I was amazed. First I asked, "How did you do that?" which was closely followed by, "*How did you do that??*" And then I became a student of magic.

15

Don't you just hate those days where you find the perfect outfit, but don't have the right pair of shoes to complete the look? For me, deciding what shoes to sport depends upon which facet of my personality I wish to reveal or activity I'm about to partake in. Each day I face a dilemma—do I show the flashy, fun side or the conservative, chic side?

16

When our family travels, my suitcase is always the heaviest, not because I pack multiple pairs of shoes, but because I bring physical books, not digital copies. This is my quirk: I don't read books electronically.

17

My mom is already telling me that I will have to clean out my room and throw away most of what fills my desk drawers. I am a very sentimental person and keep large quantities of what friends have given me over the years, so it will be hard for me to decide what to discard. The one thing I will never throw away, though, is my letters.

18

Slammed into lockers without warning for years. Verbally assaulted from Manhattan to Madrid. The constant object of unadulterated hate and derision most of my life. No matter: it has been worth the burden. A product of a mixed marriage, I should be "mauve," less red at least. But I am stolid in my defense of red principle, merit, and tradition. Go Red Sox!

19

Leaning backward in my one-man laser, I hike out hard in an attempt to keep the sailboat from capsizing, the tiller clutched hard in my left hand and the main sheet sliding through my right. These strong thermal winds are exciting yet challenging. I have been waiting for them for some time.

20

It was a thrill to land my dream job this summer as an intern with the Metropolitan Transportation Commission. As long as I can remember, I have been fascinated with everything associated with transportation. My commute to high school on the Bay Area Rapid Transit System (BART) and the city bus system puts me on the front lines as a user of public transit.

21

Every Sunday morning until the weather drops below freezing and my parents do not let me use the hose, I wash my car. This may seem like an ordinary job to some, but to me washing a car requires a distinctive technique.

22

Display dagger. Teddy bear. Cheesecake.

I love cheesecake. In fact, a slice of this delicious dessert is on my desk right now, impaled by a pair of chopsticks. These odd juxtapositions of East and West occur frequently at my house; my mother puts peanut butter into her moon cakes, and my dad uses the coffee maker to boil chrysanthemum tea.

23

When I first came to St. Andrew's-Sewanee, I had pretty much led a common life for a child in my area. Athletically, I played baseball, basketball, and soccer. There was peewee football down the mountain in the valley, but on top of our little plateau there never was much interest in getting a team together.

24

Glaring floodlights illuminated the brisk autumn night, steam rose from the sweaty players, and screams rang from the abnormally large crowd. With less than ten minutes left to play, the game remained a scoreless draw. I was the only freshman on the field, and I had been running on sheer adrenaline for nearly the whole second half.

25

After deciding it would be fun to play a sport in high school, I joined my school's water polo team as a freshman. Although I had never been particularly athletically inclined, I threw myself into the sport with total energy and enthusiasm, hoping to be a starting player.

26

A ball is rolled down the lane. Confidently, I turn around; there is no need to see the result. A perfect strike. I stroll back to the bench, receiving high-fives from not only my teammates, but the opposing team as well. Bowling has been my most satisfying extracurricular activity.

27

There I sit, just having eaten a big bucket full of butterflies. They are fluttering about inside my stomach. A warm ball of energy gathers in my chest, and all other problems of the past day, week, and year disappear. All that exists is my moment and I.

28

She whispers silent words
To the surrounding emptiness,
An emptiness that represents relationships
She has selfishly severed,
In an attempt to disappear slowly
From a world she once yearned to experience.

29

"Whenever you're ready," a voice echoes from somewhere in the seats. For the first time, I am on stage, alone, auditioning for a role in the musical *Nunsense*. Well, sort of. There are no male roles in the musical, so the directors added a chorus. I shake, and my voice quivers as I proceed with the required monologue, acting a part I have not found a way to relate to. When it is done, I nod to the accompanist and he begins to play. I sing an excerpt from "We Go Together" I have practiced for weeks. And I go off key. I leave the stage and bike slowly home, expecting to be cut.

30

All six of my elementary school years were spent in the same art room. Miniature tables and chairs sat surrounded by walls covered by prints of paintings and sculptures created by some of the greatest artists of all time. When my young eyes wandered around the room, which was often, I found my attention constantly drawn to a painting of a woman in a red hat.

31

It was the end of a lot of things. It was the end of my freshman year, and the end of my youth orchestra's concert season. It was the end of my time living in Philadelphia, right before I was to leave all my friends and the home in Swarthmore that I loved. It was the end of our last concert; it was the last page of Mahler's Titan symphony.

32

While standing backstage sipping my nth cup of coffee, forty hours awake and counting, I tried to think of what I'd do next. A year's efforts organizing Breakin' Curfew would soon draw to a close with the fall of the curtain; after this last band finished and the packed theater emptied, I'd have to begin again—with nothing.

33

Before last year I had always thought of myself as a very shy, uncreative, introspective individual. And I was happy that way. I had found my little niche in the Kinkaid society. I was the jock who excelled in sports and also managed to make pretty good grades as well. But I wasn't an artist.

34

"Let your passion rise, let your passion rise," she sang, letting her hands twirl and float up towards the ceiling. "See that beast run free, see that beast run free!"
For the first time, I was visiting Kansas City's castle of wordsmithing, the Writer's Place. It was the day after New Year's. I was barely seventeen. It was an open mic—my first—and I was nervous.

35

Two works of art have made me shiver. Chartres Cathedral in France and "Dark Star" by the Grateful Dead continue to fascinate me every time I think of them. As art, the two specimens are completely opposite to each other. Chartres is a masterpiece of human ingenuity, architecture, creativity, and order. "Dark Star" is an exercise in improvisation, a constantly evolving work of group invention and lateral thought.

36

I started playing piano at the ripe old age of ten, but there was an advantage to learning music when I became more mature. Classical music is an acquired taste, and the time to develop that taste enabled me to tolerate the unavoidable lessons on basic notes and rhythms.

37

"OH MY GOSH! I have a whole new appreciation for the art of dance!"

Who said that? The voice sounds familiar, but those words...they didn't just come out of the mouth of my dad, did they? They did, and wow, how long have I waited to hear something like that from him? Years...fifteen to be exact!

38

I tentatively grasped the plastic blue handle of the fattest brush. Its firm but compliant bristles tickled as I pulled them along my palm. I looked around nervously, waiting for my first oil painting class to begin. The intimidating, white primed canvas rested on my easel, boasting its potential. Fresh, plump paint tubes in every color but black sat in a neat line, echoing the rainbow. My water cup was half full. I was ready.

39

It has been about eighteen years since I was born in New York City, and I have spent roughly the last eight of those years in what I still call a new home, here in Charlotte, North Carolina. My life has followed the clichéd and semi-charmed life of a teenager growing up in a very nice American neighborhood.

40

I have spent the past four summers working as a volunteer and counselor at a summer camp for kids ages four to ten. Each week presents new challenges, opportunities, and surprises and I am often amazed at the wit, intelligence, and confidence that elementary schoolers can display. This year, it was the bright faces of two campers, Alfred and Bill, that provided the most humor, challenge, and surprise to me and the rest of the staff.

41

After climbing a set of dull looking concrete stairs, I entered the kitchen/dining area, a small space complete with a television and curtained windows. Two tables were set for the guests. Down a hallway were two bathrooms, one marked "Men," the other, "Women."

42

"I don't do throw-up."

My own words were coming back to haunt me as I heard one of my campers yell, "Ewww, Bridger threw up." I froze. I forced myself to turn around and look. I glanced quickly, then immediately looked away. I stopped breathing through my nose so I wouldn't be able to smell it. I was horrified.

43

The Georgia drought of 2007 set the stage. The water level at Lake Lanier was down at least 20 feet, and portions of land unexposed for years were completely visible. There were beer bottles, old soda cans, gas tanks, and even refrigerators; relics of our lives waiting for discovery by future archeologists. Interlaced among these artifacts were the true villains, mounds of plastic bags.

44

One might think it strange for a teenager to be content behind a lawn mower in his neighbor's yard, but there is something unusually rewarding about tackling the jungle of grass I face every week behind Margaret Norris's house.

45

"I do it for the joy it brings 'cause I'm a joyful girl. 'Cause the world owes us nothing, we owe each other the world."—Ani DiFranco ("Joyful Girl")

In the fall of my junior year, my mother announced that she had signed us up for a mission trip to Bolivia for Christmas break. My first thought was, "That's impossible! But I wanted a new computer and some new clothes. How will we ever get all the gifts down there? Our suitcases will be too heavy!" I was careful not to say these selfish things out loud.

46

The summer after eleventh grade represented a meaningful and eye opening experience for me. I spent the summer as a counselor at an overnight camp, Raquette Lake Girls Camp, where I had attended as a camper for four years.

47

As I am filing all those college applications, the question keeps coming back to me. Who am I? Where do I come from? Where am I heading?

48

I'm tired and a little bit desperate. My clock angrily glares at me through its neon green dial. It's 11:24. The biology exam tomorrow will be murder. I resolutely pass over my textbook, and instead return to the screen where Pandit Jasraj stares back at me.

49

"Lynching was ritualistic public square violence, part of a sordid history of white criminality." —Hakim Hasan

Looking out of the car window onto Crenshaw Boulevard, I do not see an angry mob cloaked in white, dancing on one of the street corners. Nor do I see towering willows ornamented with dangling bodies. As I look out of my window I see young African American boys flaunting diamond earrings that make their earlobes droop; young men and women bumping the latest "Jay-Z" song while bringing their twenty-inch rim-spinning Escalades to a halt at the red light.

50

"Hello 엄 마! No. I'm at the movies. 극 장! 조금있으면가." Translation: "Mom! No. I'm at the movies. The movies! I'll be home soon." If I'm with my friends, someone will ask: "What was that?" And I answer, "I was speaking in Korean to my mom." This answer is never enough, as I have learned. Only after a few rounds of saying odd phrases for their amusement is everyone's curiosity satisfied.

51

So there's a girl. You've read her application, but do you really know her? You know that she works hard and that she dreams of going to Princeton, but does that count as knowing her? I'll tell you a bit about her. Then, you decide.

52

I stood still, facing the giant bathroom mirror. *Whoosh*. The bathroom door swung open, and a group of girls came in, chatting and laughing. I stared into the mirror. A blonde, clearly more than a head taller than I, strolled past, reaching for the paper towel dispenser.

53

I have always been a very rational and logical thinker. This is why I enjoy almost all math and science courses. So here's an equation for you: $\dfrac{assumptions^2}{ignorance} + differences = ?.$

The easiest way for me to solve any problem is to put it in a form that will make it easier to understand and solve. For this particular problem I will give you a personal experience that incorporates all of the above variables and we'll find out together what the answer to this equation is and just maybe how to solve it.

54

If I were to sum up my life in one line, I would use a quote from rapper Tyler the Creator: "I am a walking paradox." I choose this line because it speaks to me of contrasting pieces that shape my personality.

55

"Ha ha! Christina is a dirty Mexican!"

Growing up in a small, conservative community, it's easy to be shoved into your own category if you don't look or act like everyone else. My hair and eyes, instead of being blonde and blue like all of my Czech classmates, were chocolate and espresso. My last name had a "z" in it, and my grandmother called me "mija."

56

There's a slender volume on the top shelf of my bookcase, nestled snugly in between *Midnight's Children* and *The Sun Also Rises*. Given a cursory glance, there's nothing extraordinary about this book—a stylized peacock in green, orange, and black is the sole embellishment on a plain white dust jacket. A title and author are printed on top of the image: *Musings of Bygone Days*, by Hari Hara Das.

57

In the beginning of third grade, I took my first standardized test where I had to fill out my full name, address, my birthday, and to shade in the corresponding ovals. My teacher then said to fill in the oval that represents our ethnicity. One of the choices was "Hispanic/Latino." I paused for a moment. I knew that I was Mexican American; my grandparents emigrated from Mexico to El Paso, Texas, where my mom and her ten brothers and sisters grew up. However, when I came across this question about my ethnicity, I never fully realized what it meant to me.

58

"A time for warm hearts and hot guts." This is the slogan of the annual Hogeye Festival in the Hot Sausage Capital of the World: my hometown of Elgin, Texas. I have lived on Pistol Hill Ranch in Elgin, population c. 5,000, for all but the first two of my seventeen years. I have grown up on small-town morals, values, and ways of life. Elgin is a place where parents still teach their children to say "yes, ma'am" and "no, sir."

59

Sometime between waking up at the crack of dawn and fourth period I became a teenage werewolf. No, wait, I mean feminist.

It's as if I didn't know until someone pointed it out to me in English class, but it was more like an "Ooh, dude, I think you just stepped in some feminist," or a "Damn! You smell like feminist," or maybe even an "I think you spilled some feminism on your shirt, and it stains…"

60

As I step up to the pulpit, I feel a familiar sense of calm come over me, the calm I always experience before singing to my congregation. Scanning the audience, I look out at the parents and grandparents, making eye contact with those I recognize and those I do not.

61

My summer job at Dunkin Donuts has taught me many things. After scooping more than 800 ice creams and making more than 1,200 cups of coffee, I've become an expert at serving all our specialties really fast. The commuters running to catch their trains and the little league teams coming in for a treat after a game can count on me and my colleagues to fill their order quickly.

62

Some nights we took the route along the Hudson River. My mom drove past the boisterous New York lights and down a few, potholed roads. She pulled to a stop in front of a small, gray building that crouched between a blinking medley of *bodegas*. The building's roof capped cracked cement walls and Pablo, a prominent preacher, stood at the doors to greet us. When a man's voice vibrated through a microphone, my mom rushed me towards the gathering room.

63

I voted on November 2nd. As an eighteen-year-old woman in America, I am legally allowed to exercise my right to vote. Although my heart beat slightly fast, and my hands shook unsteadily at the polling booth, upon arriving home from my first voting experience, I was filled with a sense of accomplishment and relief.

64

The timer emits three deafening beeps. My preparation time is up, and I gather my materials. My throat dries up; my palms sweat; my yellow legal pad quivers in my hands. Voices inside my head bombard me like anxious reporters shouting at a press conference. "What if your responses are dumb?" "This activity's too hard for you." "You're going to make a fool of yourself." I'm about to give my first speech at the beginning-of-the-year debate tournament for high school freshmen, and I struggle to find my voice, praying it doesn't crack.

65

It's 256 steps from my front door to my front door; a journey I make every other day that sparks reveries of reminiscing over the days when my parents were one. So close are the two houses that shelter me and yet so far apart are my two parents.

66

It was the action of a single moment that eventually formed many of the values that I hold today and that will continue to define me. It's not like I planned it though. Neither did I think anything of it at the time. And now, though I wish it didn't have to happen, I don't exactly regret that it did. In a way it changed me—made me who I am today—and I wouldn't have it any other way.

67

Last year I got to taste life; the lukewarm water of revival flowing down my throat. I got to feel it, in the pumping of my heart, the layers of dry dust encrusted on my hands. I got to smell it; the magnified aroma of my body fused on my clothes. I got to hear it too; the melody of zippers. And I got to see it; the orange mountains and cliffs, and sand that I thought I was used to.

68

I woke from an unpleasant sleep. As with all sleep on airplanes, it was just to pass the time; very little rest lay in the upright position. I was used to it though. Long flights have become a part of my routine, and I've grown callous enough to ignore the discomfort.

69

At seven thirty, every morning, I race down the stairs, as fast as my drowsy body permits me, and take a detour through the kitchen on my way to the door. I pick up my filled to-go cup, with the same urgency and accuracy of a relay racer reaching for the baton.

70

I won my school's Pickleball tournament in tenth grade. How many National Merit Semi-Finalists can say that?

What? That's not enough to set me apart in the massive pile of applications? Well, maybe I hold the world record for most snow cones eaten in the summer of 2004, or the record for most piggyback rides given as a camp counselor.

71

"...And finally, Stephanie Yeldell," is a phrase that I hear more than one could ever possibly imagine. One might ask "Why, Stephanie? Why is this?" The answer is simple: Our world seems to deem it entirely necessary to list individuals in alphabetical order, and by last name. For those who are alphabetically challenged, this form of listing individuals, that seems to be unbelievably prevalent, is every single shade of irritating one could possibly experience. It's annoying.

72

Contrary to what you may think, buying a bottle of shampoo is a complex and tedious process. First, I chose the five most outwardly appealing bottles, conscious that my seventeen-year-old female mind is being manipulated by blatantly false phrases like "made with real herbs so your hair will stay shiny for up to eight and a half hours."

73

Do you ever have those dreams where you've arrived at school and suddenly realize you've forgotten to wear pants? Well, for most high school seniors that dream becomes a reality, at least figuratively. We must bare our souls, not to best friends, or family, but to complete strangers who may not even want to hear about it and may even flat out reject us. What twisted institution would ever subject young adults in the formative stages of emotional growth to this experience? Oh, right. College.

74

"Try everything once." That's my family's motto, and, as mottos go, it's a pretty good one. Because of it I have played rugby, survived an incredibly painful season of track, taught Sunday school, repaired roofs and drainpipes (Appalachia Service Project), tried kite boarding, been hang gliding, moved to Costa Rica for six months, biked for two weeks in Colorado and Utah, wore a Queen Amidala costume to school, eaten raccoon, guinea pig, and iguana meat...

75

I love Perrier water with the depths of my soul. I cannot get enough of the cool, fizzy bubbles rolling on my tongue. The crisp taste is pure bliss for the palate. The bitter aftertaste is the best part of the Perrier experience.

76

Take a moment and look at your hands: their shape, texture, size, and delicacy. These parts of your body are one of the most important creations. They are the scribes of every document; the builders of homes, offices, and shelters; and what comforts many during a frightening experience. But, for me, my hands have yet to display any external similarities to the role they were created to fulfill.

77

Underwear. Say it to a kindergarten class, and they'll giggle endlessly. Write it in a college essay and…well, I guess I'll find out. But specifically I'm talking about long underwear; cozy, toasty, stretchy long underwear. I've never been much of a cold weather person, but give me a pair of long underwear and I'm "good to go."

78

It's odd how a random thought can pop into your head and completely change the way you view something. Well, I realized today that I do not want children. This revelation came to me while walking into the grocery store. An exasperated young mother was trying to comfort her child.

79

I identify Laetitia by the tights scented with French perfume in my sock drawer, her ten-pound black boots, which still live in my closet, and her beautiful laugh I hear over the phone every so often. Laetitia lived with us as an exchange student the year my youngest sister was born. She was the first and only big sister I have ever had.

80

I grew up in a brick house on Nottingham Drive, a place with old furniture and young faces, with small rooms that never seemed to be empty. I grew up with my pointy nose buried in books, wearing stretch pants and bows and listening to my father's new songs on the guitar.

81

"Alright, Snapple Cap Question of the Day: What percentage of people in the world are left-handed?" asks my dad.

"Twelve," I guess.

"Three," guesses my brother.

"Nine," guesses my mom.

"Sara wins. The answer is eleven," says my dad.

82

Toddlers with buzz-cuts. Shirts tucked in. Shorts pulled high. Matching outfits chosen by Mommy. From the beginning, my brother and I have been incessantly competing with and compared to each other. Although Bryce is nearly two years older, adults frequently thought we were twins because we were about the same height and almost identical as young boys. While I no longer have to worry about people mistaking the two of us physically, I am still ensnared by the inescapable expectations and unbelievable pressure of being Bryce Taylor's younger brother.

83

I was never really upset about it. I never resented my parents for it. I didn't ever feel unlucky because of it. My sister had Down Syndrome, and that was that. Sure, I found it a little odd that while most of my friends' big sisters secretly applied lipstick on the walk to school, mine collected worms, which she would make into jewelry. But except for the occasionally painful quarrel (one of which left a bite mark on my right shoulder) my sister and I got along.

84

"I love Winnie the Pooh! Are you related to A. A. Milne?" I can't even count on two hands the number of times I have been asked that question. "No I'm not; our last names are different. Well sort of...Well, there's a story...It's complicated."

85

A Scrabble tile skittered to the floor as Rabbi Zucker walked in. It was a freezing Shabbat with everyone practicing their various observances: davening [reciting prayers], snowball fighting, inventing a new method of playing Scrabble.

86

"The aim of argument, or of discussion, should not be victory, but progress."
—Joseph Joubert

Much of what we learn, and most of our best thinking, is not because of what is spoon-fed to us, but rather as a result of interactions with other people, including active questioning of our surroundings, beliefs, and ideas. Sometimes the best of these opportunities go unexplored. During rehearsal for an American Conservatory Theater production I was in this fall, a fellow cast member offered to tell a joke, which she warned, might offend some people.

87

"So, you want this car or not?" Dr. Matt Petrilla asked again, in his simultaneously pushy yet polite manner.

This smart, stocky man, a medical doctor and the father of a friend, had thrown me into a sudden state of blissful surprise: less than a minute before, he had offered me a free car.

88

I am in retail hell. I stand behind the cash register, palms clammy, heart pounding, my mouth curled into an effortful and thoroughly unconvincing smile. I sport a pin that encourages customers to "Ask me what's FREE!" but its bold typeface and exuberant colors cannot disguise my fear of the dreaded general public. It's noon, and the store is abuzz with chaotic consumers, hurried housewives, and troublemaking teenagers. They terrify me.

89

It was my fifth birthday. Imagine the joy that must pulse through the veins of a hungry homeless person who just happens to find a winning lottery ticket laying in the gutter. The look on that person's face would be much like the one I wore when tearing apart my present to reveal nothing more than a bag of marbles.

90

In my six-year-old mind I see the president, sitting at his plush desk chair in a navy blue suit. He's examining an important document. Or better yet, he's in the middle of a crucial meeting with leaders from all over the world. His secretary enters. She looks worried. "We've received a letter of some importance," she says. His brow furrows as she hands him a small envelope addressed in sparkly pink pen. "Anne Erickson, age six, Oakland, California," he muses, examining the careful writing.

91

I was always a chatty kid. From the time I was two, I had *Curious George* memorized and I would precociously recite it to my parents. I knew things!

92

I can't imagine wanting straight hair. People suggest it all the time, but I simply could never change my hair. It's a part of my identity, part of the reason people remember me. You see, it's not your ordinary hair—it's HUGE. And I'm not just talking curly; I'm talking mega frizzy and tangled. But no matter how difficult it is to manage, I would never get rid of it because my hair defines who I am.

93

One overpowering image appears whenever I remember my middle school years: the Dark Ages in Europe. Was I suffering through isolation, oppression, or misery? Fortunately not, yet I was, as Plato would put it, in the gloom of my cave, bereft of the light of intellectual illumination.

94

I first became aware of the transformative power of music when I attended my first live concert. This was my first weeknight excursion with my father, the culmination of many episodes of desperate begging and pleading. *Dolly Parton.* The sound of her name alone was enough to get my pulse racing, my feet tapping.

95

My junior year abroad in Germany was a very significant experience for me. At the beginning of my sophomore year of high school my family decided to take in a Japanese exchange student. Over the course of the year, Satoru became a part of our family and a dear friend. I had been thinking about going abroad even before we decided to host Sato, but by observing what a great experience his exchange year was for him, I was given the courage to go ahead and apply for a place in the Youth for Understanding year abroad program in Germany.

96

I'm somewhat used to being a part of the minority. I've always been considered the "different" child of the family, the one not quite like the others. My three older brothers and sisters were all quiet, athletic, highly motivated scholars, excelling in subjects like math and science and being awarded MVP of the team. I was different.

97

The upbeat rhythm of merengue music electrified the air. My unaccustomed feet quickly adapted to the practiced steps of my dance partner. As the tempo of the music increased, my partner swept me across the floor in a rush of quick movements that I carried out with little skill, but with all my heart. As the song came to an end, I breathlessly thanked my partner and tried to explain what a fun time I had in my slightly broken Spanish.

98

Sweltering heat, abhorrently close quarters, and short tempers. Sweatshop? No, such were the family vacations of my youth—countless hours in a poorly air-conditioned vehicle, seven traveling companions and a driver whose frustration often bordered on road rage.

99

I had never been outside the continental United States when I decided to travel to Africa. By the time I returned to school from my two-week-long sophomore spring break, I had landed in England, Kenya, Malawi, and South Africa. Maybe more people would have started smaller with, say, a tame vacation venture to Mexico or Hawaii, but since I had always planned on visiting everywhere eventually, I figured, why not?

100

I am most comfortable when I am lost. Deliberately getting lost fuels my drive for discovery. On a trip to Italy the summer after my sophomore year, I discovered the pleasure of using public transportation to get to know the city of Rome.

101

In June of this year, my parents and I took a weeklong trip to London. This trip was one my parents had been planning to take for years but had never had quite enough money before; it was to be our first real family vacation and my first time to go abroad. Such an event would, under normal circumstances, have inspired in us an unbearable level of excitement, but at the time the trip was scheduled, my grandmother was terminally ill with lung cancer and could die at any time.

102

His teeth clenched over my delicate skull, and I felt hot blood drip down my cheeks as his claws slashed at my face. My legs crumbled beneath his heavy weight as both of us came crashing down the rocky hillside. I fought to thrust myself from beneath him, remembering the mangled stuffed animals surrounding his cage.

103

I come from a long line of no-nonsense scientists, from doctors to engineers to researchers. My apple, on the other hand, fell about a thousand yards away from the family tree. For as long as I can remember, I have loved art, both making it and viewing it.

104

Rebecca Kastan's Top Ten Reasons Why Vanderbilt Is Her #1 Choice (*David Letterman* Style):
10.
Weather: I have lived in Columbus, Ohio, my whole life. Although it has been the best place to grow up, I have to admit that weather is not our forté. Weather can have an effect on people's mood and outlook. I checked out what the Nashville Chamber of Commerce says about weather, and it sure sounds good to me!

105

It was a cold day in February when I found myself in the most unusual of situations. I was happily reading the *Baseball Geek Bible* near a mountain lake when I was approached by one *anas platyrhynchos*. Curious, I looked up from my book just in time to see him bellow a 95-decibel QUACK! Its intensity shook me, and strangely, I could comprehend its meaning. He was saying "WHITMAN!"

106

I settled on St. John's a few months after I had finished applying to, visiting, being accepted by, and finally deciding not to attend three colleges. I had finished my senior year of high school by correspondence and a few classes taken credit-by-exam, so in truth my senior year was a year off. I wasn't enamored of the prospect of spending another year away from school and away from activity, but I couldn't in good conscience throw myself into a college I didn't care about. What had bothered me about the schools I had applied to was that all of them seemed to be opportunities to flounder, to waste time in a pre-adult, post-child no-man's land.

107

Upon a recent Yale visit, I conversed with a Yale senior in the admissions office about his experiences. He had only two complaints about the university: there were too many student protesters, and the university sands the roads instead of salting them in the winter. I love that Yale is a place where the students are motivated to change the world, and the faculty encourages them to act. Sanding saves the environment. What annoyed this Yale student impresses me.

108

I was getting frustrated. I knew I had a point and evidence, but I couldn't get him to agree. We were walking up the hill from New South Dorms, winding around Healy and toward the ICC auditorium. I was arguing the liberal side; walking with me was the most conservative boy I had ever met. We had been jousting the whole way, yet I couldn't get him to see why I was right. "Save your breath for the debate," he said.

109

What motivated me to apply to GW is quite simple: it is the best school to study political communications, its location is amazing, and the people/campus fit me perfectly. Because of the long list of majors and class choices, I will have the opportunity to explore all of my interests ranging from political communications to the use of technology in the media to psychology.

Acknowledgments

We wish to thank all those who assisted in the preparation of this book. Without the exceptional work of our 109 student contributors, there would be no book, and we wish them all the best in their college years and beyond. We are also grateful to the high school counselors from across the nation who connected us with our student authors. Many of these counselors give us ongoing support through our Advisory Group, and we benefit immeasurably from having them on our team.

Julie Fiske Hogan, production coordinator of the *Fiske Guide to Colleges*, has been an important source of support.

We are deeply grateful to Lindsay Newton for her skillful editing. We are also indebted to Todd Stocke, Suzanna Bainbridge, Katherine Pidde, Michelle Lecuyer, Heather Moore, and Dominique Raccah for their dedication to the Fiske guides.

We appreciate the efforts of all, but responsibility for the final product is ours alone.

About the Authors

I n 1980, when he was education editor of the *New York Times*, Edward B. Fiske sensed that college-bound students and their families needed better information on which to base their educational choices. Thus was born the *Fiske Guide to Colleges*. A graduate of Wesleyan University, Fiske did graduate work at Columbia University and assorted other bastions of higher learning. He left the *Times* in 1991 to pursue a variety of educational and journalistic interests, which included writing a book on school reform, *Smart Schools, Smart Kids*. When not visiting colleges, he can be found traveling, sailing, or doing research on the educational problems of Third World countries for UNESCO and other international organizations. Ted lives in Durham, North Carolina, near the campus of Duke University, where his wife is a member of the faculty. They are coauthors of *When Schools Compete: A Cautionary Tale* and *Elusive Equity: Education Reform in Post Apartheid South Africa*.

Since entering Yale in the early 1980s, Bruce G. Hammond has devoted much of his time to counseling others about college admissions. At Yale, Hammond was editor-in-chief of *The Insider's Guide to the Colleges*. He subsequently served as managing editor of the *Fiske Guide to Colleges*. He has been quoted in numerous national publications including the *New York Times*, the *Wall Street Journal*, *USA Today*, the *Washington Post*, *Newsweek*, *U.S. News & World Report*, *Business Week*, and *Money Magazine*. In recent years, Bruce has worked in Chinese national high schools counseling students for college in the English-speaking world.

Notes

College Counselors Advisory Group

Marilyn Albarelli, Moravian Academy (PA)

Scott Anderson, St. George's Independent School (TN)

Christine Asmussen, St. Andrew's-Sewanee School (TN)

Amy E. Belstra, Cherry Creek H.S. (CO)

Greg Birk, The American School in Switzerland

Francine E. Block, American College Admissions Consultants (PA)

Robin Boren, Education Consultant (CO)

John B. Boshoven, Community High School & Jewish Academy of Metro Detroit (MI)

Mimi Bradley, St. Andrew's Episcopal School (MS)

Claire Cafaro, Clear Directions (NJ)

Nancy Caine, St. Augustine H.S. (CA)

Anthony L. Clay, Carolina Friends School (NC)

Kathy Cleaver, Durham Academy (NC)

Jimmie Lee Cogburn, Independent Counselor (GA)

Alice Cotti, Polytechnic School (CA)

Rod Cox, St. Johns Country Day School (FL)

Kim Crockard, Crockard College Counseling (AL)

Carroll K. Davis, North Central H.S. (IN)

Mary Jo Dawson, Academy of the Sacred Heart (MI)

Lexi Eagles, Greensboro Country Day School (NC)

Dan Feldhaus, Iolani School (HI)

Ralph S. Figueroa, Albuquerque Academy (NM)

Emily E. FitzHugh, The Gunnery (CT)

Larry Fletcher, Salesianum School (DE)

Nancy Fomby, Episcopal School of Dallas (TX)

Laura Johnson Frey, Vermont Academy (VT)

Phyllis Gill, Providence Day School (NC)

H. Scotte Gordon, Moses Brown School (RI)

Freida Gottsegen, Education Consultant (GA)

Molly Gotwals, Suffield Academy (CT)

Kathleen Barnes Grant, The Catlin Gabel School (OR)

Amy Grieger, Northfield Mount Hermon School (MA)

Mimi Grossman, St. Mary's Episcopal School (TN)

Elizabeth Hall, Education Consulting Services (TX)

Darnell Heywood, Columbus Academy (OH)

Bruce Hunter, Rowland Hall-St. Mark's School (UT)

Deanna L. Hunter, Shawnee Mission East H.S. (KS)

Joan Jacobson, Shawnee Mission South H.S. (KS)

Diane Johnson, Lawrence Public Schools (NY)

Gerimae Kleinman, Shaker Heights H.S. (OH)

Sharon Koenings, Brookfield Academy (WI)

Laurie Leftwich, Brother Martin High School (LA)

Mary Jane London, Los Angeles Center for Enriched Studies (CA)

Martha Lyman, Deerfield Academy (MA)

Brad MacGowan, Newton North H.S. (MA)

Robert S. MacLellan, Jr., Hebron Academy (ME)

Susan Marrs, The Seven Hills School (OH)

Karen A. Mason, Germantown Academy (PA)

Lynne McConnell, Rumson-Fair Haven Regional H.S. (NJ)

Lisa Micele, University of Illinois Laboratory H.S. (IL)

Corky Miller-Strong, The Culver Academies (IN)

Janet Miranda, Prestonwood Christian Academy (TX)

Gunnar W. Olson, Indian Springs School (AL)

Stuart Oremus, Wellington School (OH)

Julie Rollins, Episcopal H.S. (TX)

Bruce Scher, Chicagoland Jewish H.S. (IL)

David Schindel, Sandia Preparatory School (NM)

Barbara Simmons, Notre Dame High School (CA)

Paul M. Stoneham, The Key School (MD)

Scott White, Montclair H.S. (NJ)

Linda Zimring, Los Angeles United School District (CA)

Notes

Notes